AF753590

IMAGES
of America

El Camino Real de Tierra Adentro

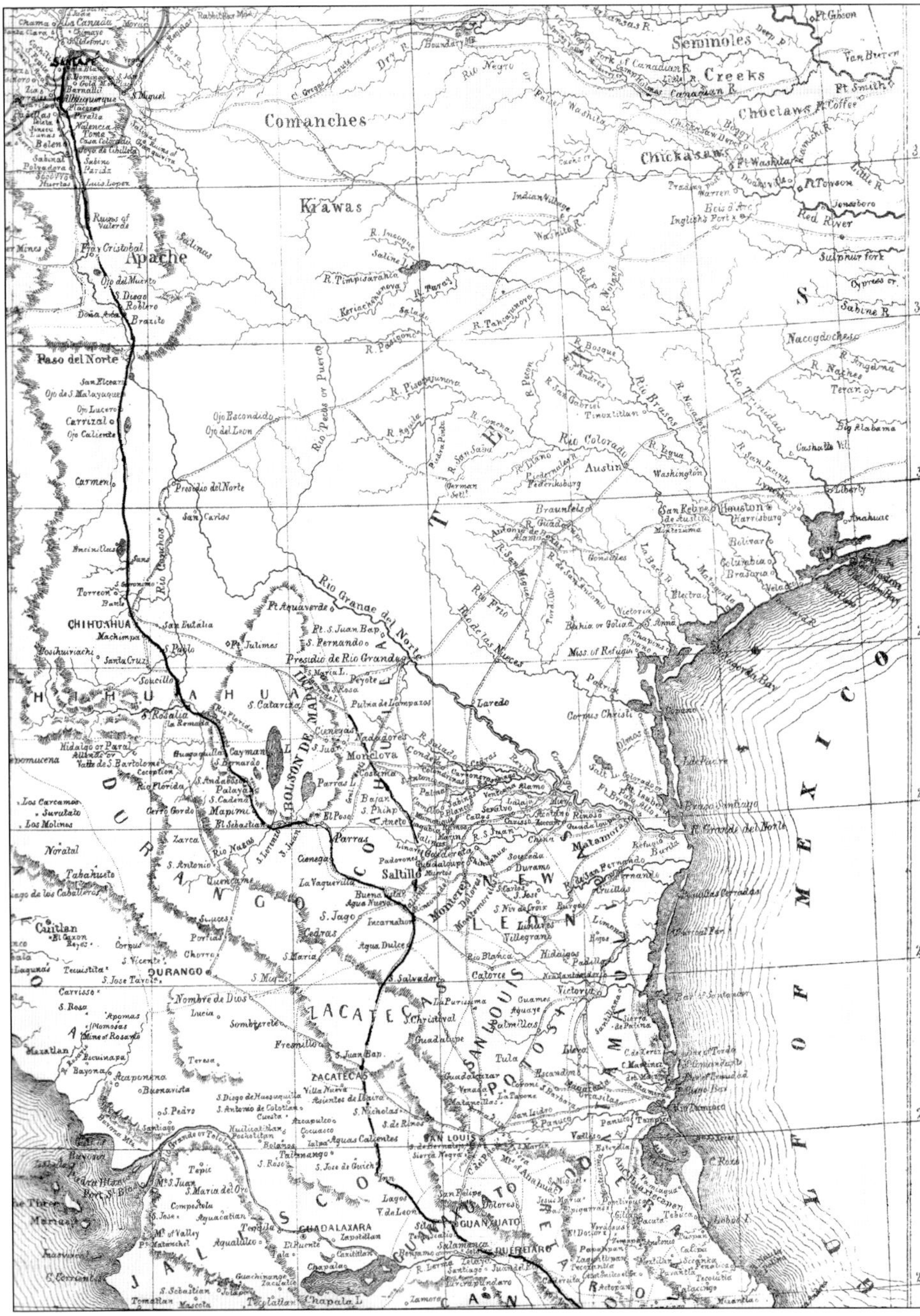

This map shows the extensive El Camino Real de Tierra Adentro from Mexico City to Santa Fe in New Mexico and its branches. The map was compiled by Jul S. Hutawa around 1850 and was printed in St. Louis, Missouri. It was included in the *Original Travel Diary of Lieutenant J.W. Abert*, edited by John Galving and published by John Howell Books in 1966. (Author's collection.)

On the Cover: Monuments to early Spanish explorers and pioneers along El Camino Real in New Mexico are seen here in the 1930s. Structures such as crosses lined with stones at the base acknowledged the important history and heritage of El Camino Real. (Author's collection.)

IMAGES
of America

El Camino Real de Tierra Adentro

Ray John de Aragón

ARCADIA
PUBLISHING

ISBN 978-1-4671-0679-5

Published by Arcadia Publishing
Charleston, South Carolina

Printed in the United States of America

Library of Congress Control Number: 2021936585

For all general information, please contact Arcadia Publishing:
Telephone 843-853-2070
Fax 843-853-0044
E-mail sales@arcadiapublishing.com
For customer service and orders:
Toll-Free 1-888-313-2665

Visit us on the Internet at www.arcadiapublishing.com

This book is proudly dedicated to our dauntless Spanish pioneering ancestors in Nuevo México who sacrificed, persevered, and survived while settling down with their families.

Contents

ACKNOWLEDGMENTS

Reflecting on my past, I was very fortunate to have attended Our Lady of Sorrows Catholic School in Las Vegas, New Mexico, during the 1950s. One of our textbooks during these early grades introduced us children to famous Spanish explorers such as Balboa, De Soto, Ponce de León, Cabeza de Vaca, and Coronado. As kids, we were taught about Spanish history and culture by the Sisters of Loretto. We learned to be proud of the heritage we have in the United States. These extremely knowledgeable nuns also taught us about other cultures and traditions that we were all told were a very important part of us.

A highlight from these years that I never forget was that we were all taken into a large room at the school. One of the sisters said we had to listen and learn. After she talked to us, as well as other sisters, we saw a movie about Hernán Cortez and the conquest of the Aztec empire. The primary focus of this motion picture was the appearance of Our Lady of Guadalupe. As children, we were awed and proud of that miraculous story of the Catholic Church.

In the following years, in public schools, our textbooks were *A Child's Story of New Mexico* by Ann Nolan Clark and Frances Carey, and *Discovering New Mexico* by Maude David Crosno and Charlie Scott Masters. We were introduced to the Spanish settlement, cowboy and horse culture, caravan trade, trail traders, and trappers, plus Indian and Spanish arts and the Penitentes. In middle school and high school, I studied El Cid and Miguel de Cervantes' *Don Quixote*.

These teachers, highlighting Spanish history and contributions to New Mexico and the United States, left an imprint on my life and career and are now acknowledged with this book.

All images are from the author's collection unless otherwise noted.

Foreword

El Camino Real de Tierra Adentro, the Royal Road of the Interior Land, is a historic route spanning 1,500 miles from Ohkay Owingeh Pueblo in New Mexico to Mexico City. Although it was widely used and expanded by Spanish colonizers at the end of the 16th century, there is ample evidence that the route was used by indigenous peoples for centuries earlier. In northern New Mexico, at the site of Chaco Canyon where the Anasazi peoples lived, macaw and other types of parrot feathers were discovered. In Mexico at various sites, artifacts were found with turquoise that has been established to have provenance in New Mexico. The resulting conclusions indicate that there was trade between the indigenous empires in the precolonial period and later. With the arrival of the Spanish colonizers, the road was expanded and more widely used.

Caravans and traders would leave northern New Mexico for points south in August or September to avoid inclement weather in the north and take advantage of the cooler weather in the south as they traveled through difficult and treacherous lands. La Jornada del Muerto, "The Journey of the Dead Man," was a particularly difficult area of arid desert, especially with the kind of entourage that was required for traveling at that time.

Ray John de Aragon is a consummate historian of the Spanish presence in New Mexico. His work on the history of the region, its people, and cultural traditions has served many in acquiring knowledge about what is perhaps the most significant early history of the United States.

—Stuart A. Ashman

Stuart Ashman is a former executive director of the New Mexico Museum of Art. He was named executive director of the Museum of Spanish Colonial Art in Santa Fe. Ashman was later appointed secretary of the Office of Cultural Affairs (2003–2010). During this time, he guided the establishment of the El Camino Real International Heritage Center and accompanying exhibits dealing with the rich history of the Spanish in New Mexico and their impact on the United States.

Introduction

The wives, children, and other relations of the soldiers comprised a significant, if uncertain, number of the expedition's colonists. . . . Juan Pérez de Bustillo was accompanied by his wife, seven daughters, and two grown sons . . . none of the females being identified by name. . . . The women were generally ignored throughout.

—Marc Simmons

Let sorrow be renewed. Let hoarse accents of weeping come with funeral sorrow.

—Gaspar Pérez de Villagrá, 1610.

Villagrá published his epic poem *Historia de la Nueva Mexico* in 1610, around the same time Miguel de Cervantes released his novel *Don Quixote de la Mancha* in Spain. Villagrá, in his monumental work, poetically recreated the colonizing expedition of 1598 with profound words for the world and future generations to read. It is recognized as a major literary work that relates the *jornada*, or journey, on what would become El Camino Real with the blood, sweat, tears, struggles, and sufferings of the Spanish pioneers who chose to leave their beloved Spain in search of opportunities and a better way of life for themselves and their families.

El Camino Real de Tierra Adentro is the oldest thoroughfare in the United States.

The ancient route extended for 1,500 miles and connected Mexico City with Santa Fe, the capital city of the northern frontier of New Spain. This highly significant road was extensively used for 300 years from the mid-16th century to the 19th century. It was recognized as a UNESCO world heritage site in Mexico City, where the road originated. Parts of the road followed Pueblo Indian trails that connected New Mexico with Mesoamerica. The Indians traded clay pots, salt, beans, squash, corn, chili peppers, medicinal plants, and other commodities. El Camino Real served as the cultural, social, and religious network of New Mexico.

New Mexico celebrated El Camino Real during the 400th centennial in 1998 with ceremonies and festivities in Albuquerque, including political speeches, lectures, entertainment, and visual and literary arts throughout the city and at the Albuquerque Convention Center. In 2000, this ancient road was officially designated a national historic trail. The legacy of the road includes a living history museum, the El Camino Real de Tierra Adentro Charter School, and the El Camino Real International Heritage Center, which continues to preserve the road's very important history.

One

Genesis of El Camino Real

It can be said with a great degree of certainty that El Camino Real de Tierra Adentro from Mexico City to Santa Fe in New Mexico began as a prehistoric Indian trail. For hundreds if not thousands of years, Native Americans lived, traveled, farmed, and traded along the tributaries of the Rio Grande. The river itself provided a lifeline for the people. A network of paths and trails led the Indians to other areas. Places for hunting, gathering, and religious rituals and ceremonies were common. Pueblo and Plains Indians, for example, traded a variety of goods and foods. Buffalo and deerskins and furs were bartered for and traded. Wood and stone implements and weapons for hunting were favored. Baskets, clay pots, weavings, berries, nuts, jerky, corn, and medicinal plants were also in high demand. Moccasins and other items made of leather, both for daily wear and cultural observance, were prized as well. However, this early state of development was about to change dramatically.

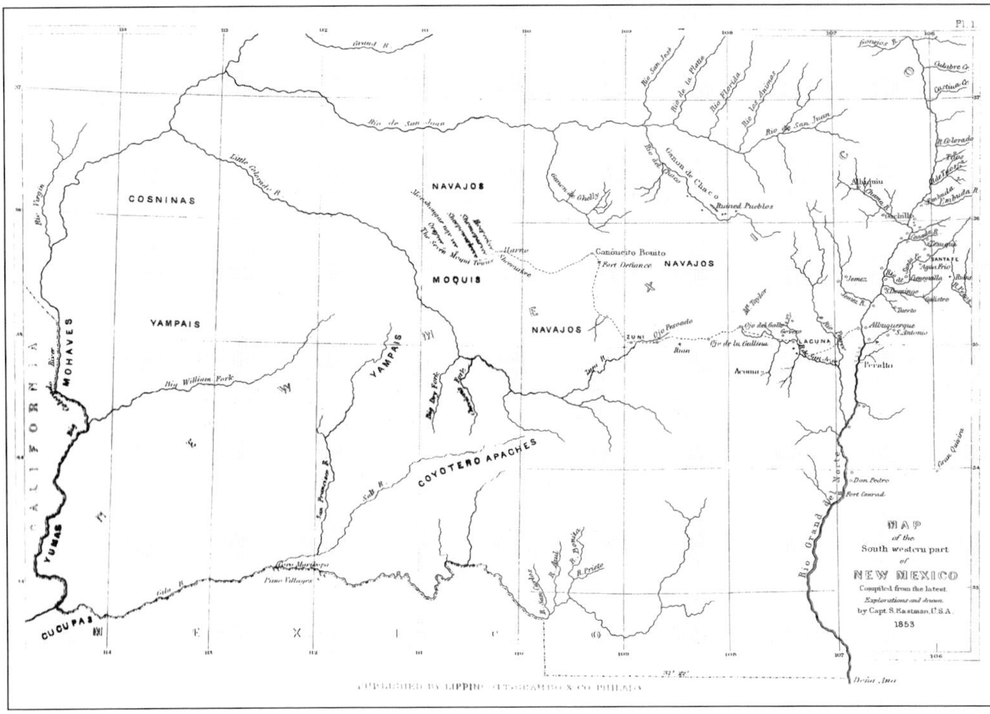

This map was published in 1853 by Lippincott, Grambo, and Company of Philadelphia from a drawing by Capt. S. Eastman of the US Army. He located all of the Indian-held lands southwest of the Spanish capital city of Santa Fe. Indians from these lands traded on what would eventually be known as El Camino Real. These lands were taken over by the US government after 1846.

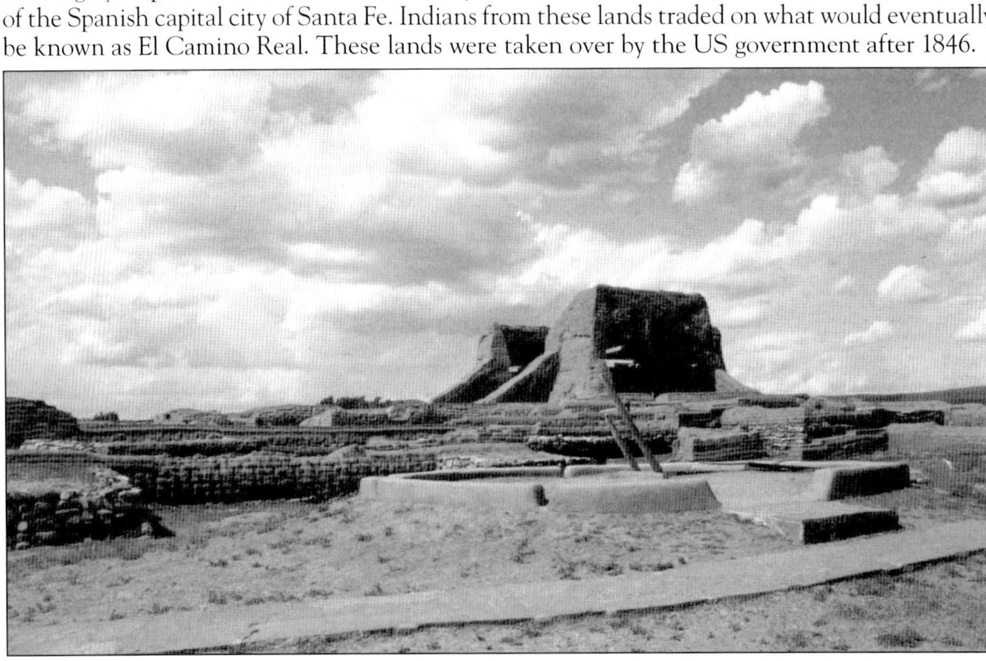

Pecos National Monument near Santa Fe is a major landmark that symbolizes La Entrada, the entry of Spanish explorers and missionaries into New Mexico. The extensive ruins are the site of a centuries-old Indian settlement and a church built in the 17th century. Spanish settlers established a community a few miles from here. (Photograph by Lucia de Aragon.)

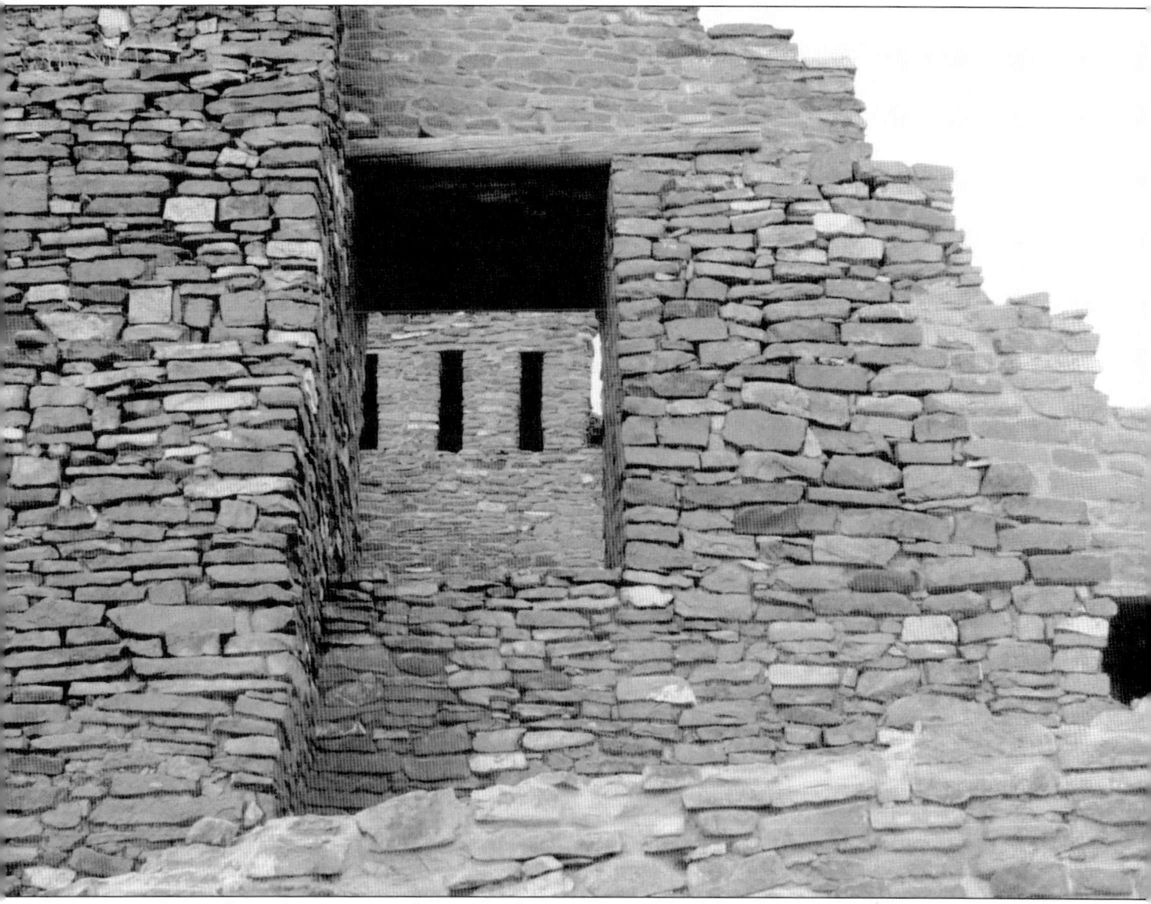

These ruins of the Abo mission church form a part of the Salinas Pueblo Missions National Monument west of Mountainair, New Mexico. Abo is one of three Indian pueblos that occupied the area; the others are Quarai and Gran Quivira. The Mogollon and later Anasazi cultures established themselves in the region. They set up a major trading center and interacted with other Indian villages along the Rio Grande. They also traded with the Plains Indians. Spanish explorers first encountered these pueblos in 1581. By 1623, the first mission church was being constructed at Abo. This original church was later enlarged and completed by 1658, when several improvements to the church and grounds were done. The area was plagued by drought, starvation, and disease. The missions and pueblo ruins were recognized as a national historic landmark in 1962.

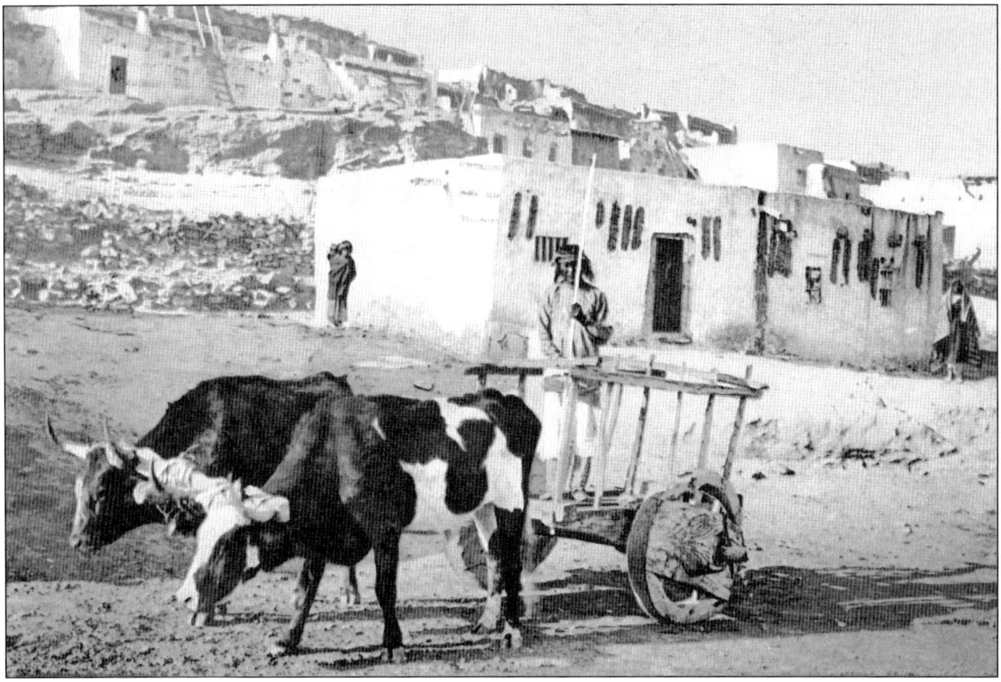

Laguna is the largest Keresan Indian pueblo and dates to 1300. It is 45 miles west of Albuquerque. The San Jose de la Laguna mission church at the pueblo dates to 1699. Native Americans adapted to new modes of transportation after the Spanish arrived. This real-photo postcard, printed by the Detroit Publishing Company around 1910, shows a Spanish cart or *carreta*.

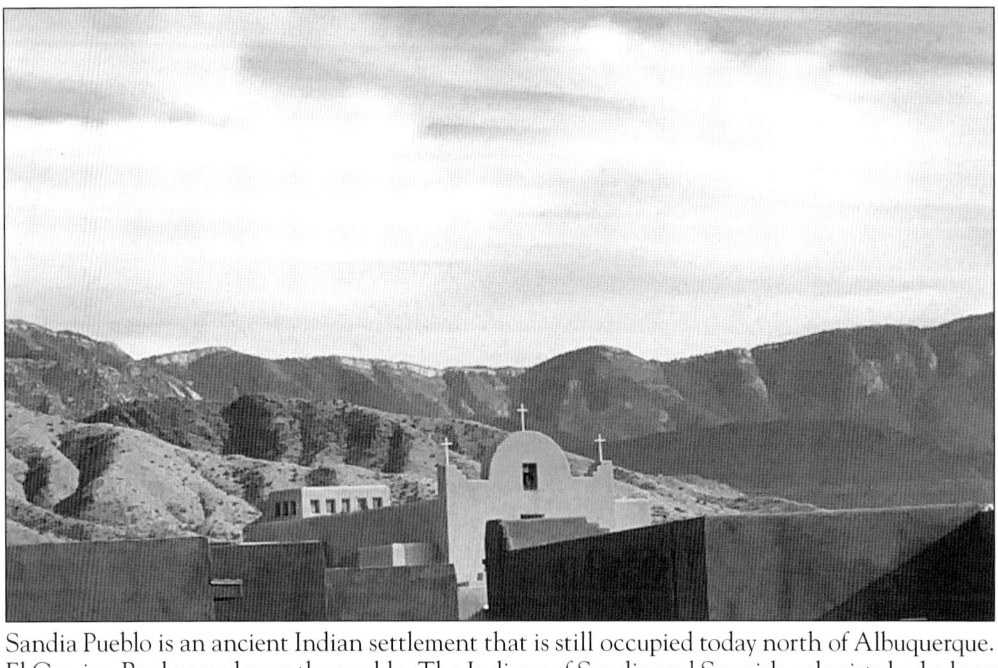

Sandia Pueblo is an ancient Indian settlement that is still occupied today north of Albuquerque. El Camino Real passed near the pueblo. The Indians of Sandia and Spanish colonists had a long history of interaction and trade. The rich, fertile valley near the pueblo was and is suitable for agriculture, and farm products were sold or traded. (Photograph by Rosa Maria Calles.)

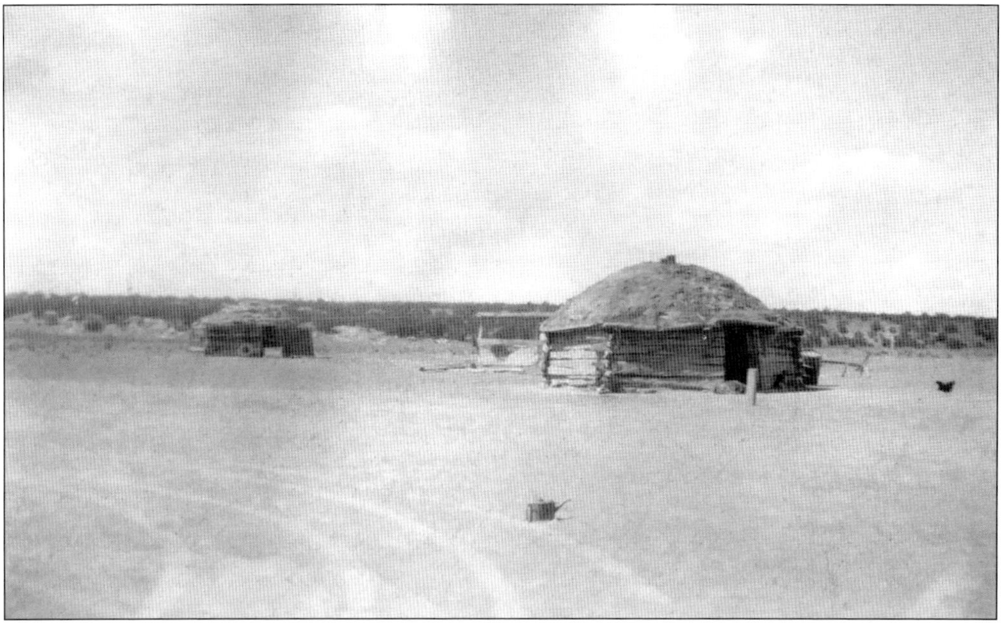

Hogans were Navajo dwellings built with logs and mud. The ones pictured here around 1935 were located near Gallup, New Mexico. After the Indian wars in the 19th century, the American cavalry led remaining Navajo on the Long Walk to a reservation through bitter heat and cold. Many died from starvation, thirst, and disease while walking through areas such as La Jornada del Muerto, dreaded by travelers on El Camino Real.

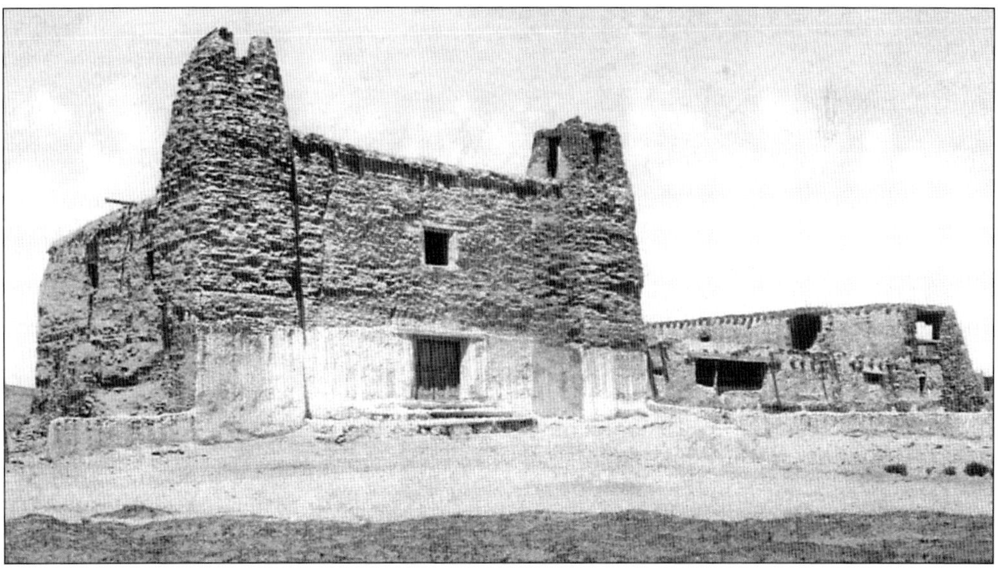

This real-photo postcard of the Acoma Pueblo Spanish mission church, built during the 17th century, was taken about 1906. This deteriorating centuries-old church was lovingly restored by Acoma Pueblo Indians. These Indians acknowledged a strong connection between themselves, Spanish culture, and Catholic beliefs. However, Acoma Indians helped to precipitate the Pueblo Indian Revolt, which took place in 1680. Other Indian pueblos have also restored their Spanish mission churches.

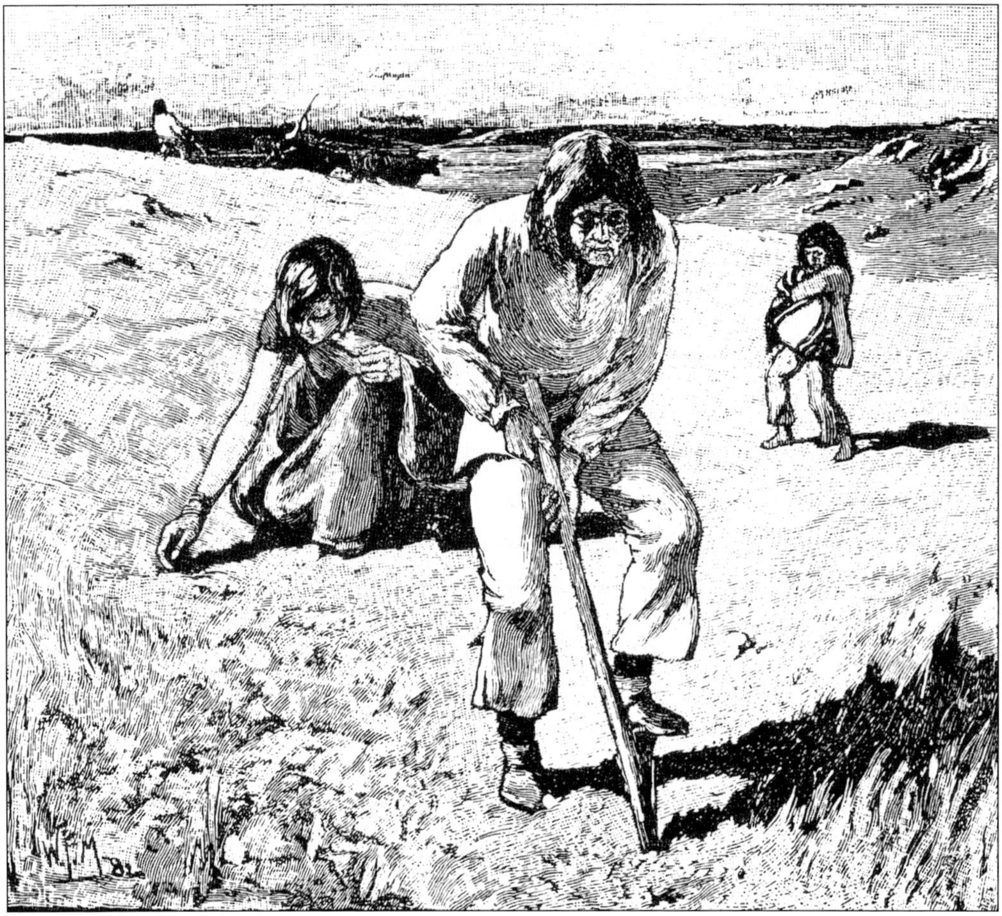

Native Americans in New Mexico and the Southwest prior to the arrival of the Spanish had very crude methods of agriculture and transporting goods. They either walked, carrying baskets on their backs, or used a travois, a rough contraption made with long trailing tree branches. These travois were either pulled by dogs or women. The men had to protect the caravan or hunt game. This was a method used for centuries. Indians readily adapted to the use of mules, horses, and oxcarts with the arrival of the Spanish. Natives became so adept at horseback riding that they often rode bareback while accompanying the wagons. This illustration from an 1882 *Century Magazine* issue shows seed planting.

A Comanche chief is pictured around 1890. Comanches traded with a group of Spanish who became known in New Mexico as "Comancheros," those who traded with Comanche Indians. Comancheros were instrumental to the survival of the colony, securing vital goods to supplement their own. Most often, the Comanches wanted iron implements and iron arrowheads, plus tools, iron tomahawks, and other items used for hunting and protection.

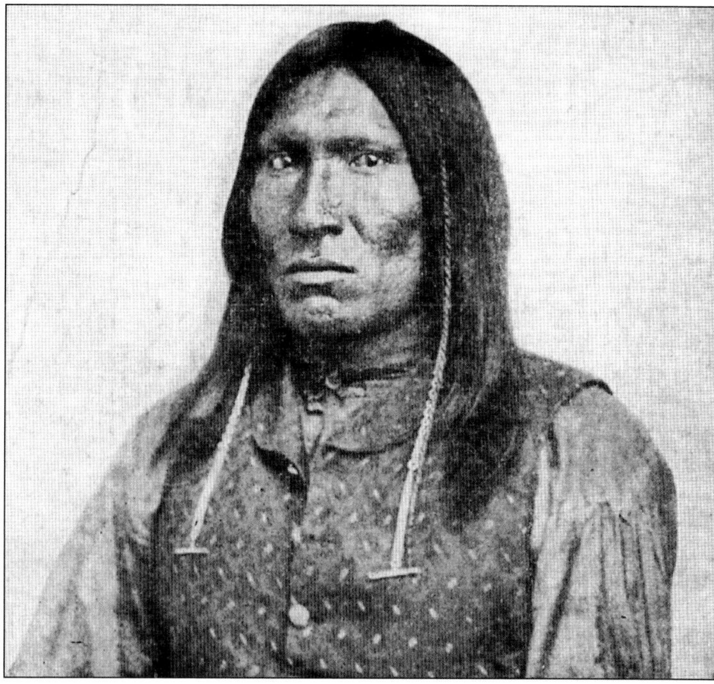

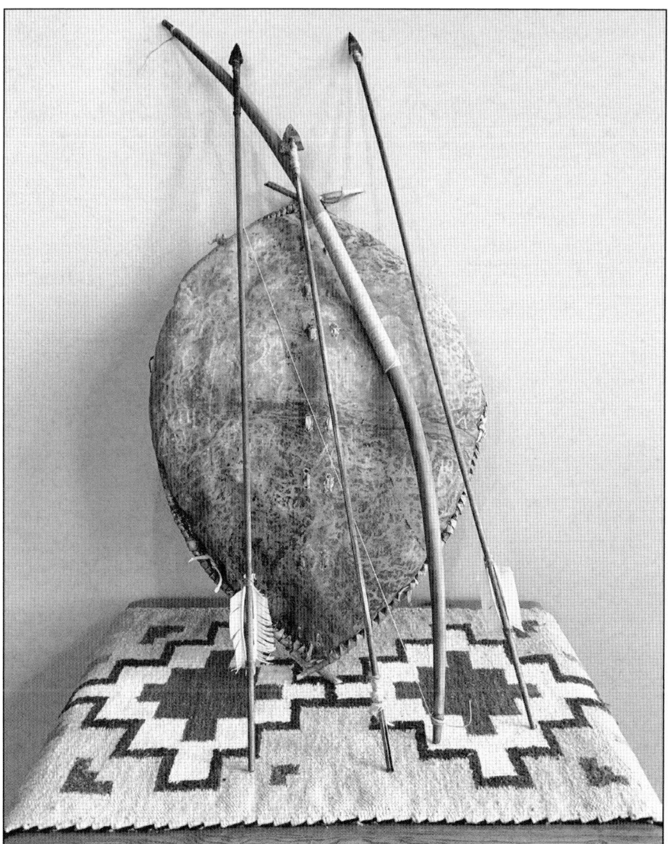

One of these Comanche arrows has an iron point. Spanish colonial blacksmiths produced iron points for arrows that became popular with the Indians, who previously used flint arrowheads. The Comanches were nomadic Indians who followed buffalo herds and other game, which they often traded. Comanches attended trade fairs in Spanish villages such as Taos during peaceful times.

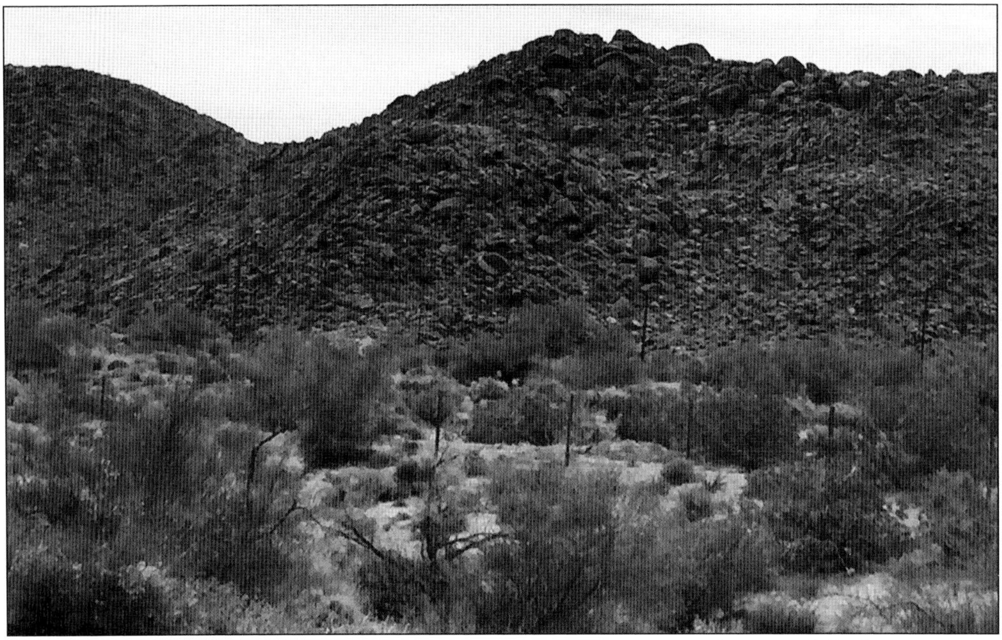

La Jornada del Muerto (Journey of the Dead Man) is a continuous arid area with little vegetation. This was the most dangerous and lengthy region experienced by travelers on El Camino Real. Added to the danger of traveling through here was the threat of sudden Indian attacks. When someone died, the remains were buried and marked with a cross. (Photograph by Rosa Maria Calles.)

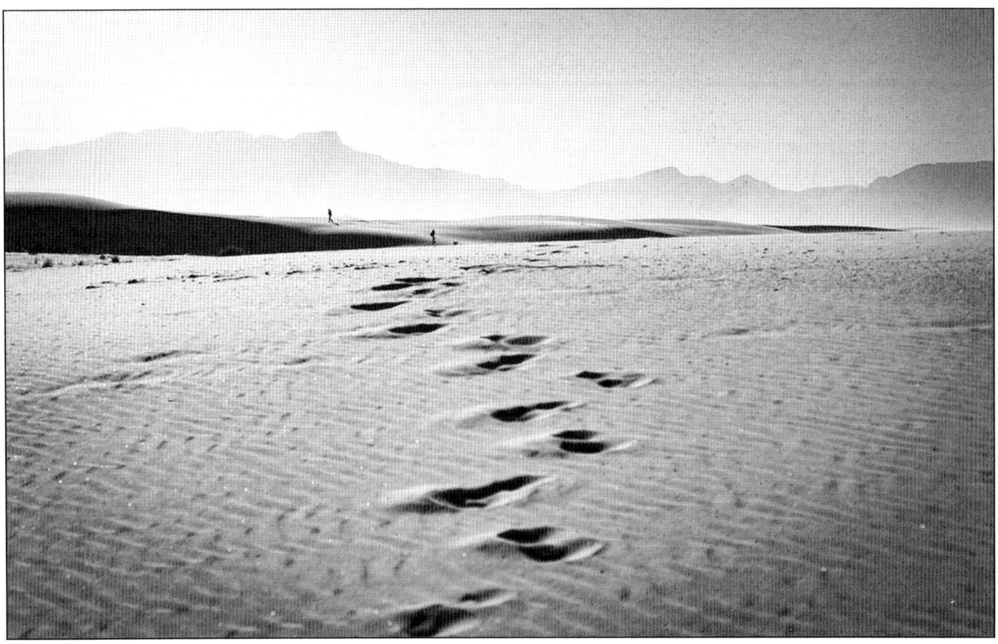

White Sands National Monument is a vast area of white gypsum. Paleoindians hunted and gathered in this area. Their projectile points have been discovered along with a trackway of footprints dating back to at least 11,700 years ago. Approximately 700 years ago, Apache hunters and gatherers established themselves in the region. This area is associated with various Spanish explorers. (Photograph by Ramon Juan Carlos de Aragon.)

Two

Spanish Explorers, Settlers, and a Royal Road

Interest in a vast unknown territory that would eventually be called New Mexico began at an early date. There were nearly 20 explorations of the land sponsored by the Spanish government and church. One of the earliest, and considered the most important, was the Francisco Vásquez de Coronado expedition of 1540–1542. Historians credit him with pioneering a route to and through New Mexico along the Rio Grande. This large party of Spanish soldiers, accompanied by some of their wives, discovered many multistoried Indian pueblo settlements along the way. One was Kuaua Pueblo west of Albuquerque, which is now a national historic monument called Coronado National Memorial.

Don Juan de Oñate y Salazar is credited as the trailblazer and father of El Camino Real de Tierra Adentro. He was the first governor of New Mexico in 1598 and led an indomitable group of hundreds of pioneering settlers with many soldiers, Franciscan friars, and families of men, women, and children. They took along approximately 83 loaded wagons of personal belongings and provisions to establish a colony. They also had around 7,000 head of cattle, flocks of sheep, horses, fruit tree saplings, seeds, and flower bulbs. This group founded the capital city of La Villa Real de la Santa Fe de San Francisco de Asís, the Royal City of the Holy Faith of St. Francis of Assisi. In 1680, a Pueblo Indian revolt against the Spanish settlers took place. This was the second revolt by Native Americans against Europeans in North America. The first was a massive revolt by various tribes against the English on the East Coast in 1675.

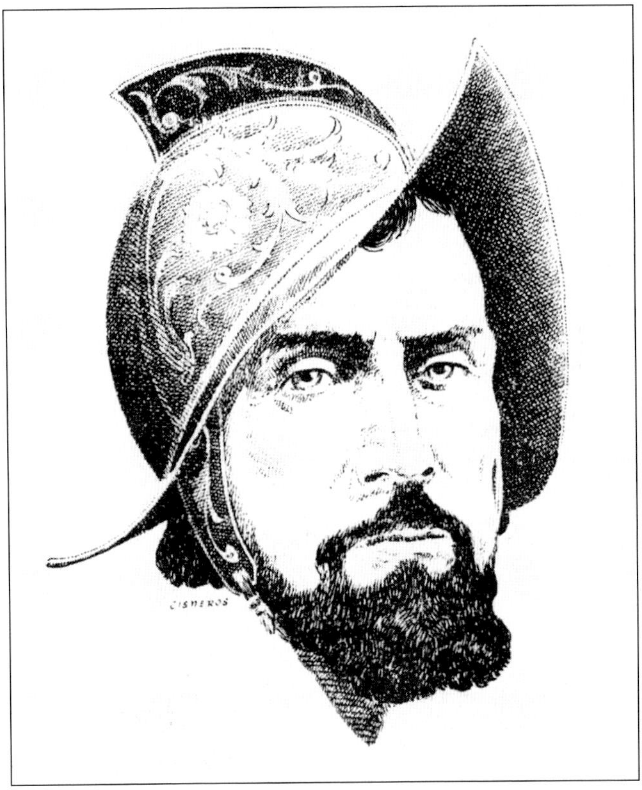

Don Juan de Oñate y Salazar, the colonizer of New Mexico, is the recognized father of El Camino Real. He primarily used his own wealth to finance a massive settlement on the northern frontier of La Nueva España for the Spanish crown. Oñate succeeded in convincing Spanish families to resettle and begin a new colony. (Courtesy of José Cisneros.)

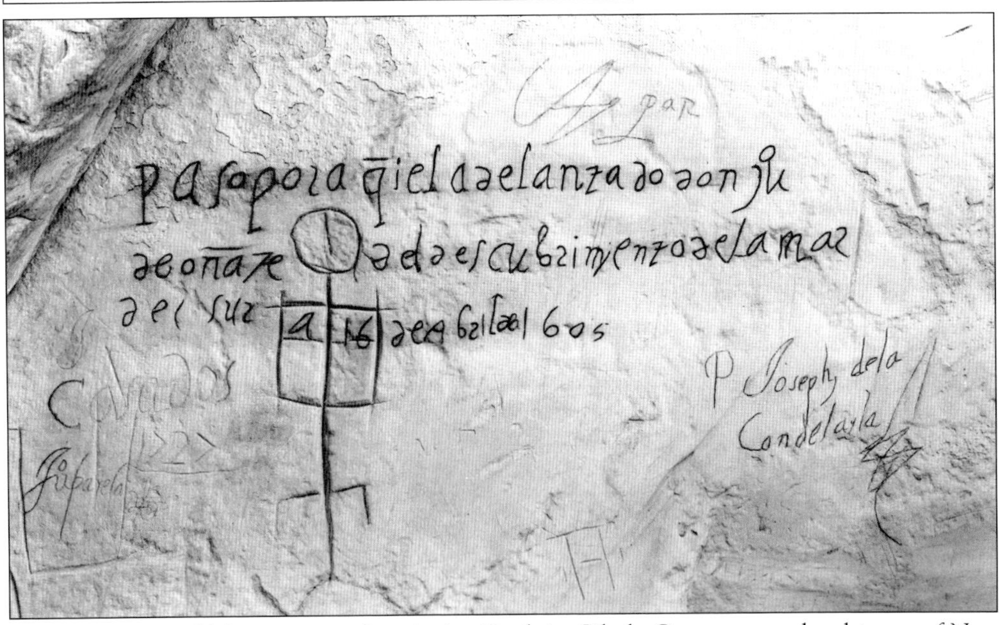

El Morro National Monument or Inscription Rock in Cibola County records a history of New Mexico. The area preserves the remains of a prehistoric pueblo that sits atop a sandstone promontory. Ancient petroglyphs are nearby. At a spring-fed pool of water at the base, Spanish and American explorers and travelers carved historic inscriptions. Gov. Don Juan de Oñate left this engraved memorial in 1605.

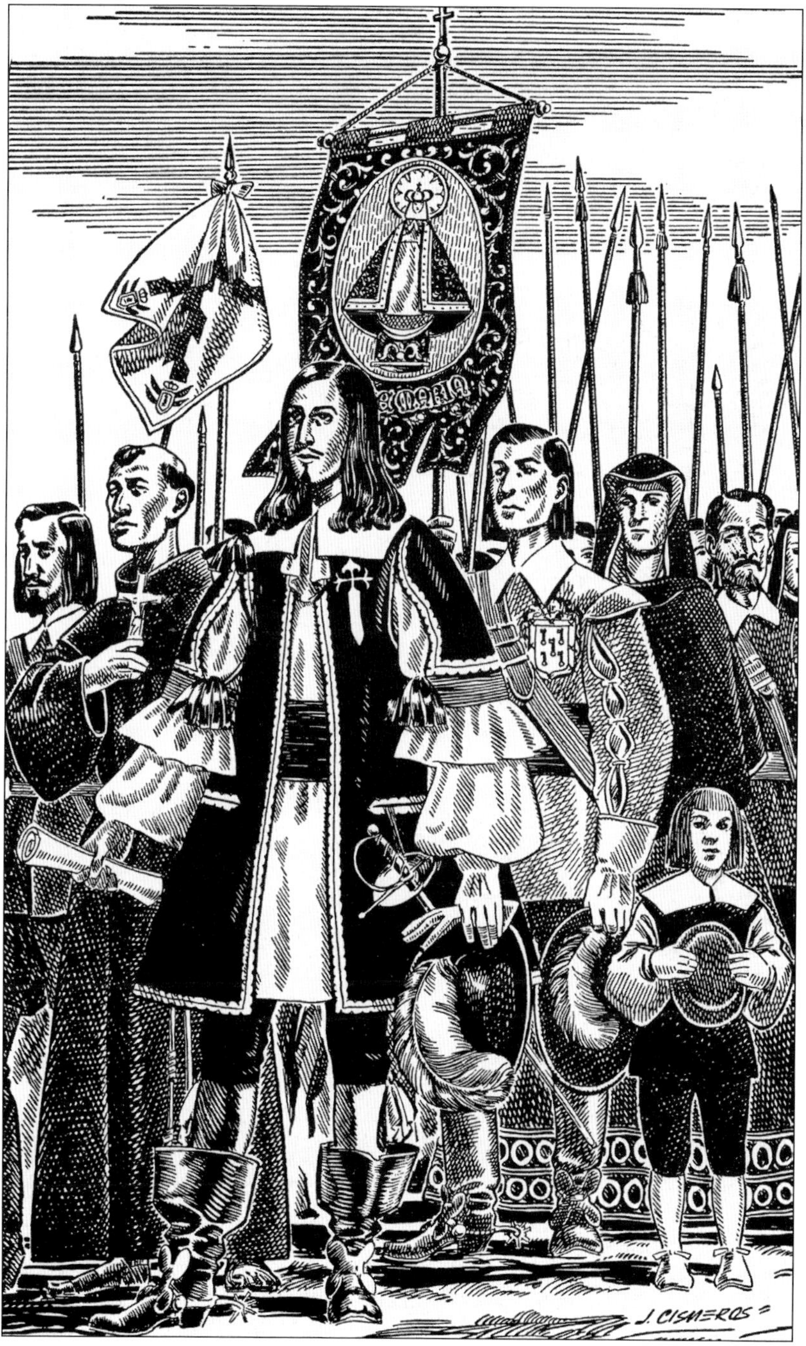

Gov. Don Diego de Vargas and the Spanish colonists are shown entering Santa Fe in 1692. The artist captured the vibrance and feel of this historic event by recreating the styles of dress, Spanish banners with one representing the mother of Christ, and other details he spent countless hours researching. De Vargas is credited with the peaceful reconquest of New Mexico. After the Pueblo Indian Revolt of 1680 and the massacre of many Spanish colonists, priests, and Indian supporters, those remaining escaped to El Paso del Norte. De Vargas succeeded in returning 12 years later. His leadership led to the success of the colony for Indians and settlers. (Courtesy of José Cisneros.)

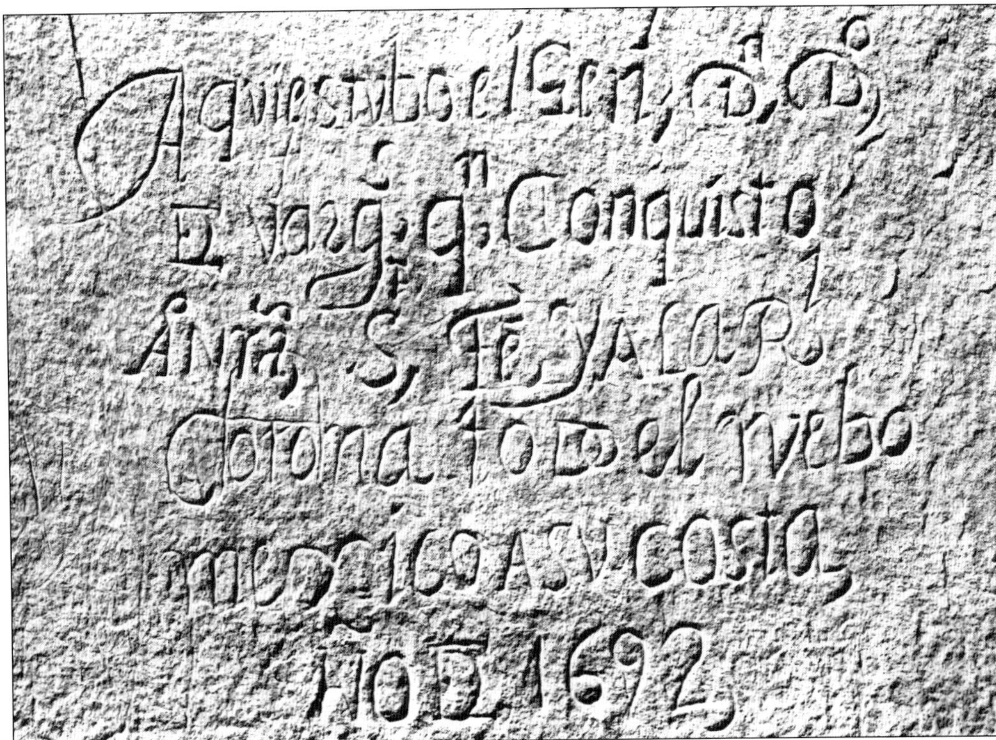

This inscription by Gov. Don Diego de Vargas at El Morro National Monument is dated 1692. The Native Americans were first to make inscriptions on the massive rock with petroglyphs and drawings. Others, including the first Spanish leaders, added their names and the dates they passed through. A few included several other details on this historical record.

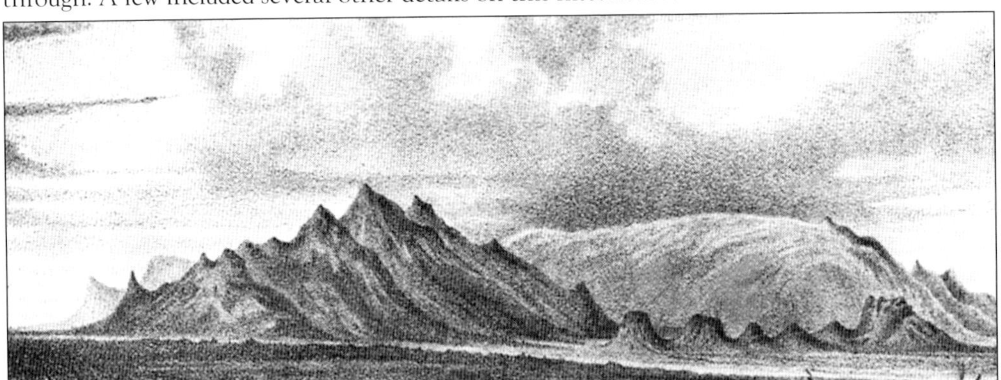

This is a very early engraving of El Camino Real de Tierra Adentro, possibly near the Organ Mountains by Las Cruces, around 1839–1840. A colonial carreta is being pulled by oxen. The man at left carries an ox goad. Another traveler rides on the wagon. A cross at left graphically displays the dangers encountered on the trail.

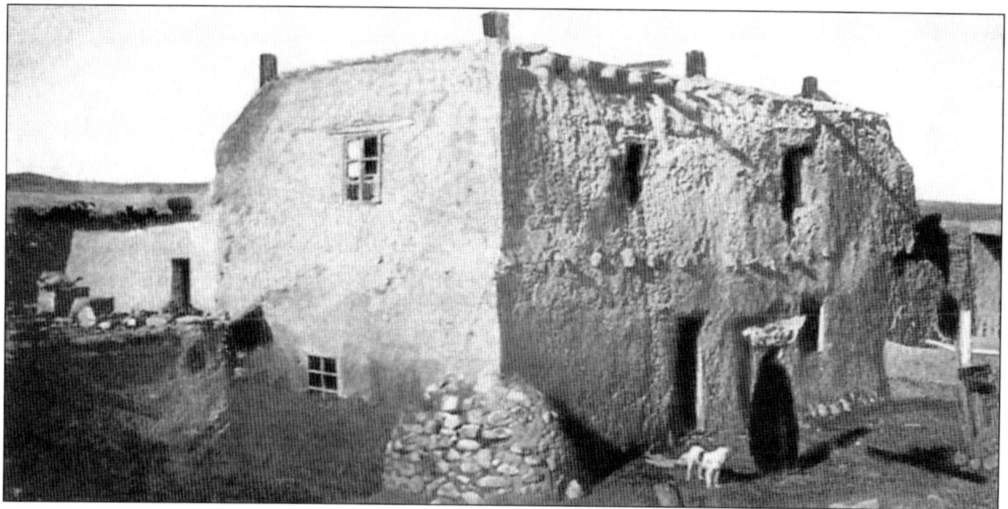

The oldest surviving house in the United States is on De Vargas Street in Santa Fe. It was built by the Indians in the 13th century. At one point, the building housed Spanish governors and government officials. The dwelling stands at what would be recognized as the end of El Camino Real in an area that was known as El Barrio de Analco, the District of Analco.

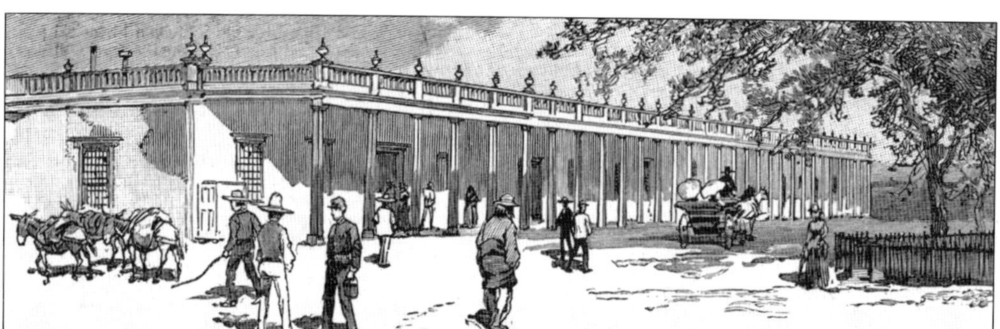

The Palace of the Governors in Santa Fe is the oldest government building continuously used in the United States. It was built around 1610 and served the Spanish, Mexican, and American administrations of the territory of New Mexico. It was controlled by the Confederates for a short time during the Civil War. Now it houses an extensive museum and a gift shop.

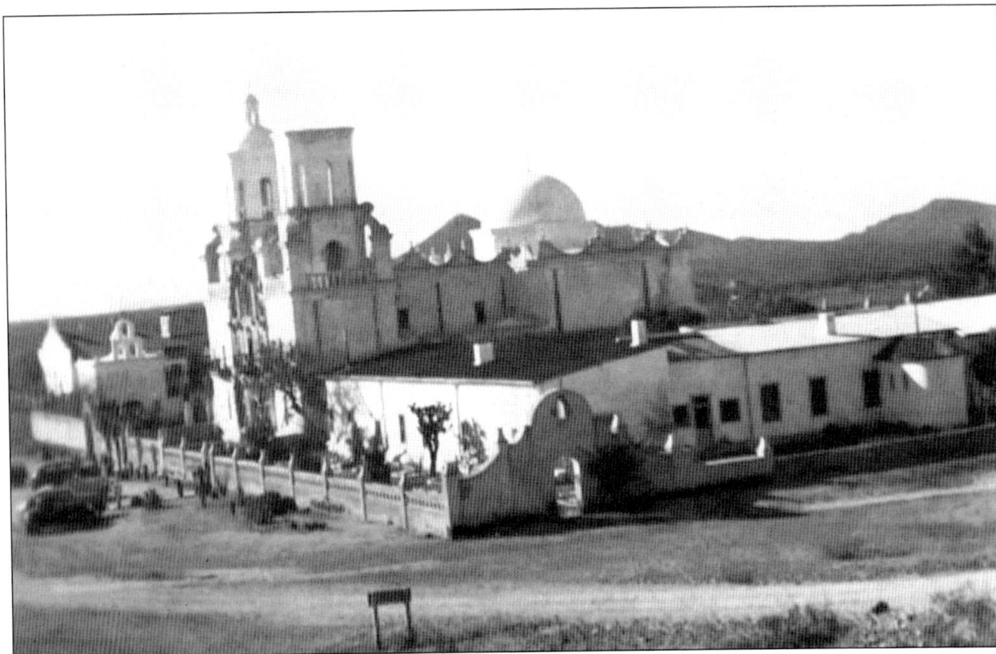

There were scattered settlements on El Camino Real from Mexico City to Santa Fe. Some of these communities were among the oldest founded in North America. Included were San Luis Potosi, Zacatecas, and Queretaro in Mexico. These Spanish colonial centers, such as the one pictured, provided many of the goods that were necessary to sustain the frontier colony of New Mexico. Zacatecas, for example, shipped silver to the colony.

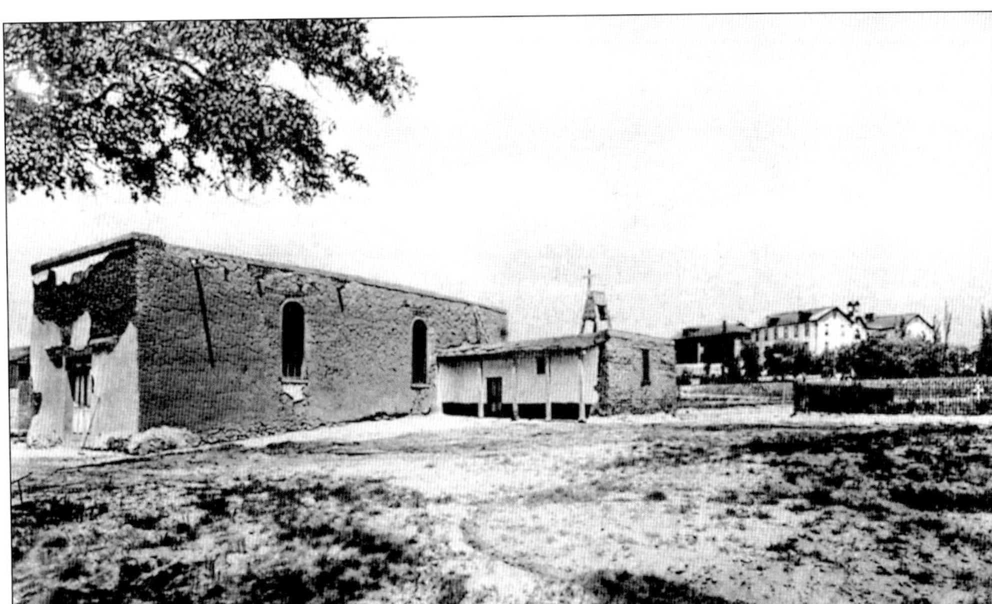

A section of Santa Fe is pictured as it appeared at the beginning of the 20th century. El Camino Real leads up to this area. Rosario Chapel, built in the early 19th century, is seen here. It was built on the site where Don Diego de Vargas presumably honored the Virgin Mary in 1692 for a peaceful reconquest of the territory.

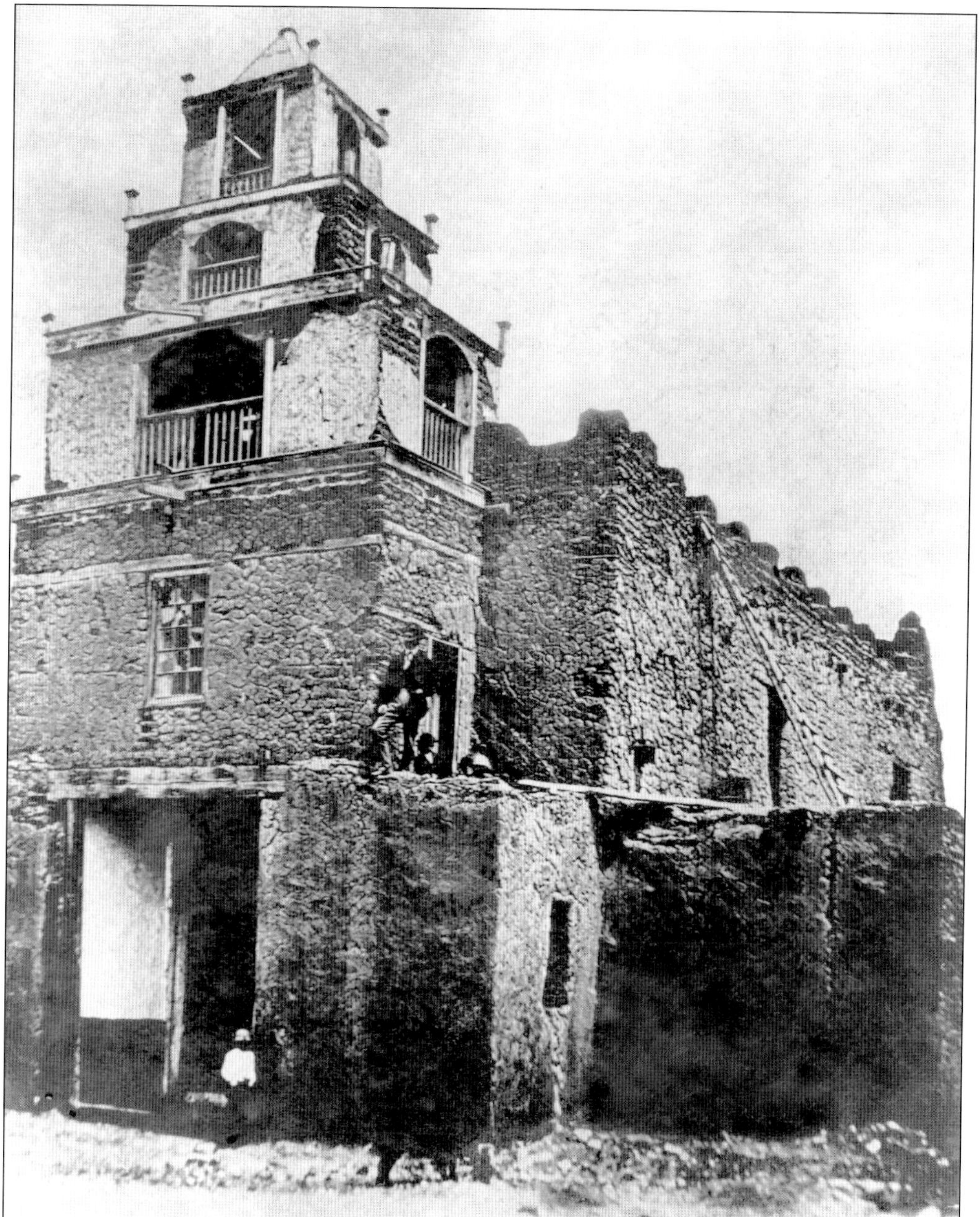

This c. 1870 photograph shows the San Miguel Church in Santa Fe. It is in El Barrio de Analco Historic District. It was the first church built by the colonists, around 1610. Natives, including Tlaxcalan, who accompanied the Spanish in 1598 lived in this area and helped with the construction. It was built with adobe. The Spanish colonists used this church across from the Santa Fe River as their parish until another, larger church was built. San Miguel experienced some damage during the Pueblo Indian Revolt of 1680. Governor de Vargas initiated repairs in 1693. After that, the San Miguel Church went through various restorations. It is a national historic landmark and is considered the oldest church in the United States.

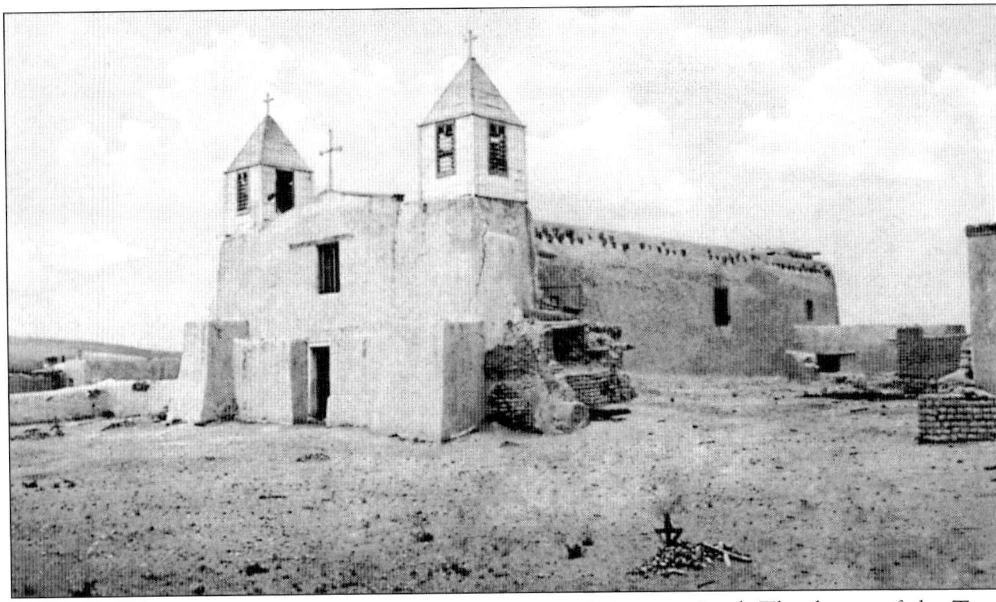

Isleta Pueblo is 13 miles south of Albuquerque along El Camino Real. This home of the Tiwa tribe was established in 1200. The Spanish mission of San Agustín de la Isleta was built here in 1629–1630. Isleta Indians sold what they produced. It was an important stop on the Royal Road. This real-photo postcard shows the church and other buildings at Isleta.

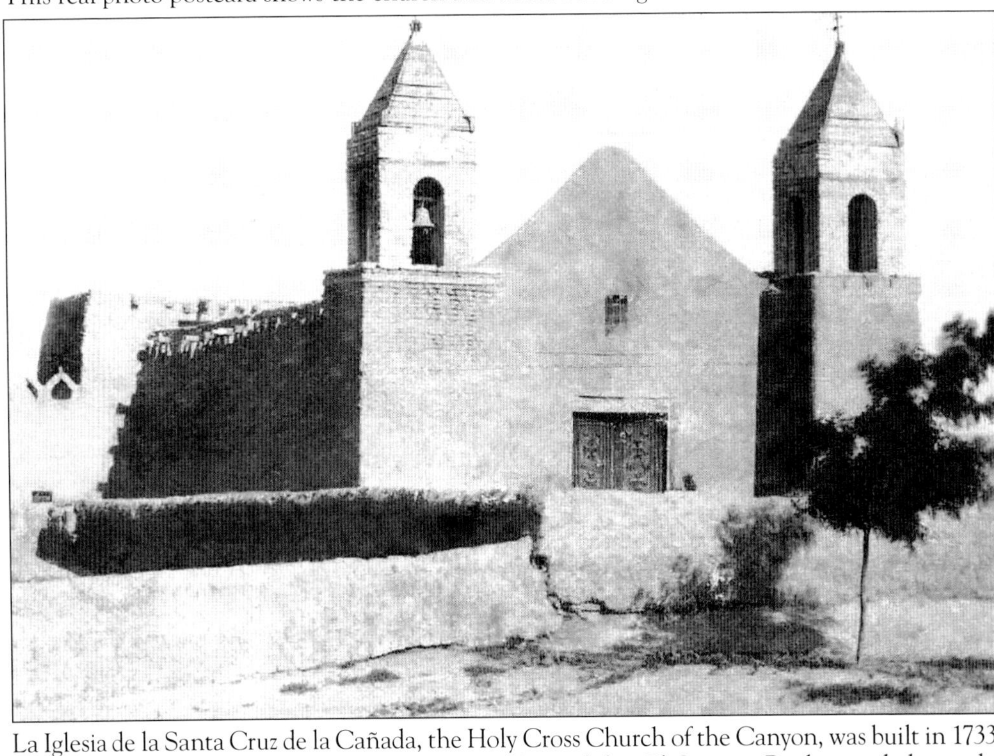

La Iglesia de la Santa Cruz de la Cañada, the Holy Cross Church of the Canyon, was built in 1733. During the earliest period of colonization, it can be said that El Camino Real extended past the area of this church and plaza to the first Spanish settlement of New Mexico at La Villa de San Gabriel. The area of San Gabriel was occupied until 1617.

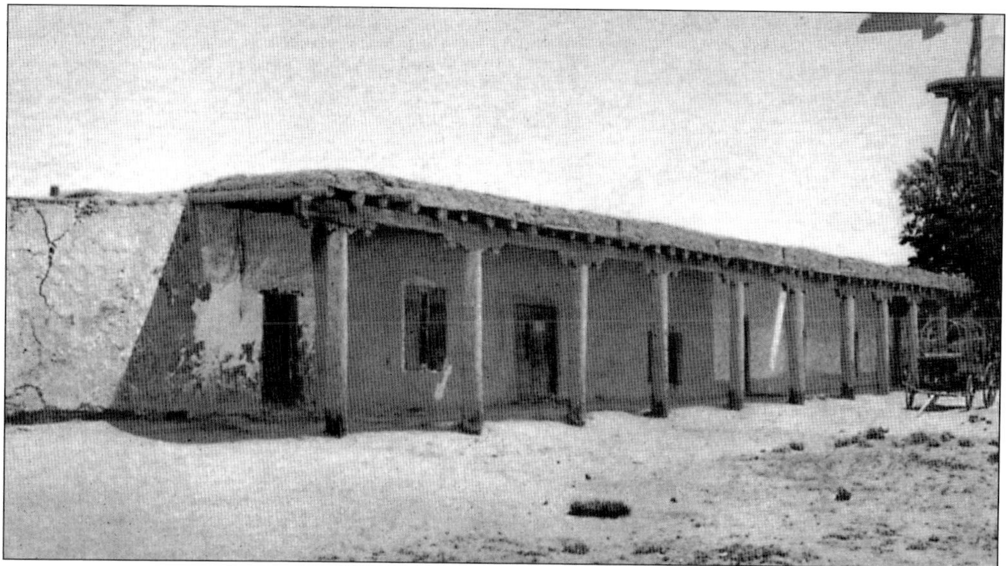

This adobe hacienda at the Old Town Plaza in Albuquerque was built in the early 18th century. It is thought that this property once belonged to Gov. Manuel Armijo's family and later served American military officers during the Civil War. The building also served as a headquarters for Confederate forces for a short time and may have served as Gen. Henry Sibley's offices.

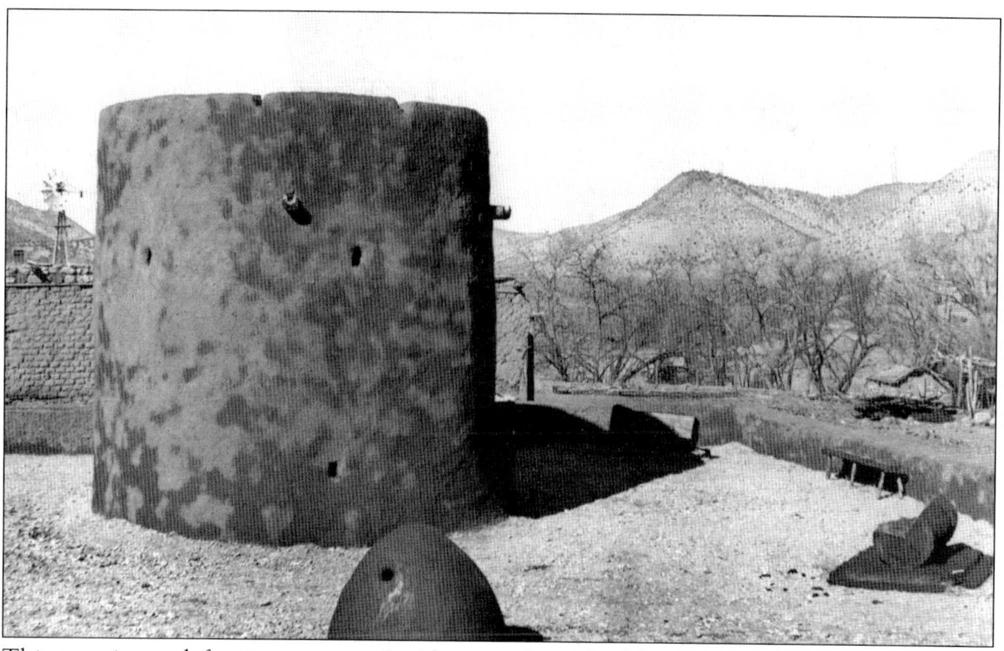

This *torreón*, or defensive tower, at La Placita in Lincoln, New Mexico, has been restored. It is an excellent example of a fortified building erected by Spanish settlers around New Mexico during the colonial period. These buildings were entered through an opening on the roof. Ladders could be pulled up once people were inside during attacks. A beehive oven used for baking bread is nearby.

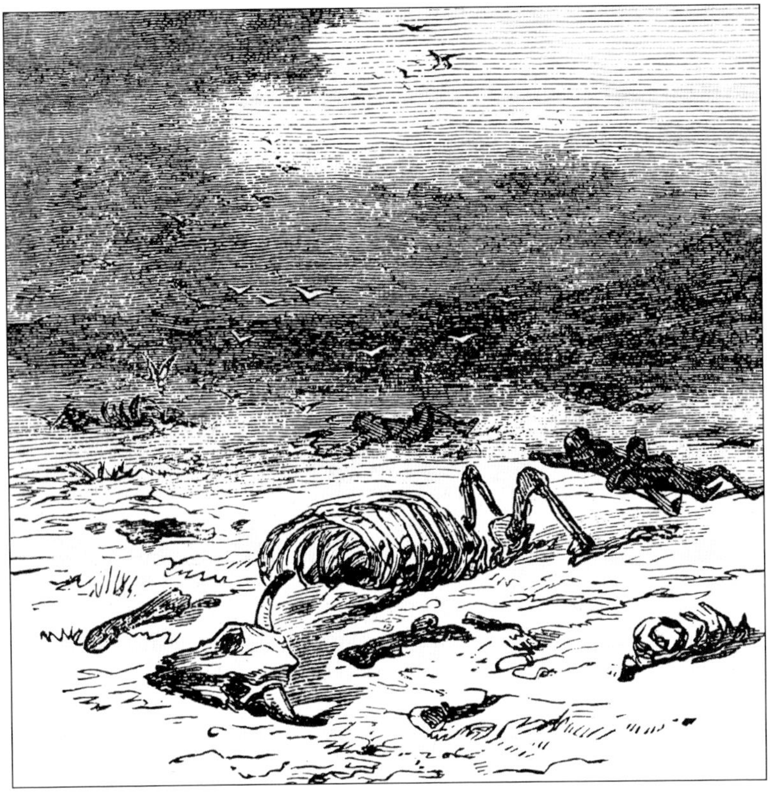

This depiction of La Jornada del Muerto is from *Beyond the Mississippi* by Albert Richardson, published in 1867. Some of the travelers on El Camino Real and their livestock perished here. The artist shows a very graphic representation of remains along the trail, including human remains.

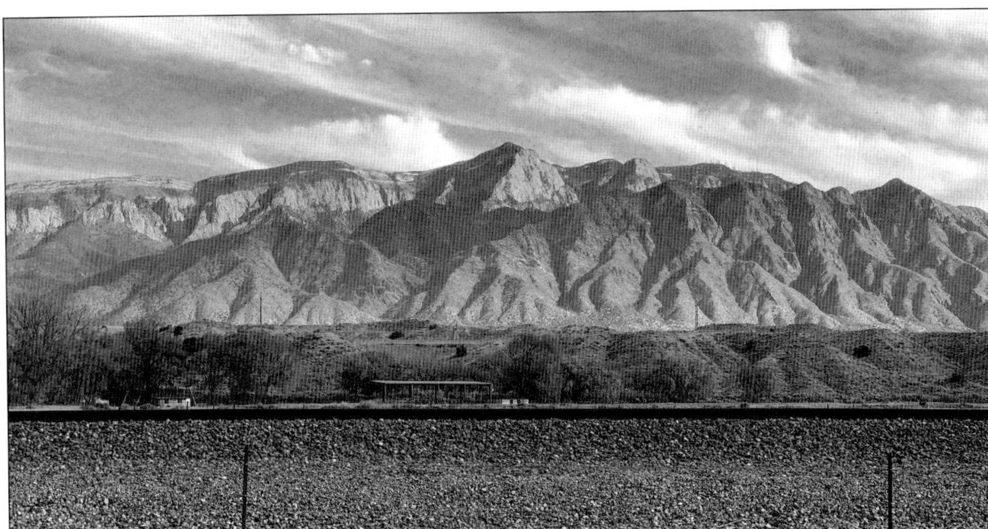

The Sandia mountain range near Albuquerque was a natural landmark and a welcome sight for travelers on El Camino Real. This marked a farther journey of about 60 miles for those traveling from the south to the capital city of Santa Fe. The mountains were probably named *sandia*, watermelon, due to their color as seen from a distance. (Photograph by Rosa Maria Calles.)

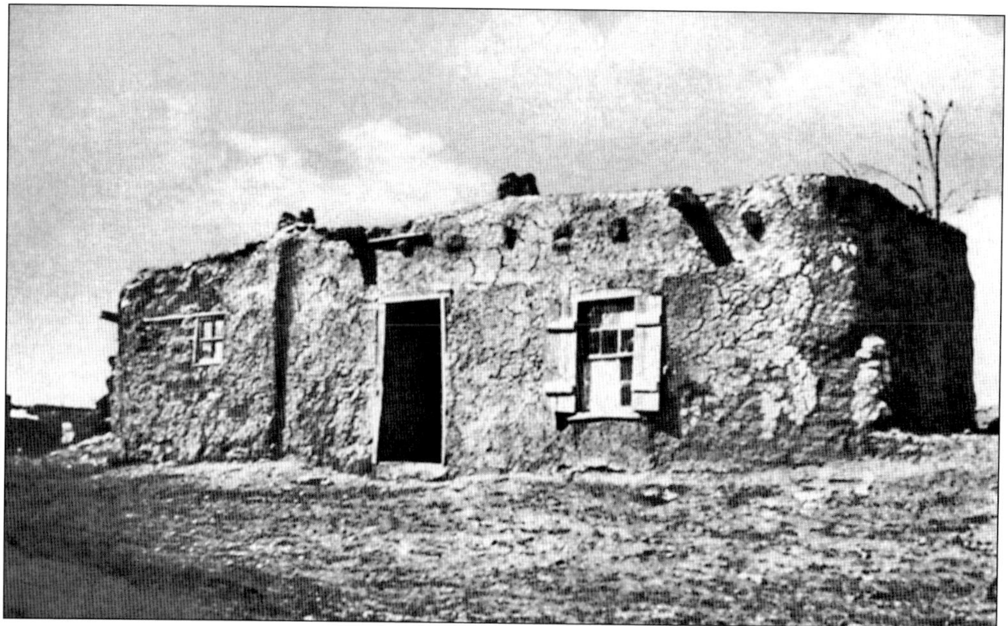

An early photographer captured this 18th-century adobe structure at the beginning of the 20th century. This house was in an isolated section of Santa Fe. The historic dwelling was typical of many others built throughout the territory. It was torn down to make room for progress.

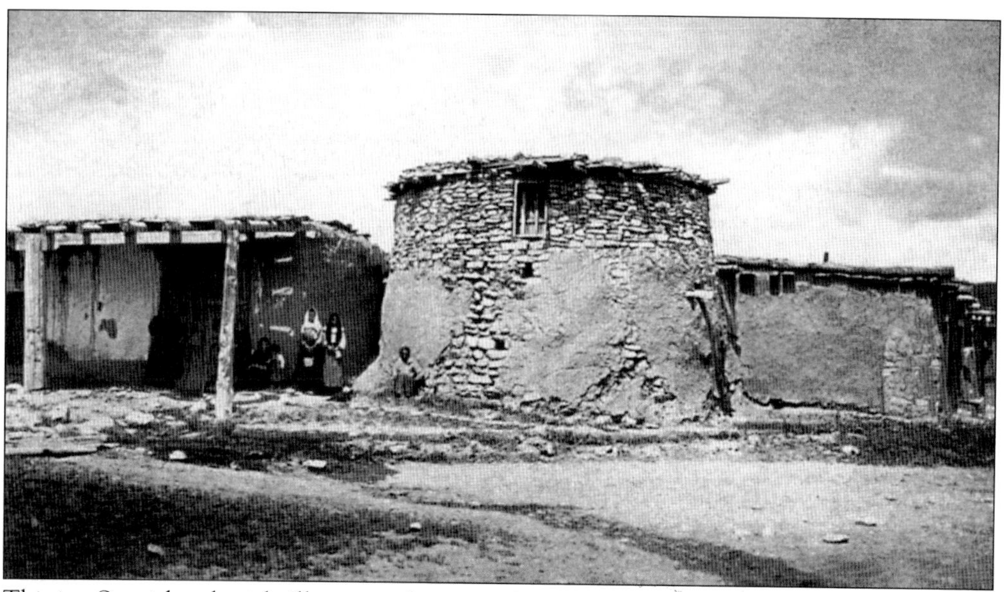

This is a Spanish colonial village once known as Manzano. It featured a torreón at the enclosed entrance. The circular torreón was common in Spanish colonial villages in New Mexico. These defensive structures with origins in early Spain provided protection for the inhabitants but were eventually brought down by American howitzers. The early village of Manzano no longer exists. This Detroit Publishing Company real-photo postcard was published around 1908.

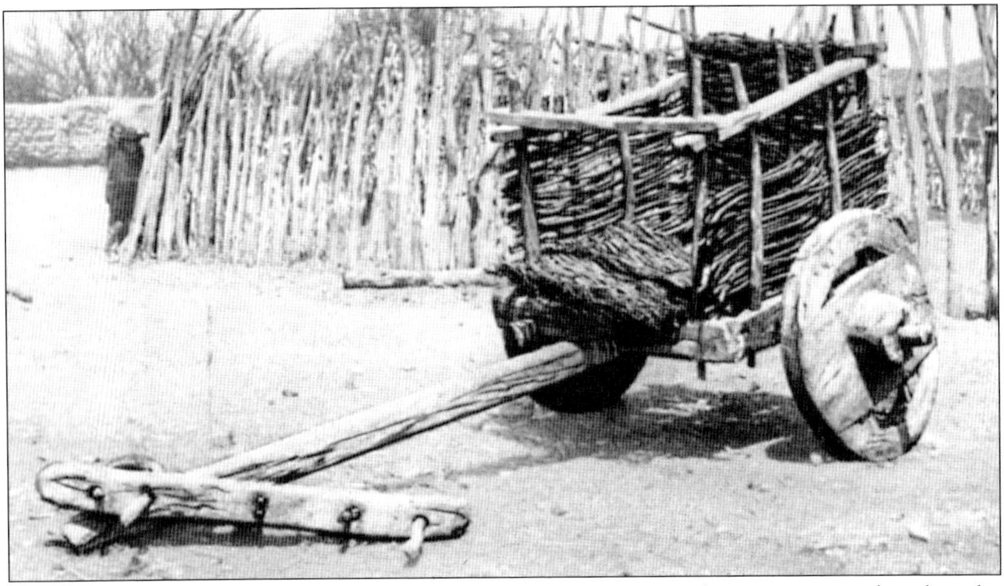

The Spanish carreta transformed the landscape of New Mexico when it was introduced in the 16th century. Peasants in Spain since Roman times had used this strong, open wooden vehicle. The New Mexico State Monument System has sponsored the reconstruction of the carts while preserving and interpreting their history. The indispensable carretas could navigate curves, rocky mountain terrain, and even muddy and swampy areas.

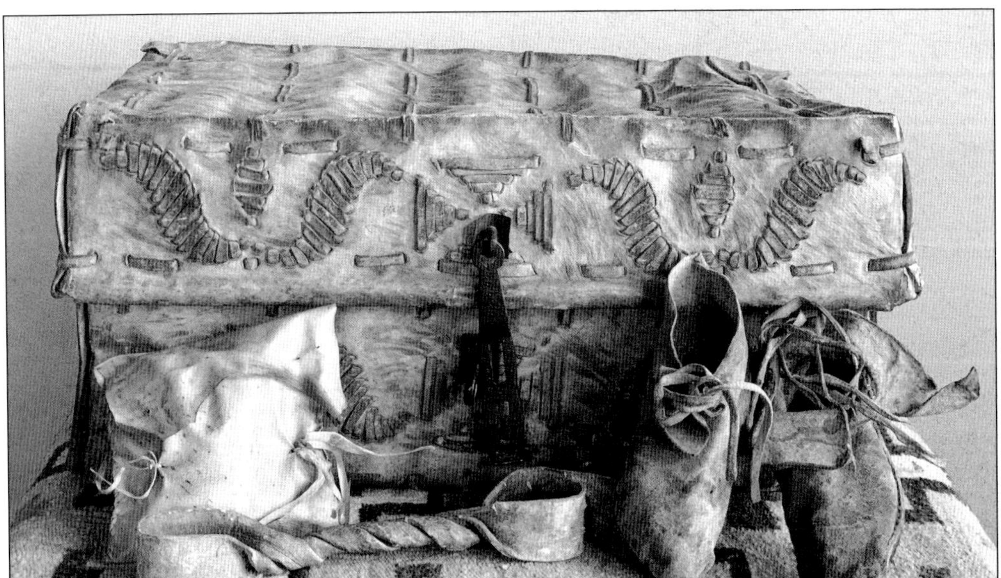

This is an 18th-century leather traveling trunk along with *guaraches* (Indian moccasins) and other leather items, including a pouch that was used for medicinal herbs. These trunks were packed with prized possessions on long trips. The production of small leather chests and trunks was a major business. Those who made them either obtained and processed the leather themselves or purchased it from others.

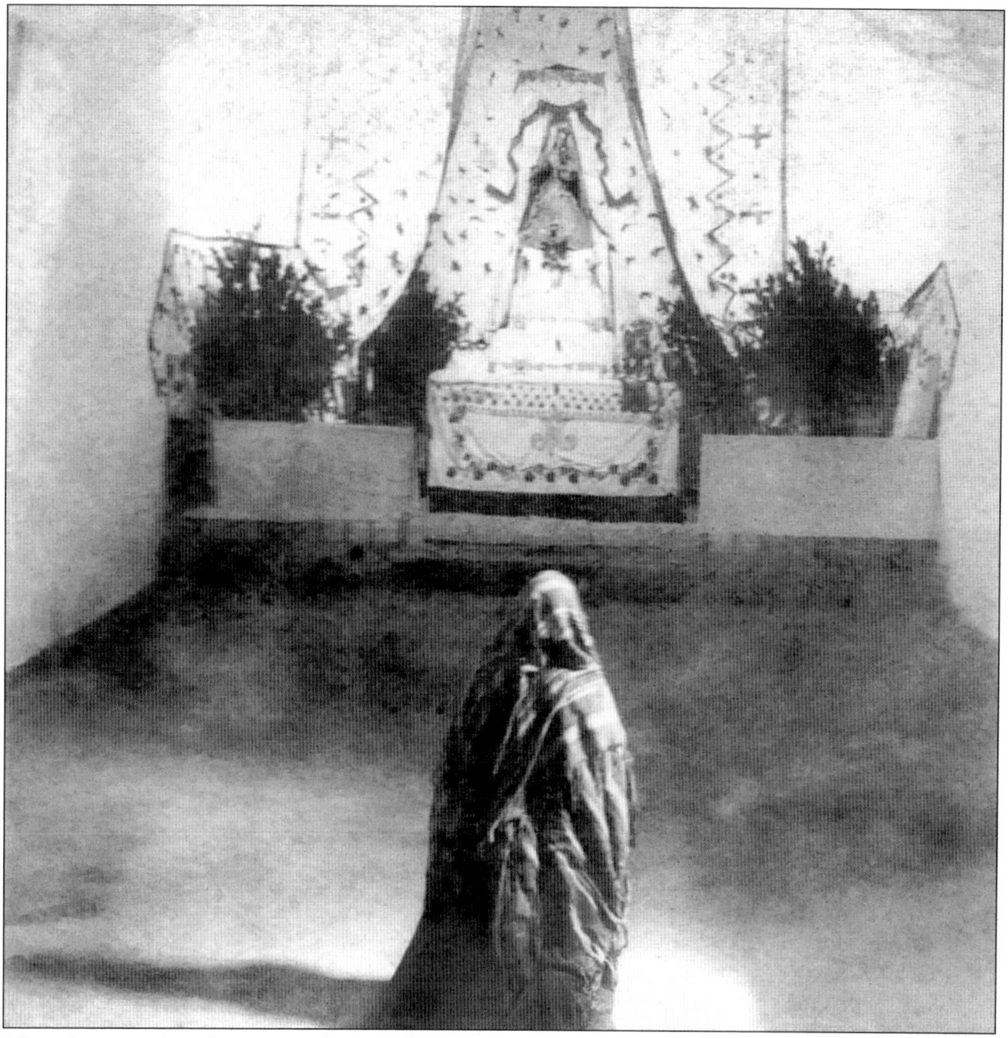

This photograph, taken around 1860, shows a woman kneeling in the interior of a chapel before an altar. Chapels, *capillas*, and oratories were found in all Spanish colonial villages and towns. They were normally dedicated to the patron saints of the settlements. This one features a wooden image of Mary, the mother of Christ, and native weavings. Spanish colonial women spent countless hours weaving and embroidering altar cloths and other decorations for chapels and churches. This woman is kneeling on a dirt floor that was packed down and smoothed with sheep's blood. This gave the floor a sheen and the appearance of cement.

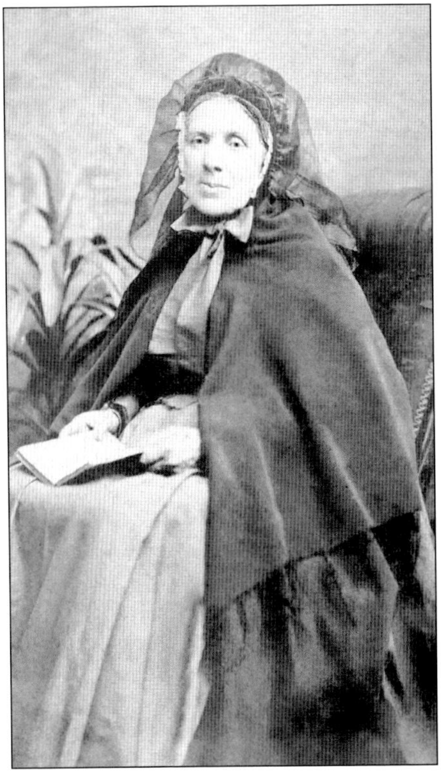

This mid-19th-century photograph shows a woman cradling her book. Many of the settlers and their descendants were literate in Spanish and later also in English. Books and printed materials were readily available to the colonists. These were brought in on El Camino Real and later through other roads such as the Santa Fe Trail from Missouri to Santa Fe.

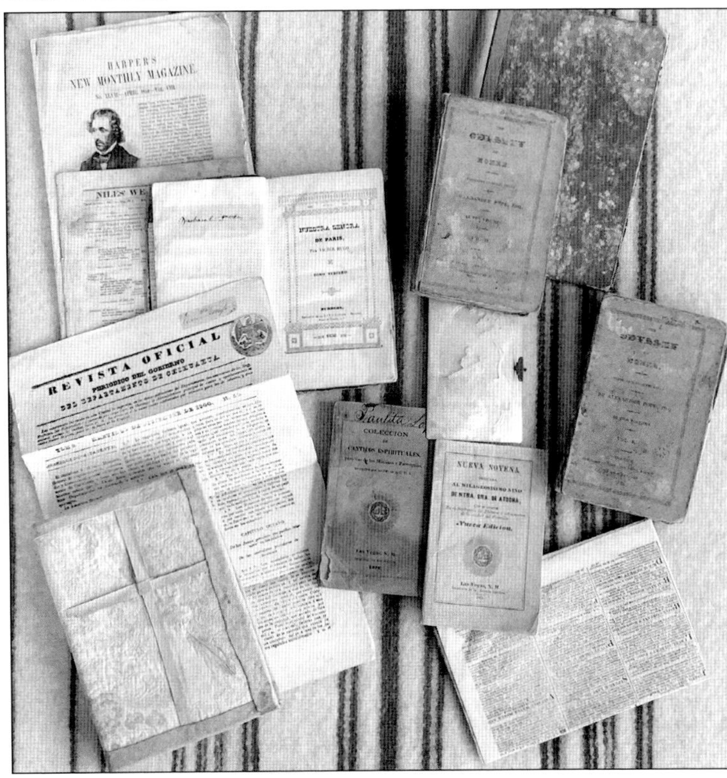

Contrary to what has been popularly written, many New Mexicans were highly literate in Spanish. Books, newspapers, and other periodicals and publications were available. These were in Spanish, since it was the language of the territory. There were Spanish printing presses in most of the towns by 1890. There were also some publishing houses and an association of Spanish publishers and Spanish literary clubs.

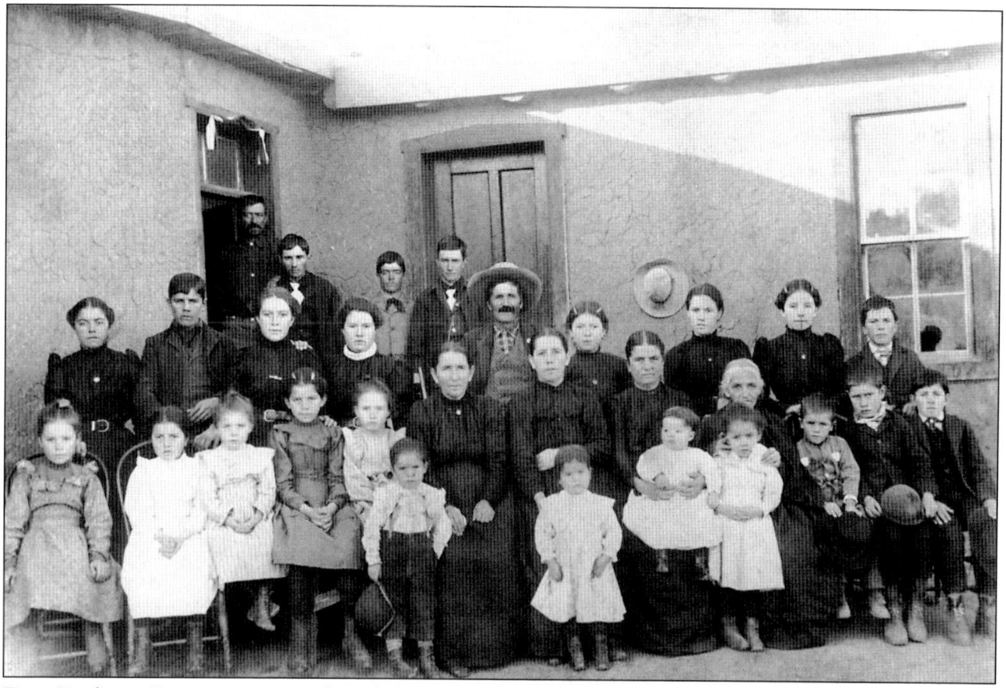

Don Perfecto Romero, pictured with his extensive family around 1896, was an early merchant on El Camino Real. They pose in front of his home at Los Poblanos, a community of farmlands and ranches on the trail eventually absorbed by Albuquerque. Los Poblanos was settled in the 18th century.

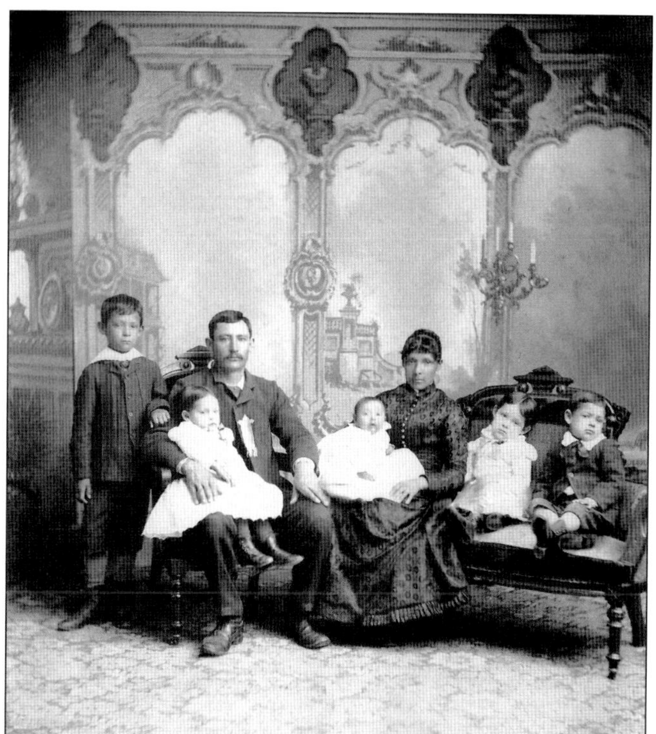

A well-dressed couple are pictured with their children around 1880. Photography became popular in New Mexico as itinerant photographers traveled throughout the territory. Some also set up studios. At one point in the 19th century, almost every town had one or more resident photographers. Photography became an art, and residents were more than willing to have a picture taken.

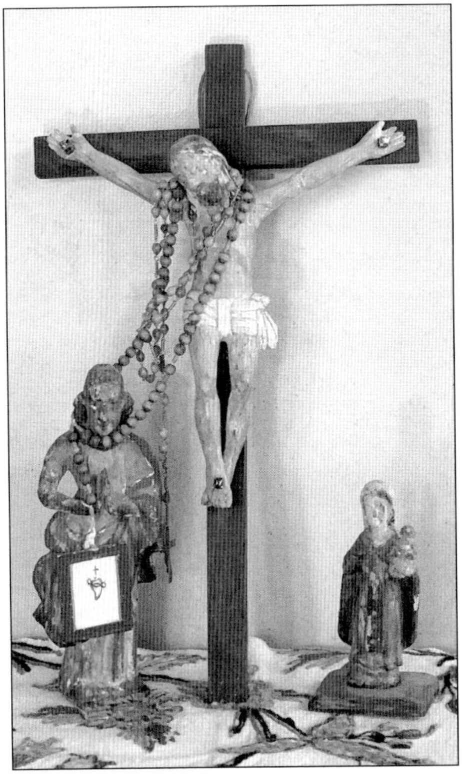

This is an early- to mid-19th-century New Mexico pinewood crucifix with gesso and natural pigments by an unknown maker. The images of Mary with Jesus and a prayerful Mary are Latin American in origin. Often, carved wooden and tin religious images from Mexico and elsewhere made their way in and out of New Mexico as trade items.

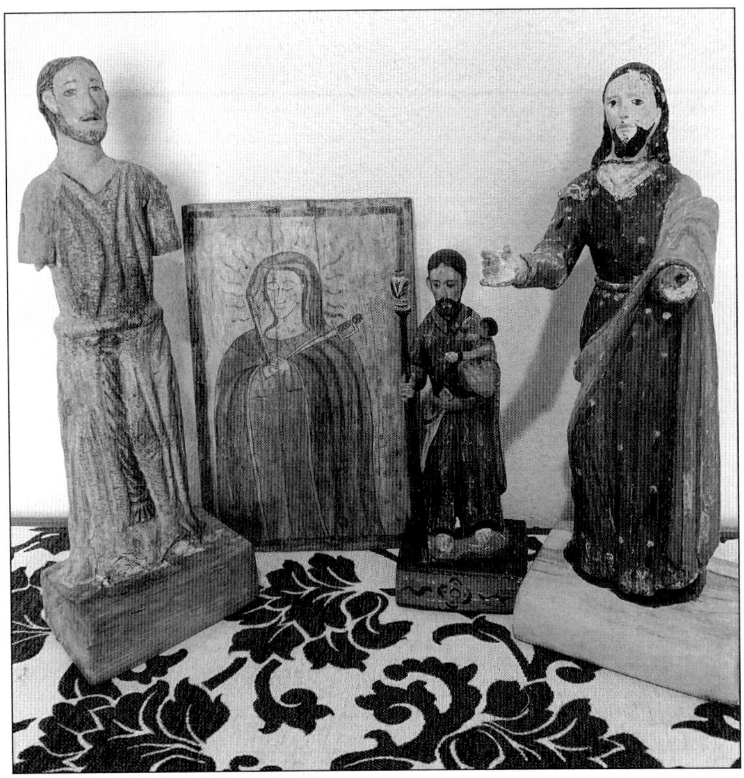

Representative New Mexican Spanish colonial art from different periods is seen here. From left to right are San José (St. Joseph) by Antonio Molleno (1800–1830s), a retablo (painted wood panel), by an unknown maker; San José by José Rafael Aragón (1796–1823); and San José by Franciscan priest Fray Andrés García (18th century). Fray García was assigned to various Indian missions, and like other Franciscan missionaries, he produced artwork for his churches.

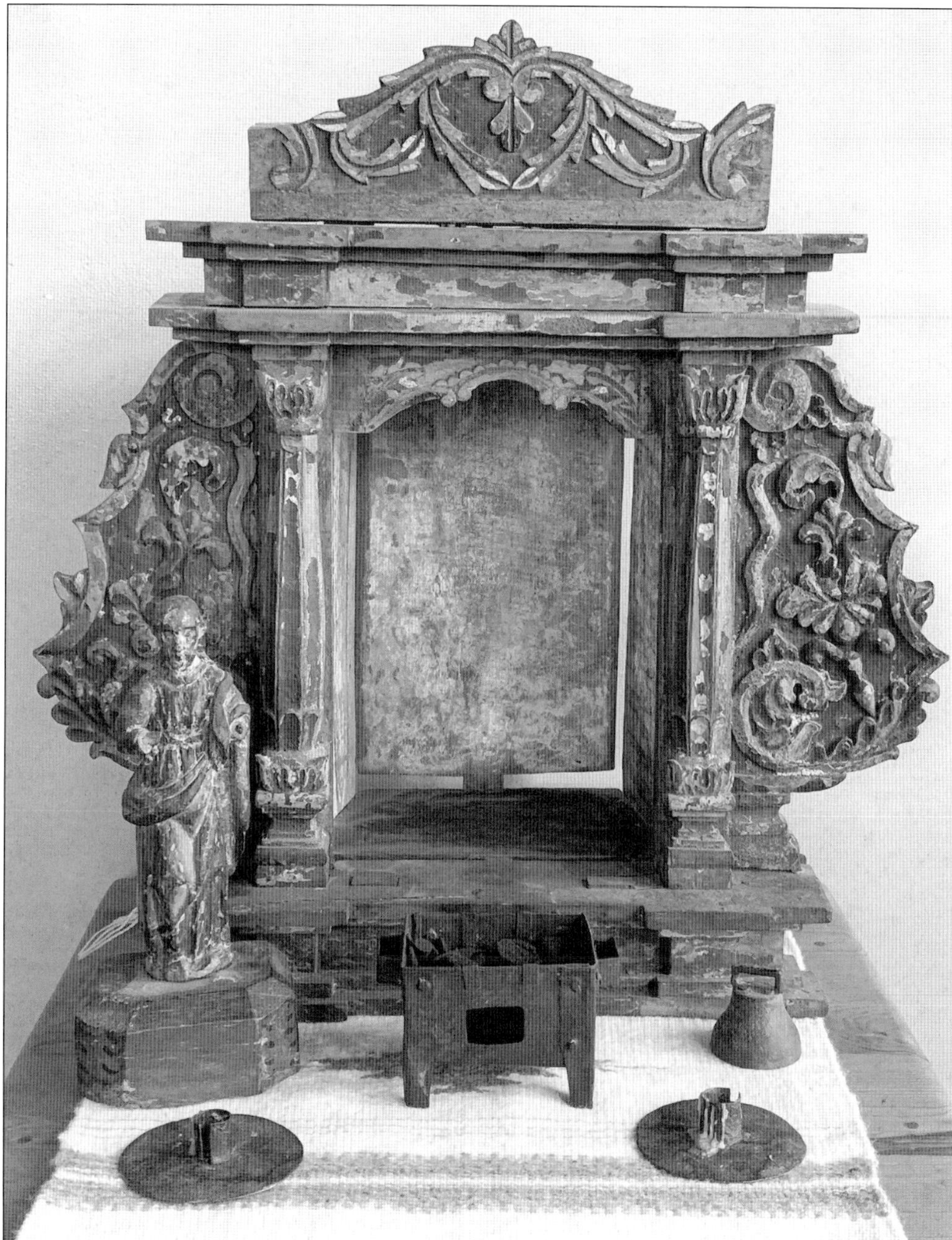

Spanish Franciscan Catholic missionary friars during the 16th to 18th centuries could set up and perform their religious services at any time and any place. This 18th-century portable tabernacle was transported in parts. It fit together like a puzzle with pieces that simply snapped into place. A makeshift altar could be set up on a wooden table. This was vital for the devout settlers on the long and treacherous journey. The tabernacle was used to hold the consecrated eucharistic host for mass. This photograph also shows a *bulto* (carved religious image) of St. Joseph, an incense burner, iron candleholders, and an iron bell.

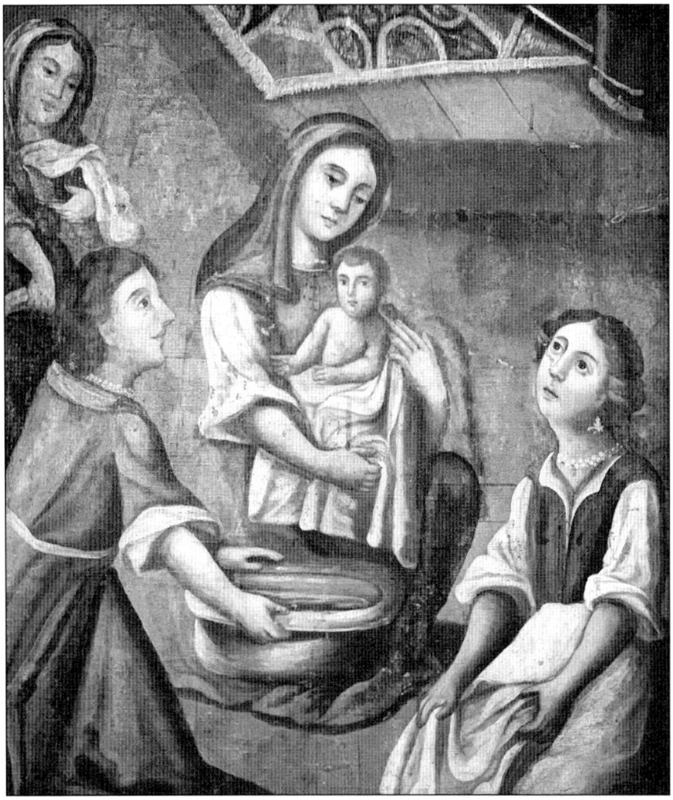

This 18th-century oil painting by Gullin Mero, *El Baño del Santo Niño*, the Bathing of the Christ Child, is an example of artwork that was brought into New Mexico during the Spanish colonial period. Spanish missionary priests transported various religious items including paintings on canvas to set up their mission churches.

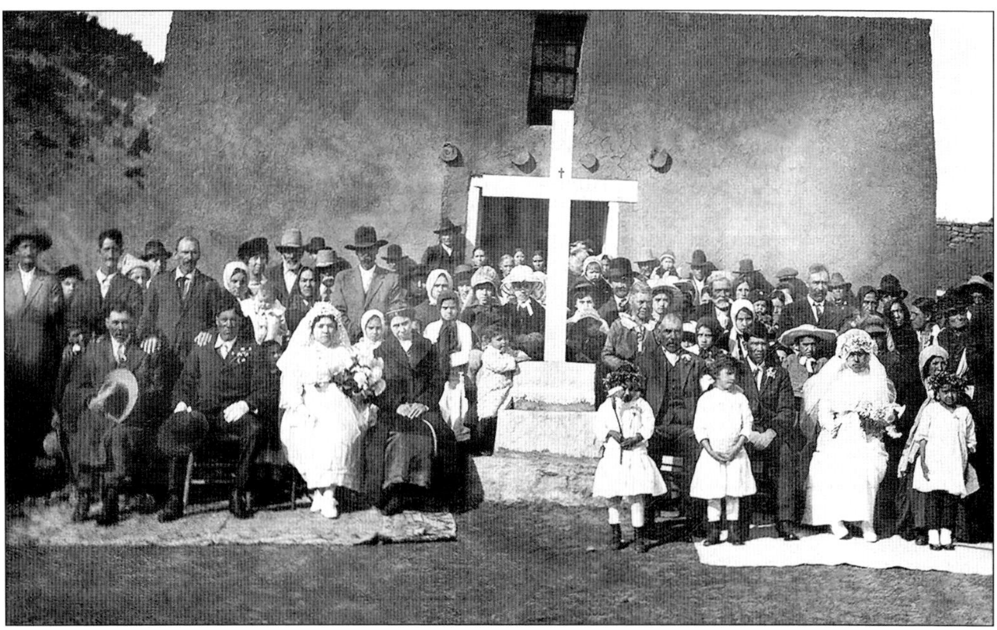

It seems that everyone appeared for a double wedding in this photograph taken in a New Mexico village about 1889. In Spanish settlements, baptisms, weddings, and funerals were large affairs. In some cases, most residents were somehow related, as might be seen here. Everyone gathered to enjoy traditional food and music.

An assortment of typical items that were carried by women on El Camino Real is shown here, including a wood comb, a tortoiseshell holder for face powder, a silver perfume bottle, and a curling iron. Other items include scissors, an iron, a weaving instrument, a silver rosary, a mirror, and a silver reliquary.

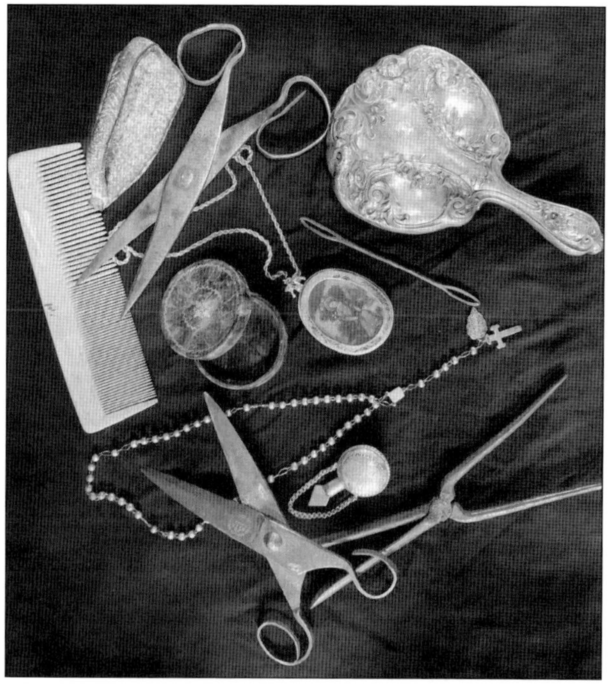

Cooking areas in Spanish Colonial homes held a variety of iron and wood cooking utensils. Iron trivets like those shown here were popularly used on the trail, on the range, and in homes. They consisted of a flat iron ring, three legs with feet, and a handle with a rat-tail finial. A trivet only required a copper pot for cooking pinto beans, dried red and green chile, vegetables, or meat.

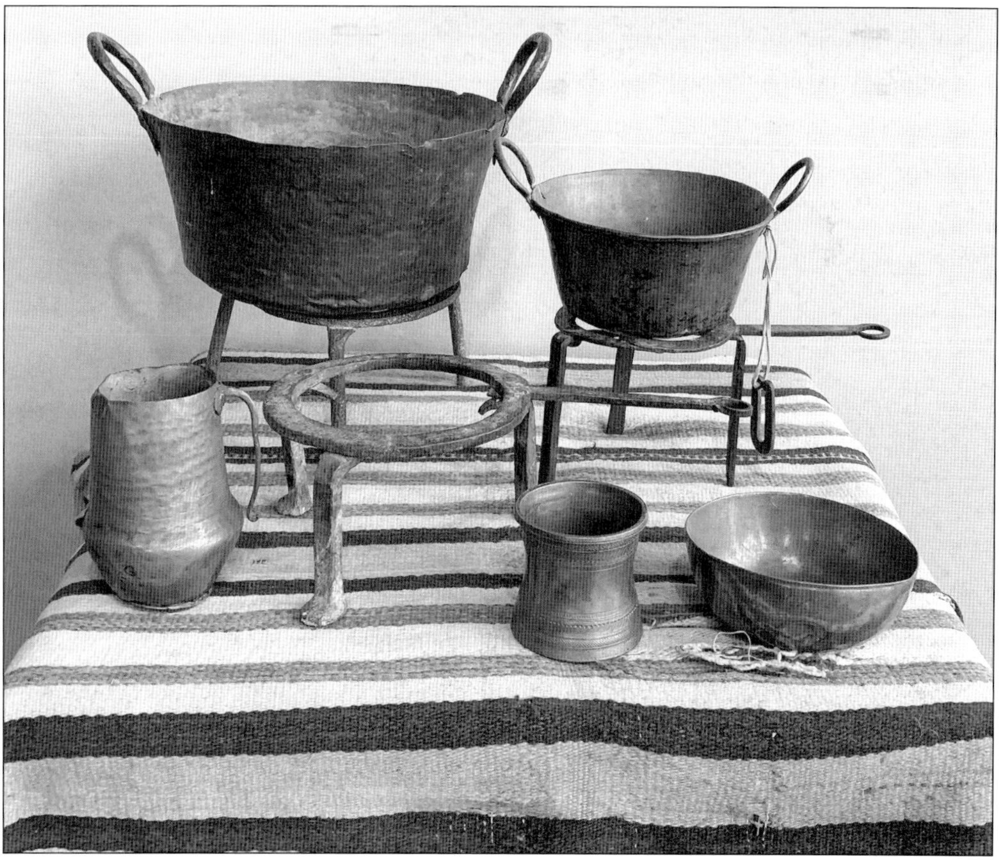

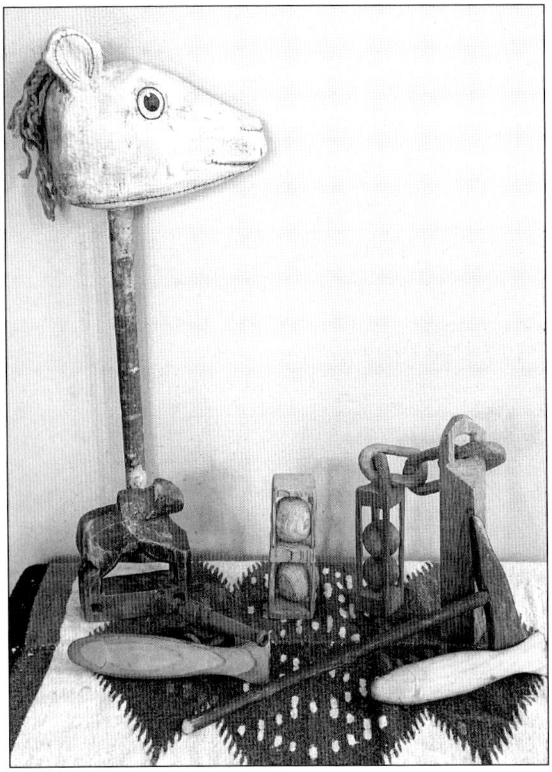

It is not generally known that New Mexico woodworkers who fashioned furniture and other items also made toys like these for children. In this display is a toy horse with a stretched and painted leather (pigskin) head, a toy cannon, carved fish, a ball in a cage, a bird attached to a stick with wheels that could be rolled, and a ball in a cage with a chain.

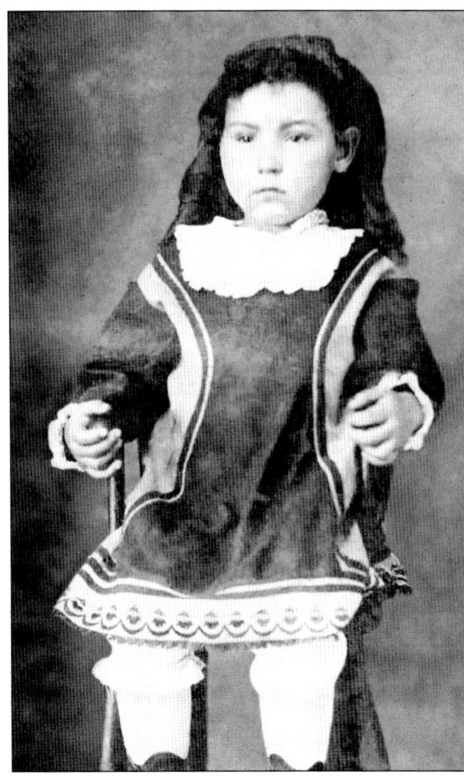

Before the United States took over New Mexico in 1846, colonial styles of dress were prevalent in the territory. This was true throughout the Spanish Southwest. Whatever was in vogue in Mexico was also introduced into New Mexico. This little girl poses proudly in her beautiful outfit in an early tintype photograph.

Three

A Farming and Ranching Frontier

The massive caravan of Oñate settlers began their journey into the virtually unknown territory of New Mexico to establish a colony on January 26, 1598. The preparation had taken months, a much longer time than had been anticipated, and they headed out during the dead of winter. These dauntless pioneers faced unimaginable deprivation, hunger, thirst, hardships, and even death on this very long journey. They agonizingly transported wooden ploughs, countless iron tools, and building and farming implements. Spanish women and men even transported toiletries, soaps, washboards, shaving tools, medicines—anything and everything they believed would be necessary to start a new life in an unknown land. Faith came first to them, with wooden images of Christ, Mary, and saints. Franciscan frays carried along portable altars and tabernacles they could set up immediately for prayer and devotion depending on the hardships encountered along the way. Once settled, fearless Spanish adventurers sought to set down roots. They did so by establishing ranches, farms, and military posts along El Camino Real de Tierra Adentro. Noted scholar Felipe R. Mirabal wrote, "The best part of my job as former curator of collections at the celebrated El Rancho de las Golondrinas Living History Museum, was to see families visiting the beautiful farmland and spectrum of exhibits in historic adobe structures. This ancient rancho was the last stop on El Camino Real which ended at the plaza of the Villa de Santa Fe."

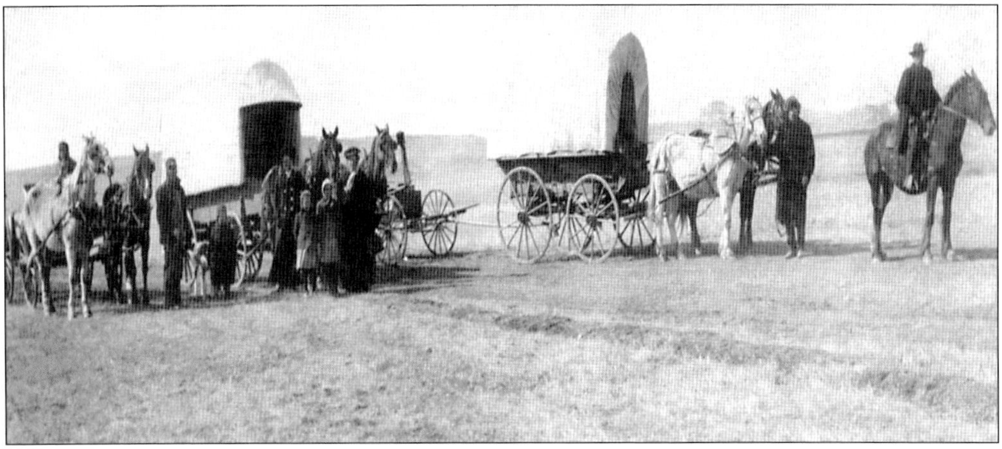

Caravans were guided by wagon masters on trails and roads leading to the Spanish capital city of Santa Fe. For generations, travelers depended on the men who knew about springs, artesian wells, and other sources of clean water for themselves, their horses, and their livestock. These wagon masters also knew about places for fishing and the natural habitats of wildlife that could be hunted for food.

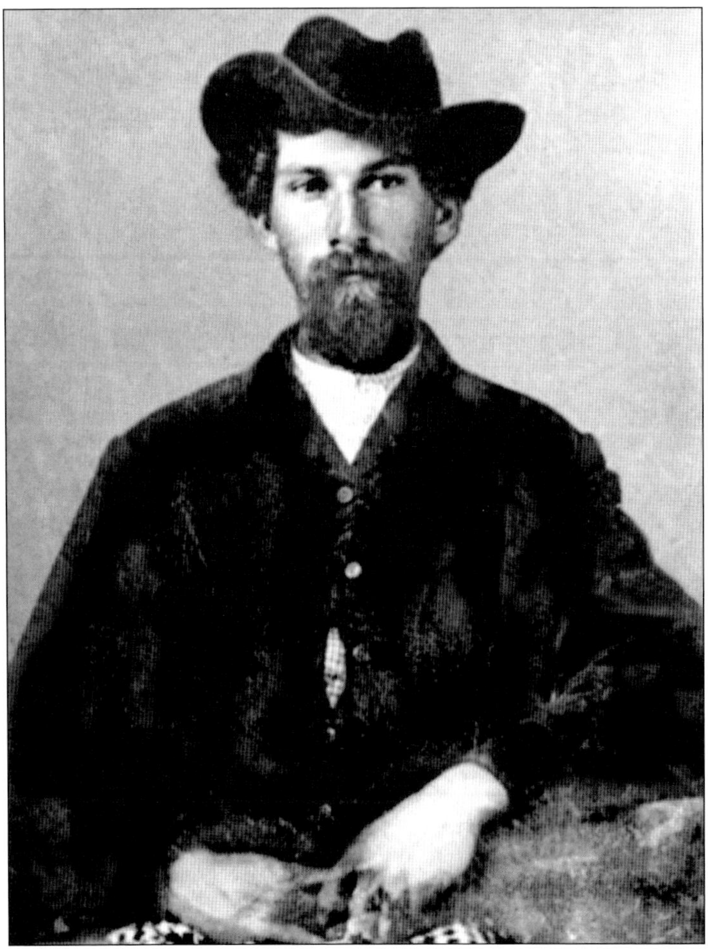

This is a rare photograph of a trader-merchant on El Camino Real. These traders purchased and sold merchandise to make a profit, but they also provided a much-needed service for the settlers. Sometimes they made their trips on El Camino Real twice a year and secured merchandise that was not readily available locally from distant places.

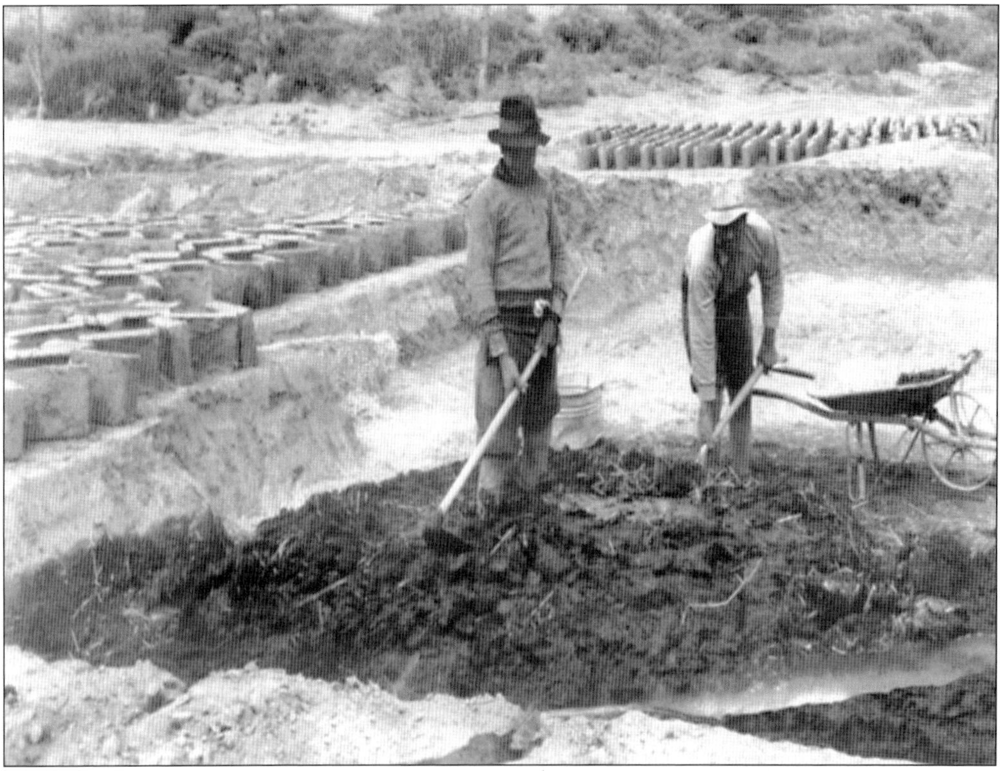

Spanish settlers used adobe bricks made from mud and straw. This form of building was introduced into Spain from the Mediterranean, where the technique was used in ancient Egypt and elsewhere. The conquering Moors introduced beehive ovens constructed with adobes into Spain for baking bread and meat. Adobe making was an art that became an essential trade.

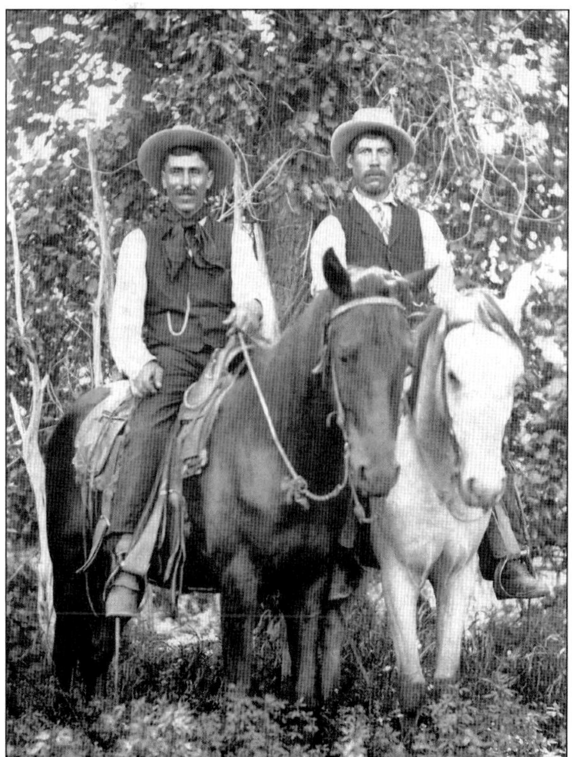

These men, pictured around 1889, show how proud they are to pose with their horses, which were indispensable to their livelihood, transportation, and daily lives. El Camino Real would not have survived as a major route for trade and transportation without horses, mules, and oxen. Horseback riding also became a popular sport in New Mexico.

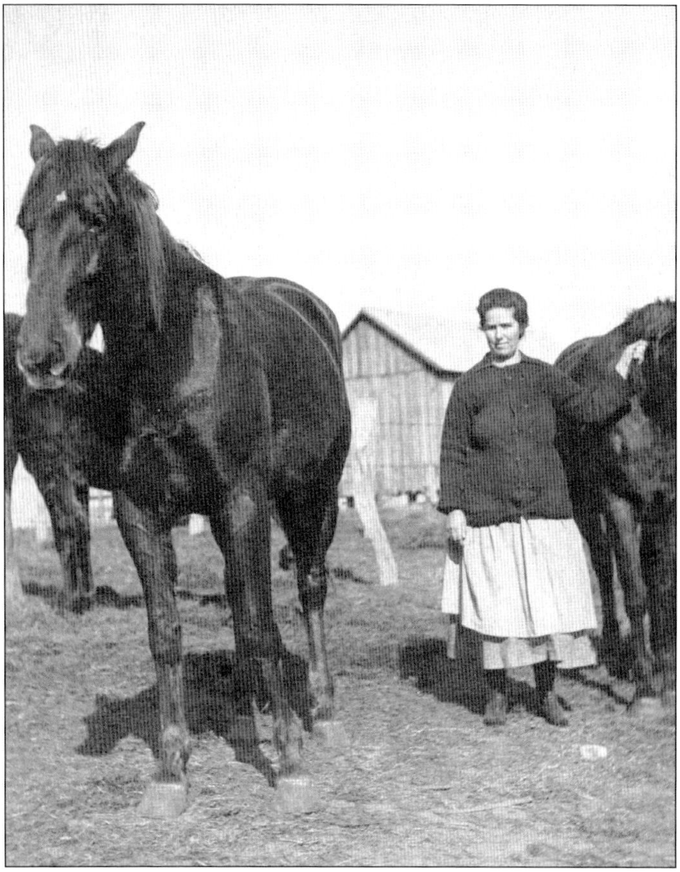

Women participated in all activities on farms and ranches alongside raising their children. They also cultivated vegetable gardens, fruit trees, and medicinal herbs. They were responsible for the medical care of their families and sometimes their neighbors using folk remedies passed down in their families for generations. Sometimes, they joined their husbands to defend their homes. This woman stands proudly with livestock around 1890.

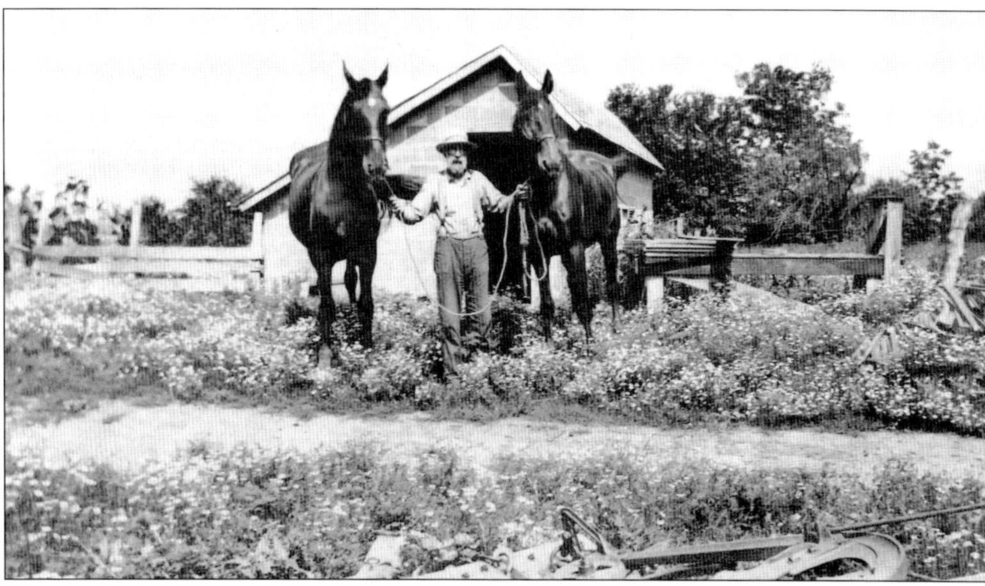

This rancher poses proudly with his prized horses in 1899. Farmers used horses to till the soil for planting. Horses were so vital in the daily lives of people that they commanded high prices. Because of this, horse rustling was commonplace, especially in 19th-century New Mexico.

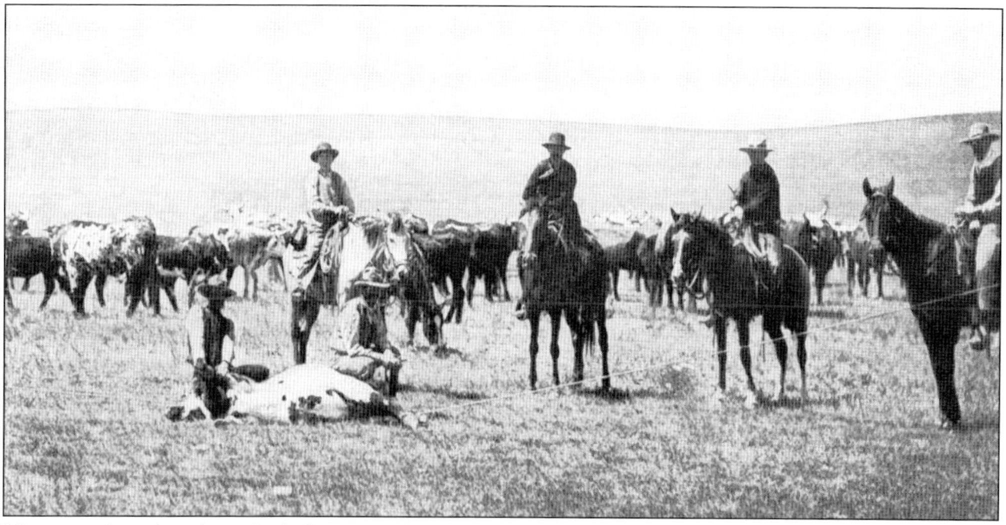

Vaqueros (cowboys) worked the range from sunup to sundown, branding calves and rounding up cattle. The Spanish introduced cowboy culture into New Mexico in the 16th century. It spread throughout the Southwest and was adopted by the Indians and, later, the Americans. Farmers planted fields and harvested crops. Communities regularly held fiestas called *matanzas*, wherein fattened pigs were slaughtered and barbequed.

The adz (*azuela*) at upper right was used during the colonial period to dress lumber, hollow out troughs, and make plow frames. Colonial-style hoes, at lower right, were grubbing tools used for breaking the soil and weeding for planting. Ox goads were used for prodding oxen for plowing and pulling wagons. A New Mexico mission brand and other colonial branding irons with rat-tail finials are also shown.

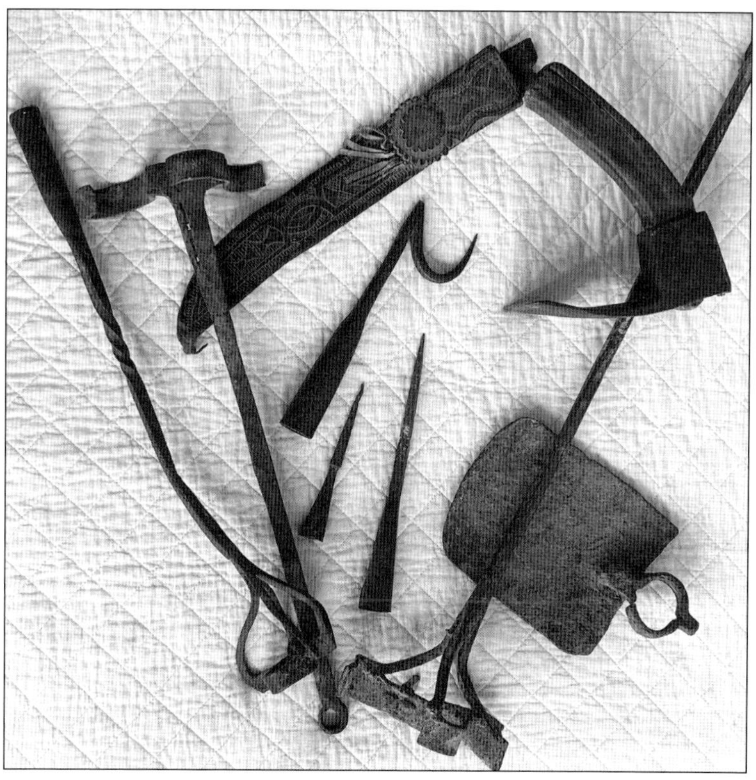

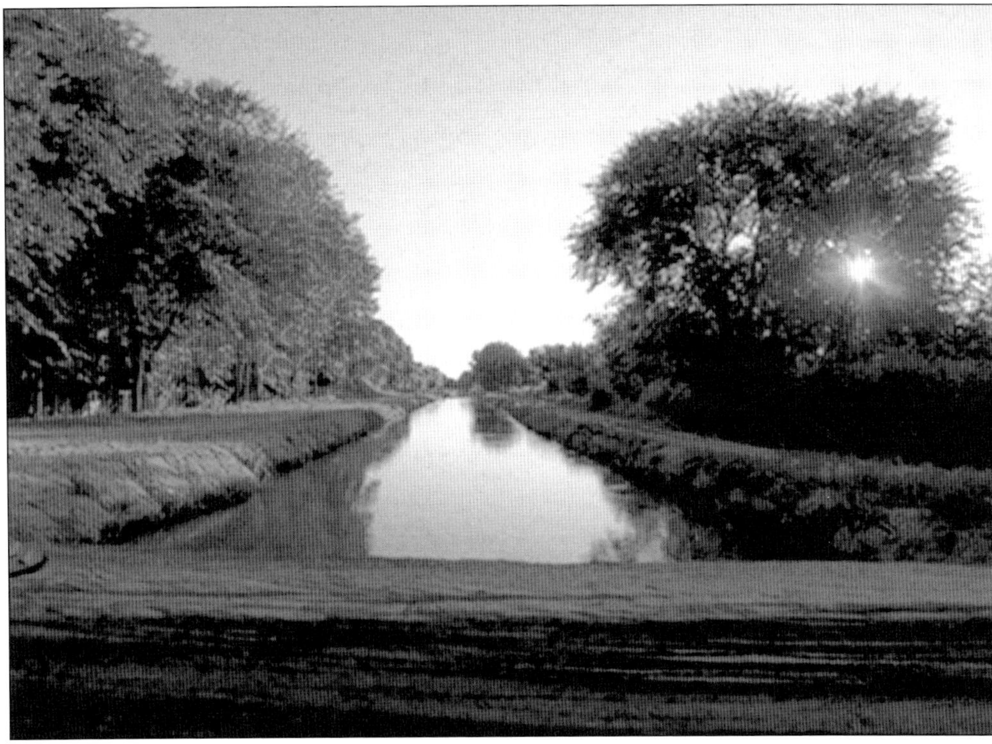

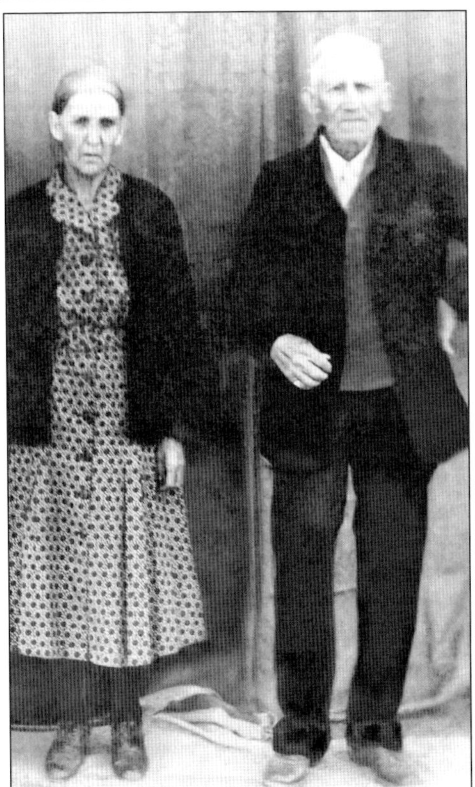

Irrigation canals (*acequias*) and ditches were introduced by the Spanish settlers into New Mexico. This extensive system for directing waters from rivers and other sources provided farmlands for both the Indians and Spanish colonists. With the changes in climate, some rivers became dry beds. This so adversely affected the lives of people that they were forced to move. (Photograph by Ramon Juan Carlos de Aragon.)

Don Enrique Calles and his wife, Felicitas Vallejos Calles, stand at the doorway to their home at La Ladera, New Mexico, in 1940. Enrique was born in 1859. He was best known for his vineyards, which produced fine wines. He delivered his wine in a horse-drawn wagon north and south on El Camino Real.

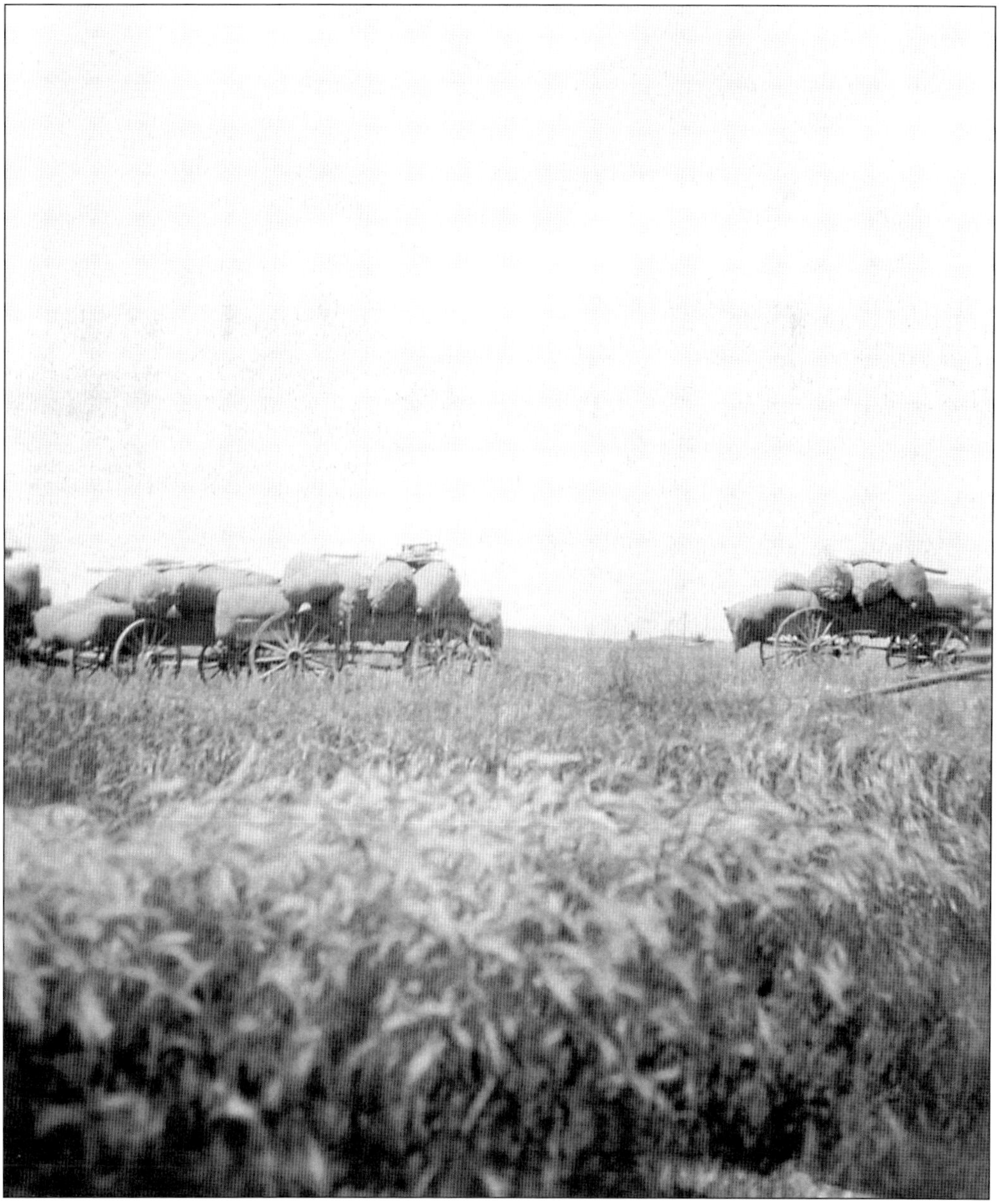

Burlap sacks, coarse bags made with hemp or jute, were filled with wheat, piled into wagons, and readied for transportation in this undated photograph. This cereal grass was widely cultivated in certain areas of New Mexico. The wheat was taken to mills, where the grain was ground into flour for baking. Cotton sacks of flour were then traded or sold. Indian lives substantially improved with bread and other baked goods, such as cakes and cookies. Harvests on farmlands included wheat and other grains that would be shipped in gunnysacks like those pictured here. Spanish colonists introduced wheat into New Mexico as well as horses, cattle, swine, and chickens.

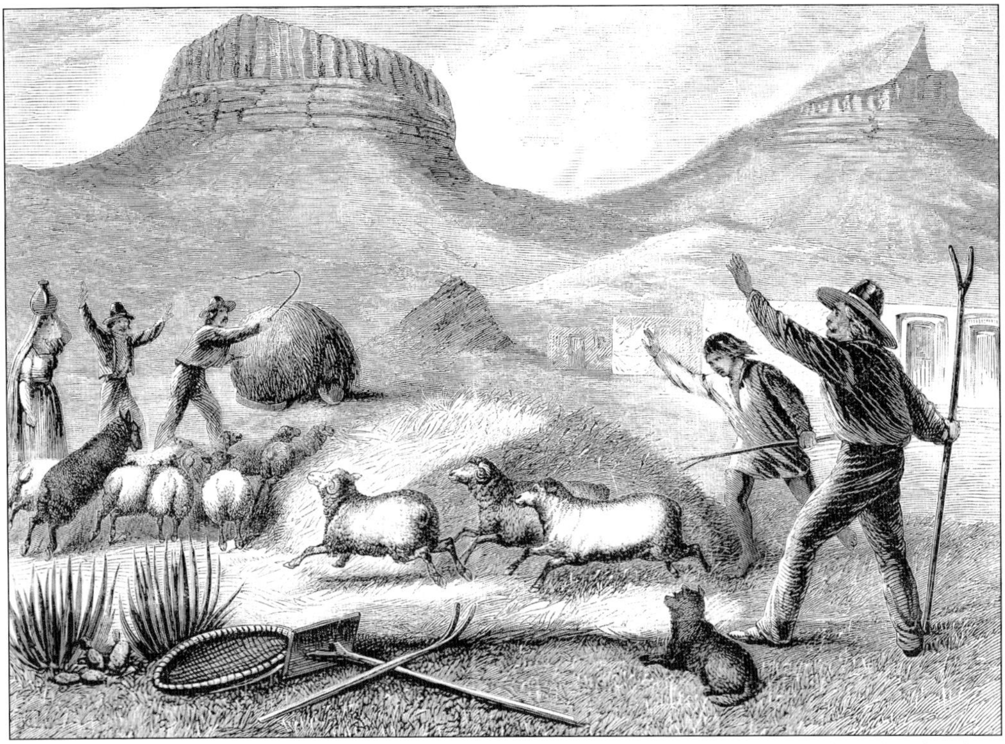

An 1870 issue of *American Agriculturist* featured this engraving by H.W. Elliott called *The Thrashing Machine of New Mexico*. It states, "In proceeding to thrash, a ring is made, and the earth within smooth and hardened; then a pile of shock wheat is put in the center and from this supply the surface is covered from four to six inches in depth with the wheat straw."

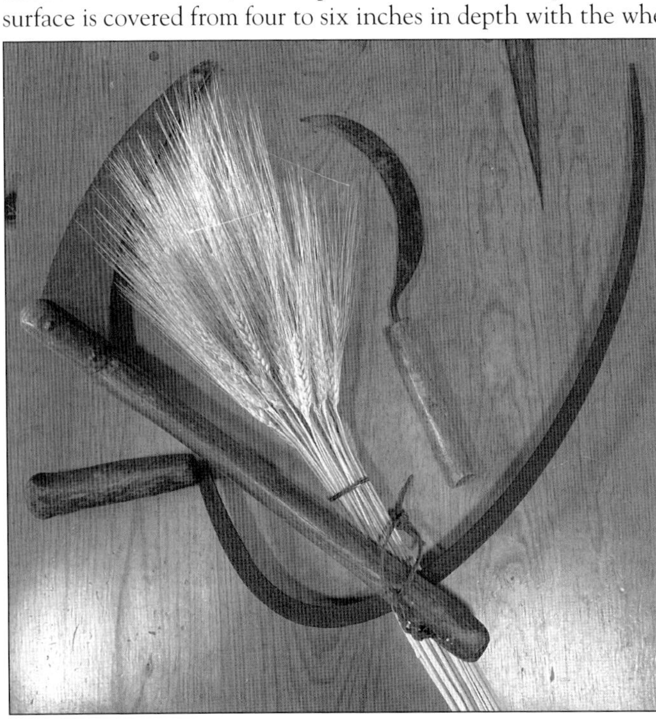

The main harvesting implement was a sickle (*hoz*). Farmers held the sickle and cut off clutches of ripe grain. This assortment of sickles dates from the late 18th to the early 19th century. Not much changed in the style of the implements that were used, nor in the methods used for cutting grain.

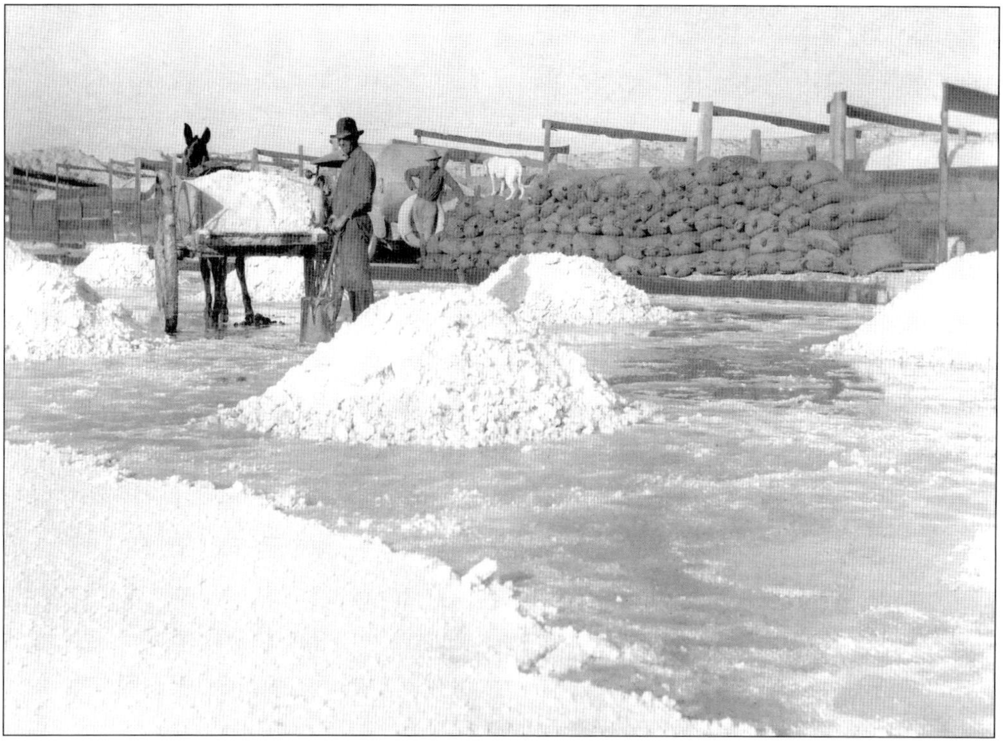

Traders, merchants, and residents received shipments of salt from the salt lakes called Las Salinas near Willard, New Mexico. This area had been mined for centuries by Indians, who traded the salt far to the north and south. Rights to the salt deposits and other minerals became the Las Salinas Grant.

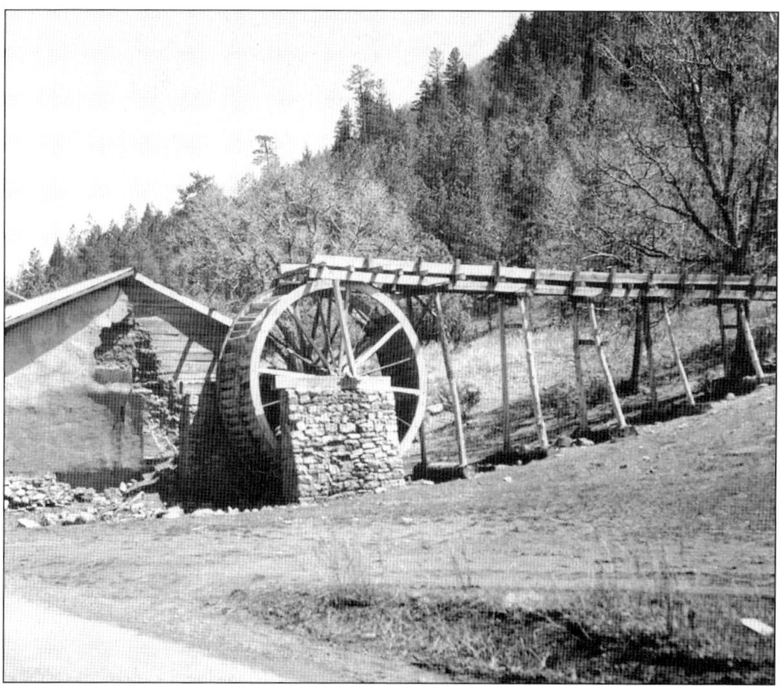

This mill was used for grinding grain. These mills, run by spring water, were once prevalent in most areas to grind flour. A historic mill that was saved and restored can be seen at the living museum of El Rancho de las Golondrinas near Santa Fe.

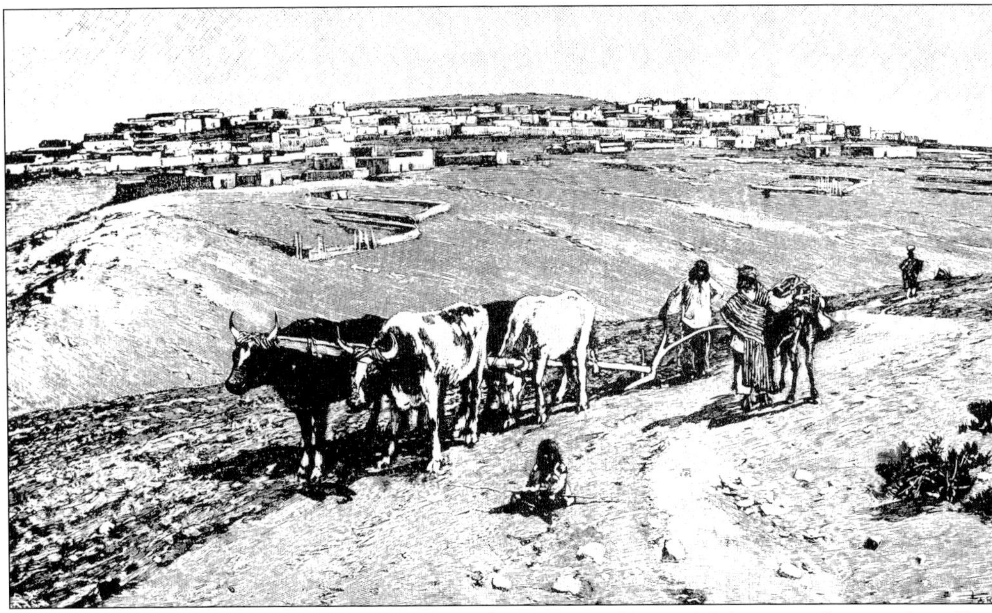

This engraving of Laguna Pueblo from the February 1891 *Harper's Magazine* depicts the tilling of fields with an ox and plow on Indian land. The Spanish introduced extensive technological improvements, including horses and mules, to the Indians, among whom the agricultural technology spread.

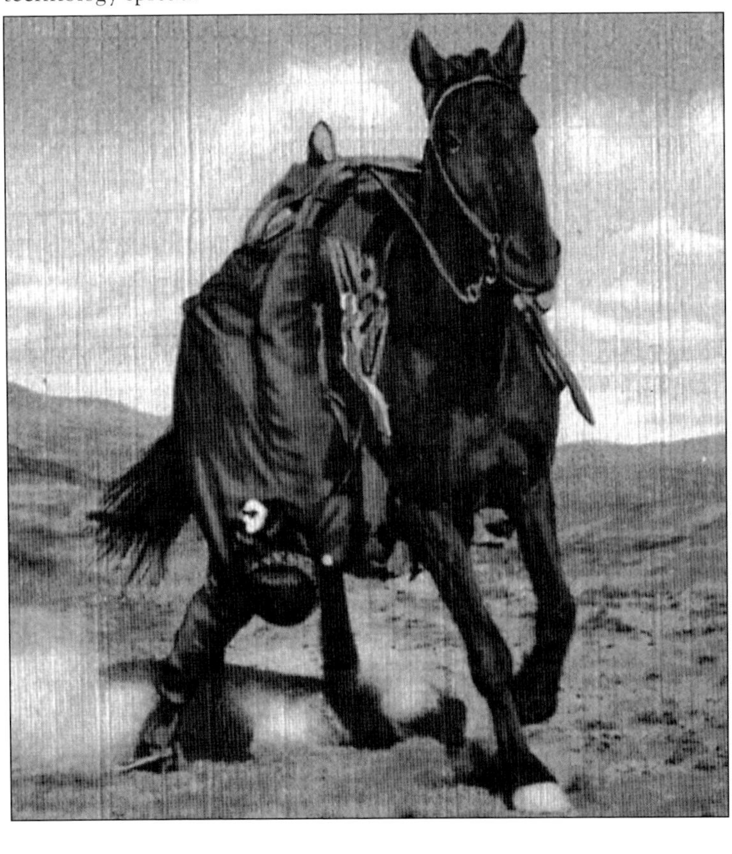

The Spanish settlers entertained themselves with rodeo competitions and horse races. They also had events called *las corridas del gallo*, or "rooster pulls." A rooster was buried in the ground with only the head showing. Riders on horseback lined up. At the sound of a pistol, they rode off, and the first one to pull the rooster out of the ground won. Indians, like the one pictured here, took up this sport.

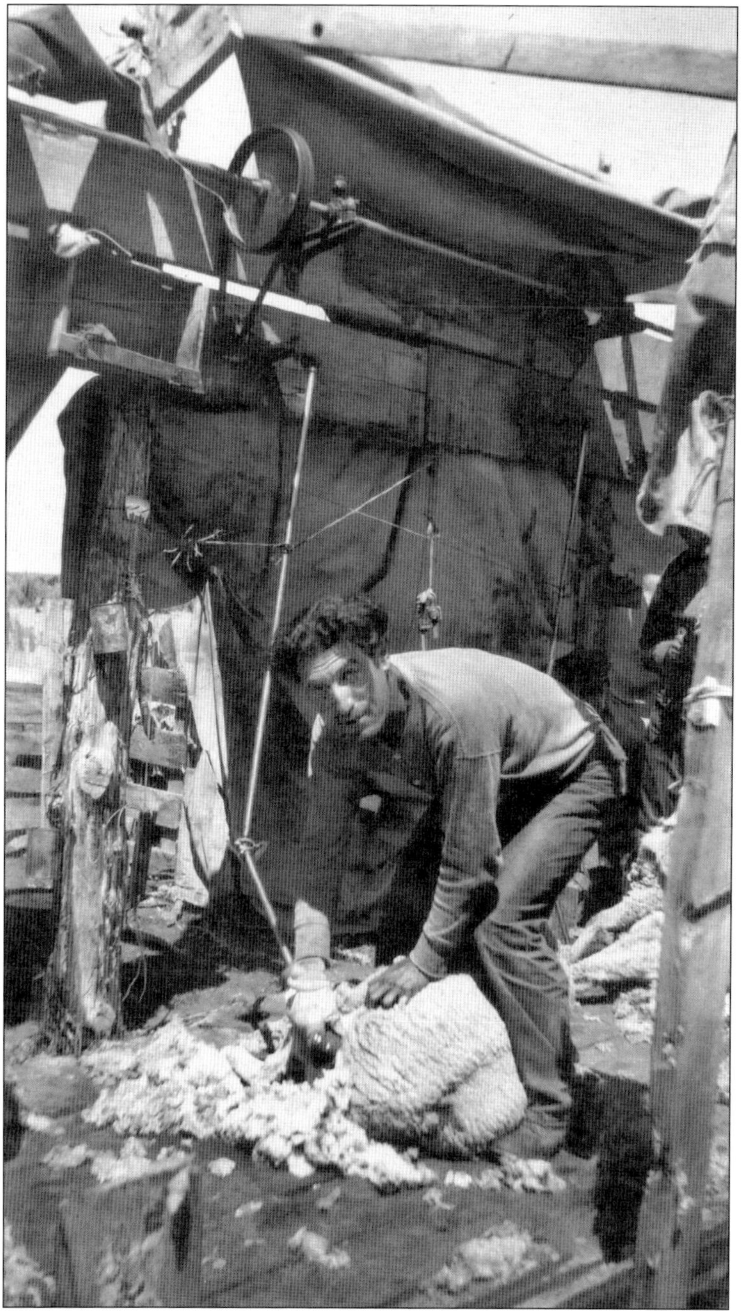

Shearing was a skill that was in demand on sheep ranches. Sheepmen like the one pictured were either hired or volunteered on ranches for days at a time during shearing season. The thick wool was used for mattresses or was carded for weaving clothing and blankets. Sheepskin was used for velum that covered books. Velum was also used as a writing surface. This was a major industry. Wool is one of the oldest trade commodities in New Mexico. The shearer cut the woolen fleece from each adult sheep in about two to three minutes. He began by removing belly wool with blade shears or machine shears, such as the shearer seen in this photograph. This was normally done during the warmer months before lambing. Shearing became a competitive sport.

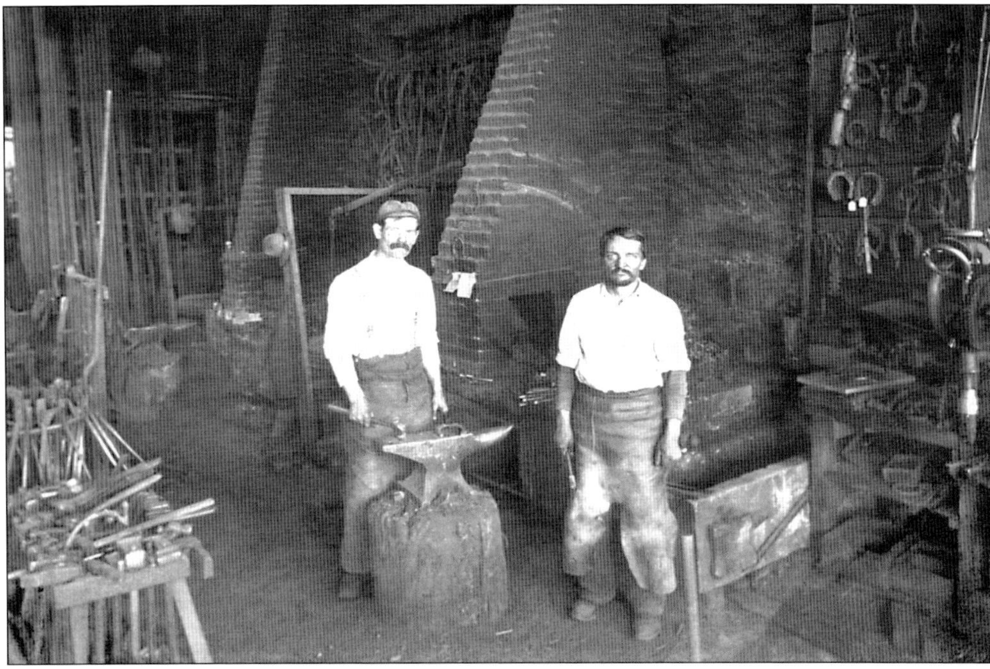

Blacksmiths C.S. Rogers, left, and Epigmenio Valerio repaired wagon wheels and produced iron horse, mule, and ox shoes. They did other ironwork that was in demand, making nails, farming and ranching implements, cooking ware, and weapons. Blacksmiths arrived early during colonization and their skills were extremely important. They were treated with respect and honor. Spanish blacksmiths trained Indians in their craft.

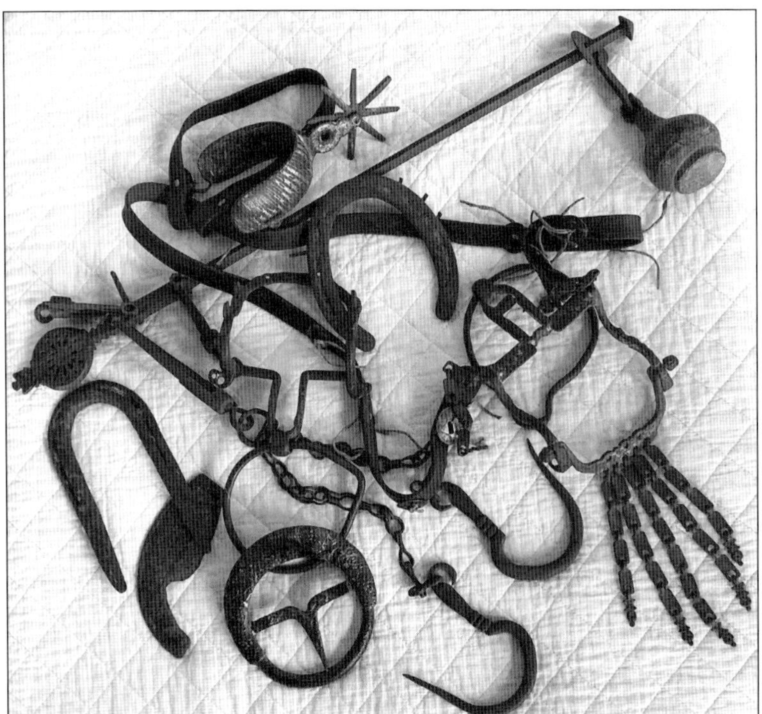

Horse gear for 18th-century Spanish vaqueros included an iron bit that applied pressure to the tongue and bars of a horse's mouth. The one pictured is heavily ornamented with a variety of decorations such as jingles and an engraved bridge. Spurs, some with fine damascening using silver, and a cinch ring (*argolla de hebijón*) adorned with silver for use on saddles are also shown.

This c. 1782 San Isidro Labrador bulto was made by Bernardo Miera y Pacheco, a Spanish cartographer who documented New Mexico on maps. It has replacements of a tin symbol of the sun and leather seed bag. St. Isidore is a patron of farmers. The *nicho* is by a Taos Serrate tinsmith, and the tin frame is by a Rio Arriba tinsmith; both are from around 1870.

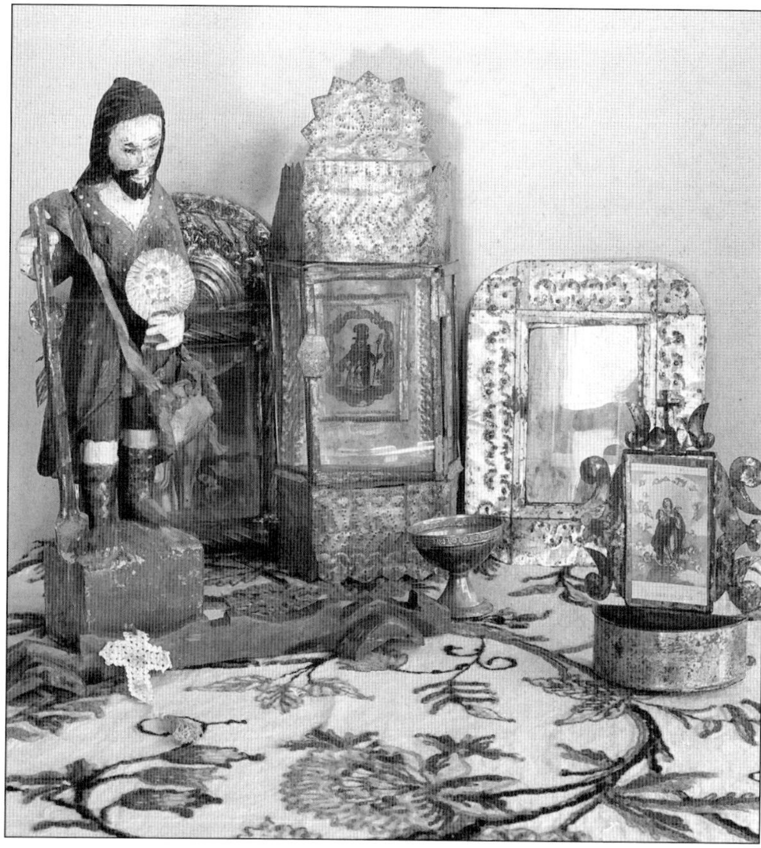

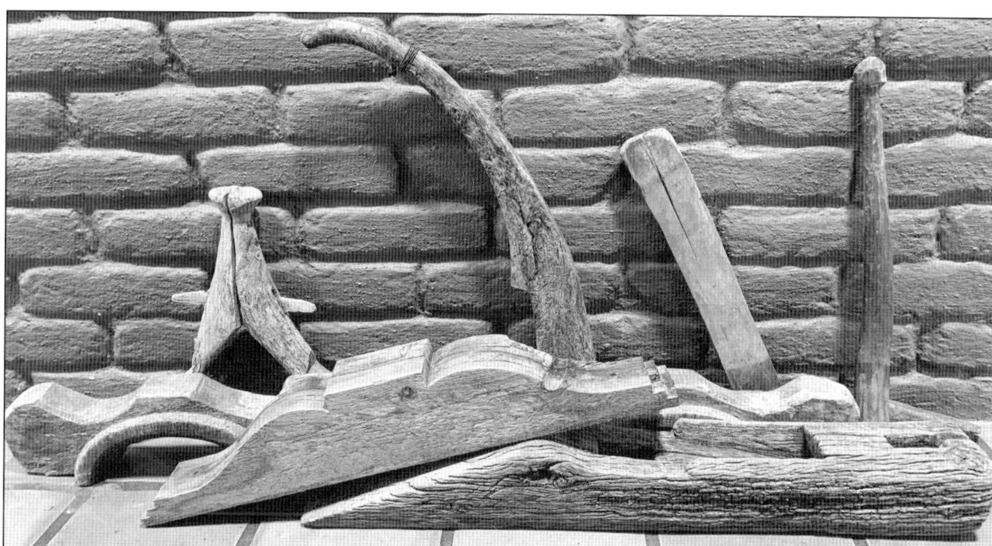

Farming, ranching, and building implements included ox yokes, wood saddle horns and saddles for mules and horses, and architectural corbels, as seen in this assortment, mostly from the 18th and 19th centuries. There were many essential items used by the colonists to establish settlements. Most of what was needed was made by the settlers themselves, including the items in this photograph.

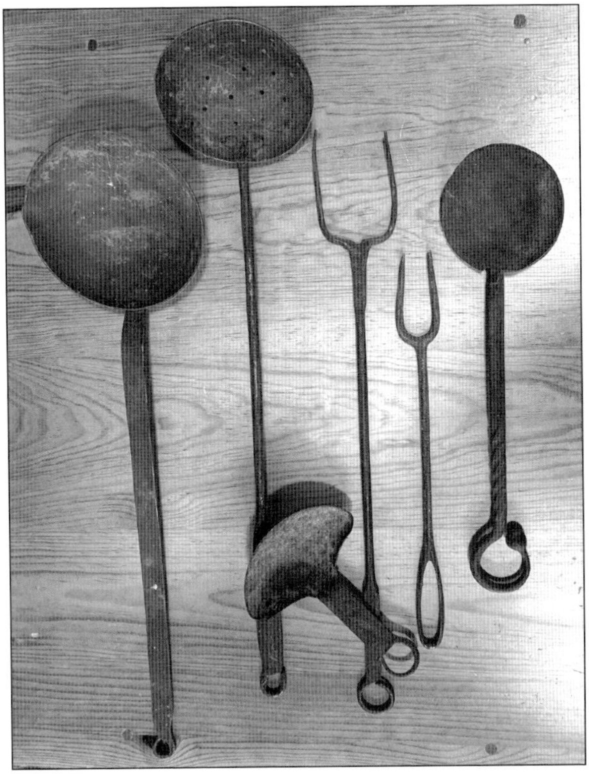

These Spanish colonial forks, skimmer, and spoons are from the 18th century. New Mexico blacksmiths were kept quite busy producing essential cooking and eating supplies. Blacksmiths were not only located in towns but also traveled and sold their wares in Indian villages.

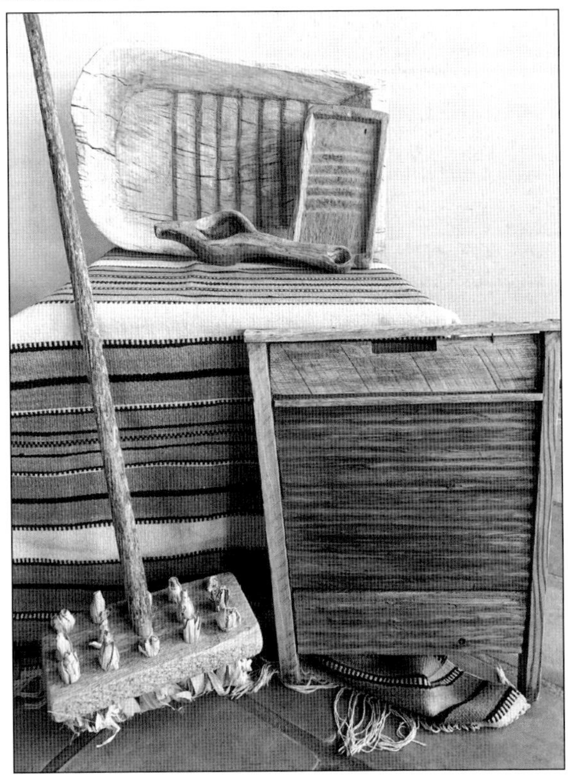

Wooden washboards were necessary not only in homes but on the trail. When clothes needed to be washed, women took handmade soap and simply washed them on the side of streams or rivers. At residences they used well water. A handmade broom like this one, fashioned from corn husks, served for sweeping floors.

Fired clay pots of various sizes were important trade items for the Indians. Some villages became well known for the clay work they produced, at times with ancient origins. With the establishment of El Camino Real, these clay pots were in demand by Spanish colonists. They were traded and purchased by the hundreds through the centuries.

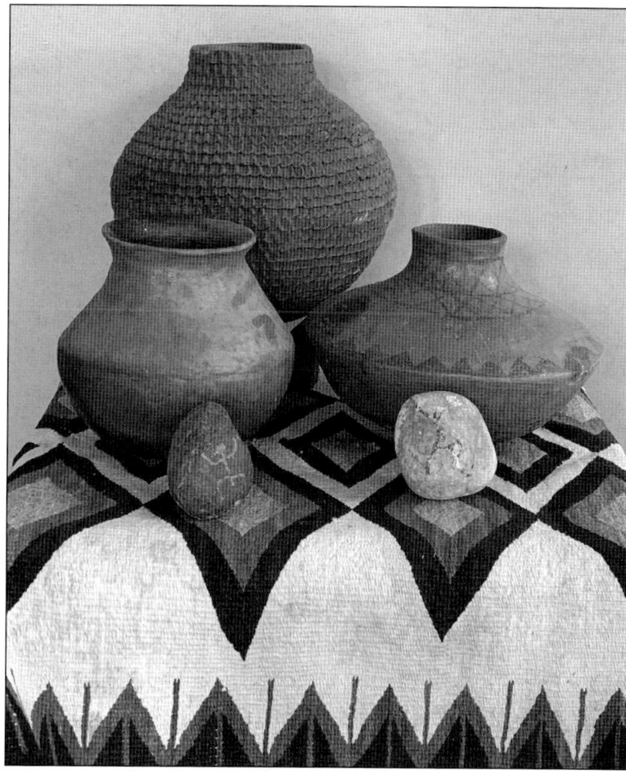

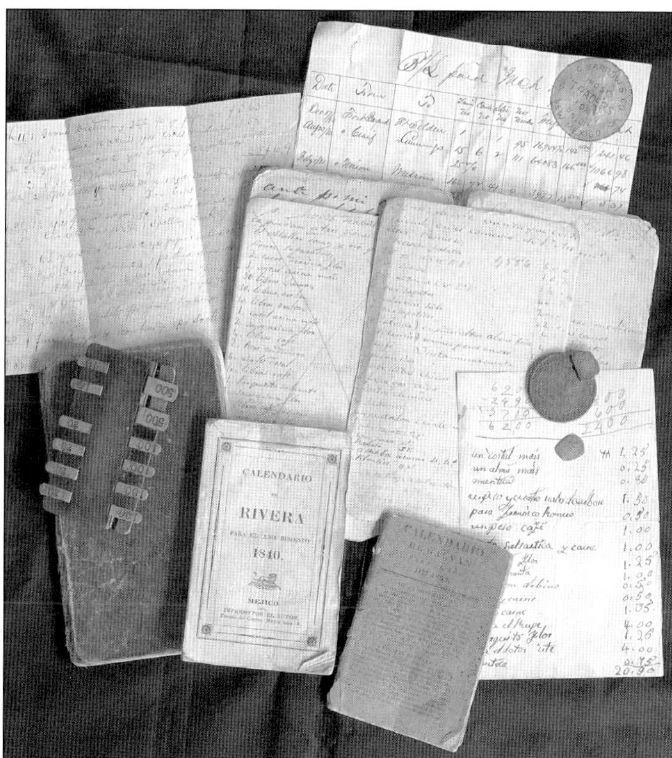

This photograph includes account books of merchant Perfecto Romero, early-19th-century calendars, colonial coins, and an object for manual counting, most probably used for livestock. Merchants like Romero kept meticulous accounts of purchases and sales. Account books continue to survive in archival collections.

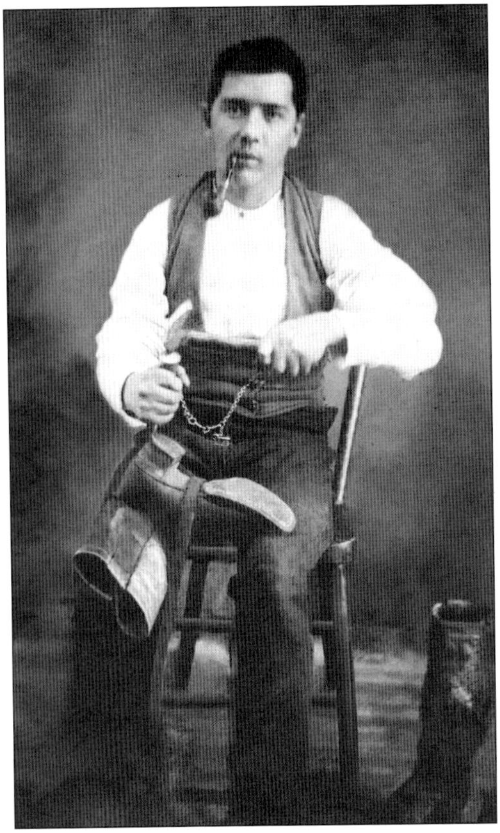

This is an early photograph of boot and shoemaker Pedro Mondragón. He is shown repairing a pair of boots with an iron hammer and chisel. Leather bootmakers were essential to the taming and settling of New Mexico. They produced a variety of leather goods other than footwear. Mondragón as well as others in this business served cowboys and ranchers, the Spanish and Mexican military, and later the American soldiers.

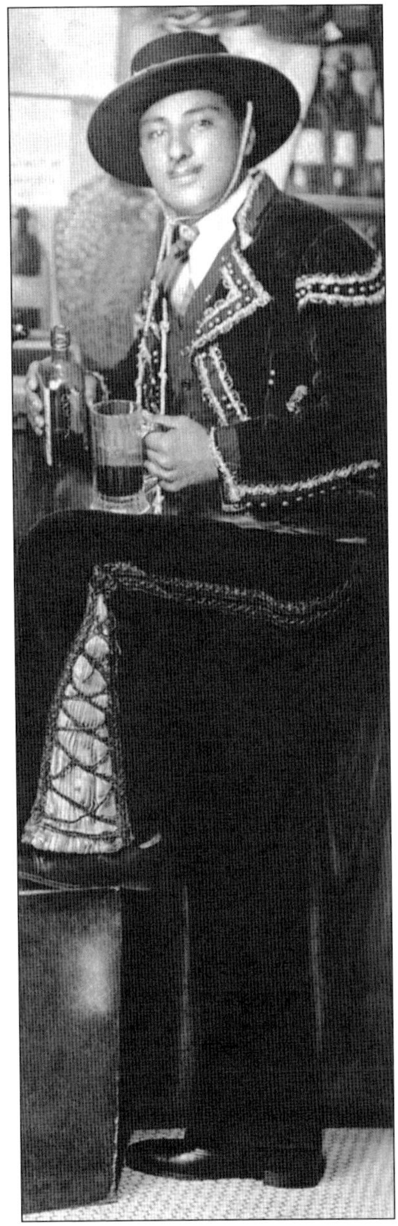

This c. 1940 photograph shows a Spanish colonial outfit being worn for the Santa Fe Fiesta. It is the earliest celebration by Native Americans, held jointly with descendants of Spanish colonists, in the United States. This very popular annual event brings visitors from across the state.

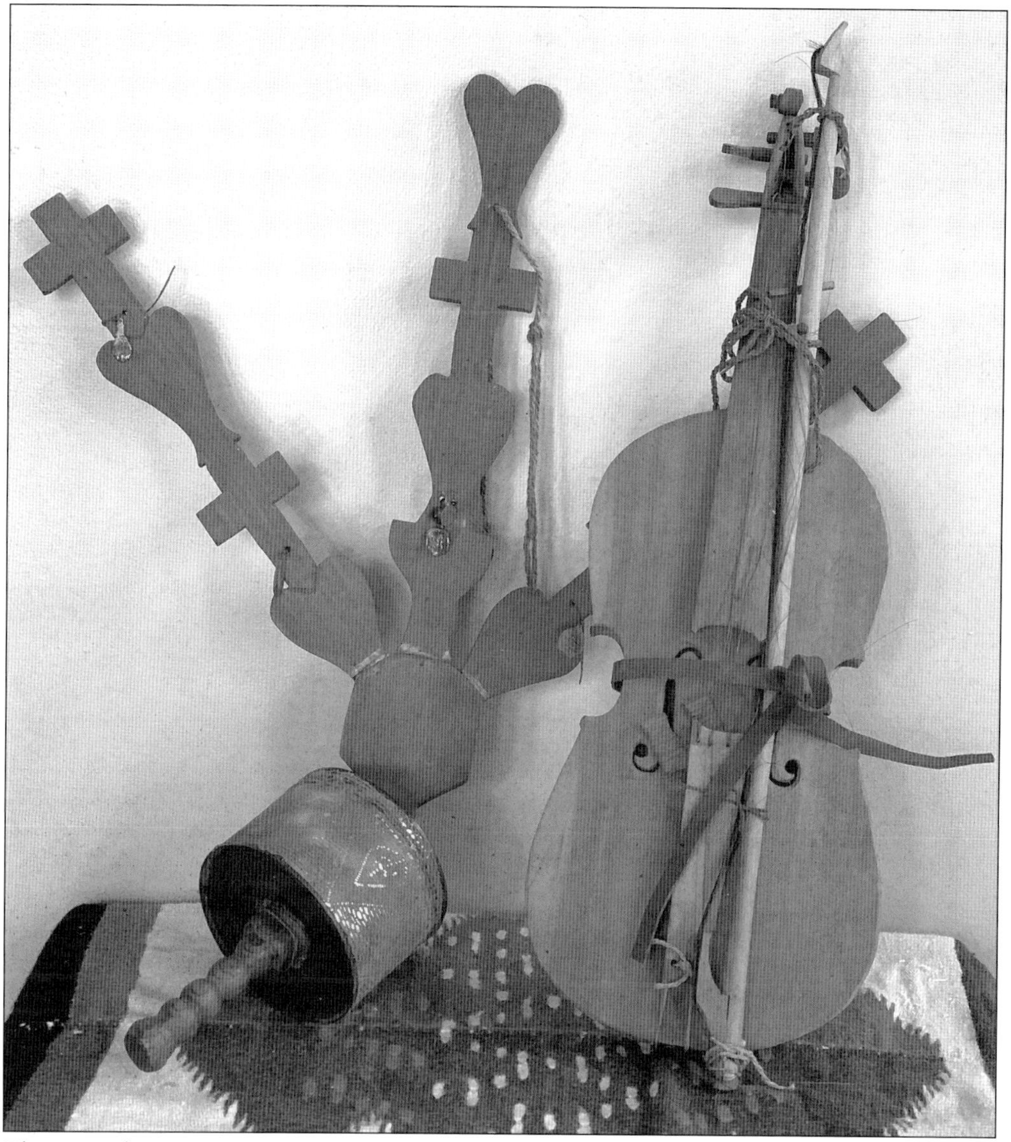

These ritual instruments are associated with the Matachíne dance in New Mexico. The origins of this ancient dramatic dance lie in obscurity. The important pieces used in its performance include a violin, tin or gourd rattles, and a striking wooden article called a *trinidad*, or trinity. This unusual thin, three-stemmed board carved in pine is swung during the dance. Some older individuals say this piece represents La Santisima Trinidad, the Holy Trinity, with God at center, the Holy Spirit at left, and Christ at right. The dance features a person dressed as a bull, another who represents a king, and a young girl dressed in white. The orderly marching dancers wear an Arabic inspired headdress. The dance appears to represent a battle between good and evil and is performed on Roman Catholic saints' feast days in some villages.

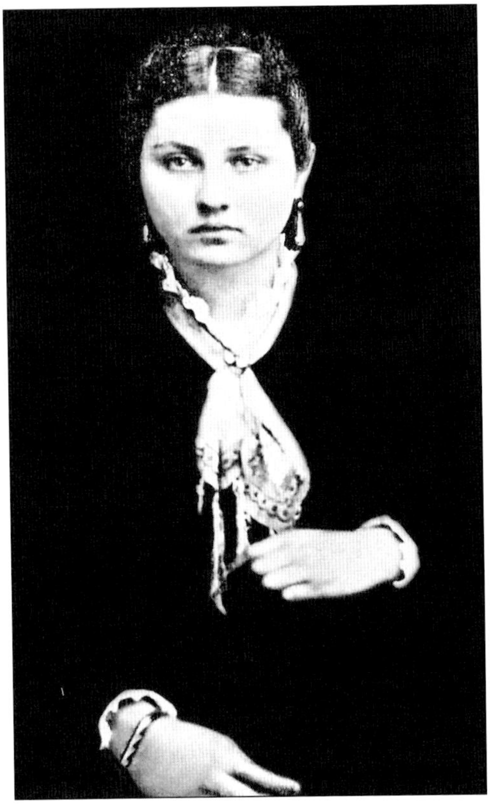

Once photographers arrived over various trails, photography became an artform in New Mexico. Politicians, outlaws, lawmen—everyone wanted to have their picture taken. Itinerant photographers plied their trade on the Royal Road into all corners of the territory. They were also amazed at the landscape. This beautiful c. 1870 tintype shows the skill of New Mexico photographers.

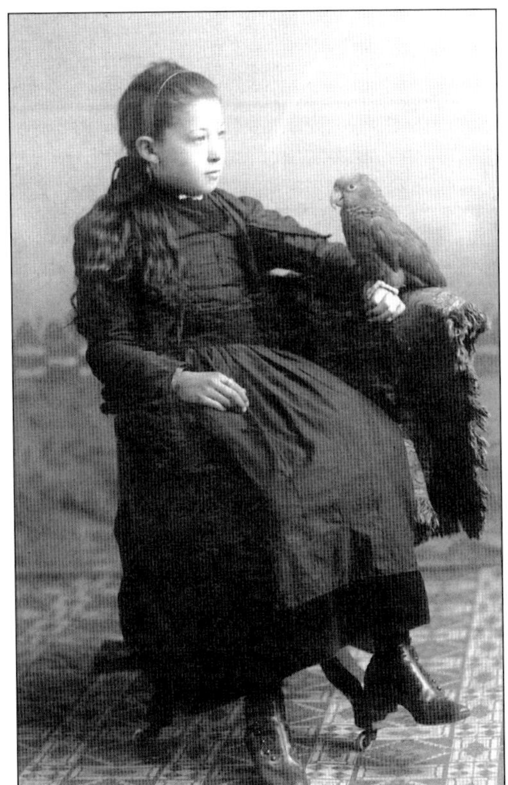

In this c. 1879 picture taken in Santa Fe, photographer T.J. Curran captured a serene scene of a young lady and her pet parrot. Macaws were a popular trade item dating back centuries. Their feathers have been found in prehistoric Native American sites. This trade continued on El Camino Real.

Four

Military Excursions and Campaigns

During the early history of New Mexico, Indian trails were used to harass, circumvent certain areas, and attack unsuspecting victims. Apaches, Navajos, Comanches, and other nomadic tribes used ancient beaten tracks to attack Indian pueblos. Spanish presidio soldiers attempted to maintain the peace along the trail. During the Civil War, Confederate commanders used El Camino Real to attack New Mexico. Major battles were fought along the road, such as the well-known Battle of Valverde and others less known such as the Battle of Albuquerque and the Battle of Peralta. The Union garrison at Albuquerque was taken over by Confederate troops as well as the capital city of Santa Fe. This took place after the horrendous Battle of Valverde. One early American traveler stated that the place was in ruins during the 1840s, though this may or may not be true. Mailed postcards from here are still extant from the late 1800s. What is known is that hundreds and perhaps thousands of Hispanic Union volunteers from New Mexico and Texas Confederates fought, were maimed, and died here. The Union troops were winning the battle and distinguishing themselves in combat, but for an unknown reason, the Union commander, Col. Edward Sprigg Canby, ordered a retreat. His singular move gave the victory to the Confederates, who continued their invasion, causing many more casualties. Colonel Canby was only 24 years old. He was promoted to general after his stint in New Mexico and became the only American general killed during the Indian wars. The famous "Gettysburg of the West," fought at Glorieta, was won by Lt. Col. Manuel Antonio Chaves and his New Mexico Volunteers. He had a well-known hacienda, trading center, ranch, and farm near El Camino Real. Years after the American takeover in 1848, El Camino Real served American forces in continuous battles against the Indians. The famous Long Walk of the Navajos took place along El Camino Real after they had been subjugated by Christopher "Kit" Carson.

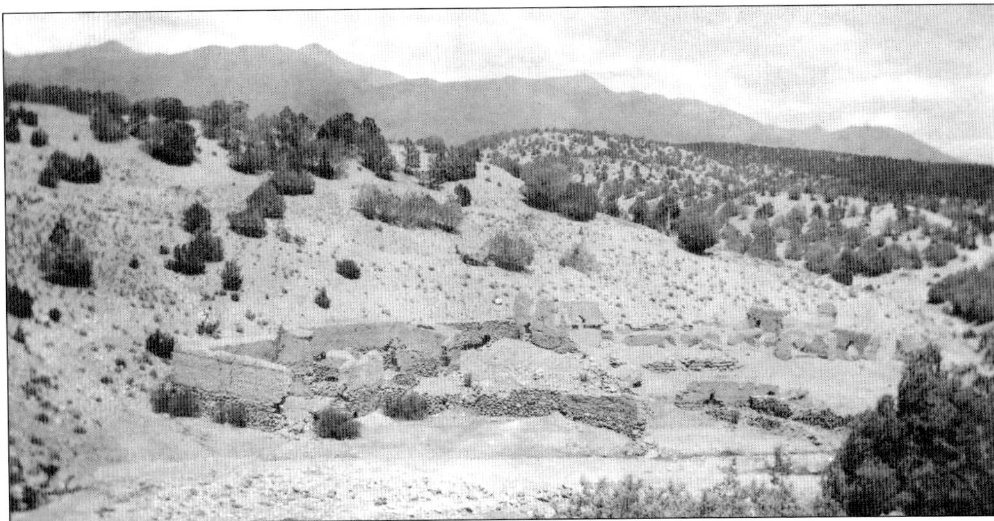

Military presidios, outposts meant to protect travelers, merchants, and traders on the Royal Road, were located in many areas. These were established in the 18th century. This photograph shows a no-longer-extant compound with clearly visible lookout towers and remains of other structures at the military site.

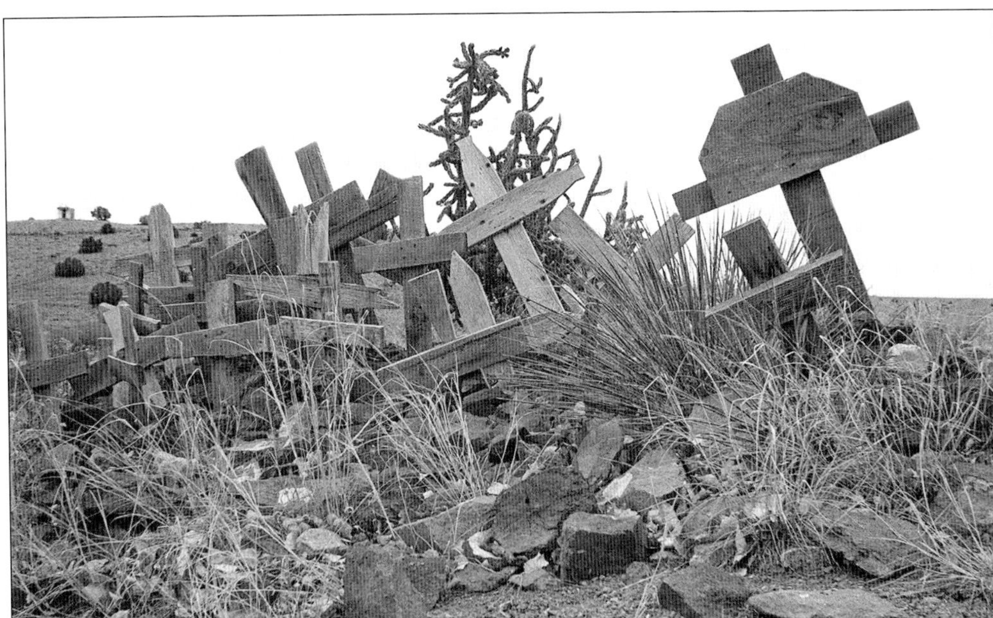

Roadside memorials with crosses to mark where someone died have a very long history in New Mexico. This beautiful commemoration may very well have marked where a person died and was buried while traveling on El Camino Real. Engravings dating from the early 19th century show these crosses. These *descansos* (resting places) and *memorias* (memories) continue to dot roadways even today.

This is an 18th-century Spanish shield from New Mexico made from buffalo hide, cowhide, or a combination of both. These rare shields helped to protect *soldados de cuera*, Spanish presidio soldiers. These indispensable troops patrolled the frontier borderlands and trails. They were ready to ride wherever they were needed. These men were well armed and fearless in battle.

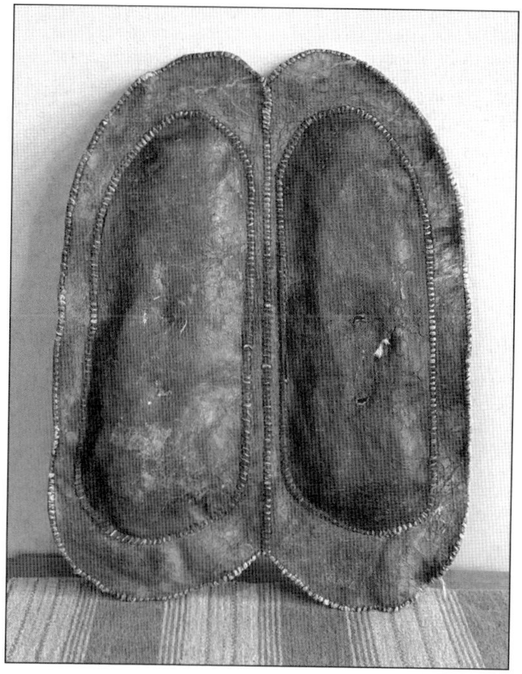

Pictured in this group of Spanish colonial artifacts is a portable traveling desk that was carried on the trail. There are also two leather document holders and a sample document plus a leather map case. The elaborate case is unusual and rare. A cartographer would have used this while traveling, identifying, drawing, and documenting landmarks. This one is attributed to Bernardo Miera y Pacheco. (Photograph by Rosa Maria Calles.)

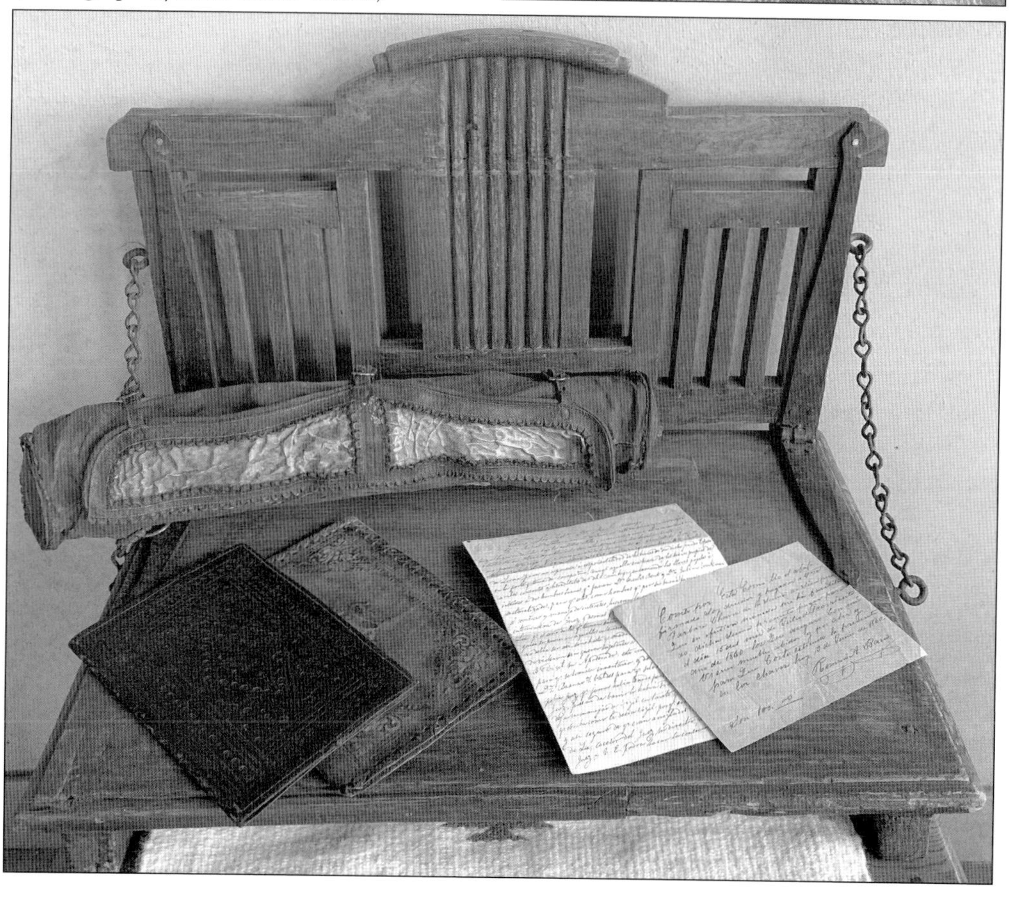

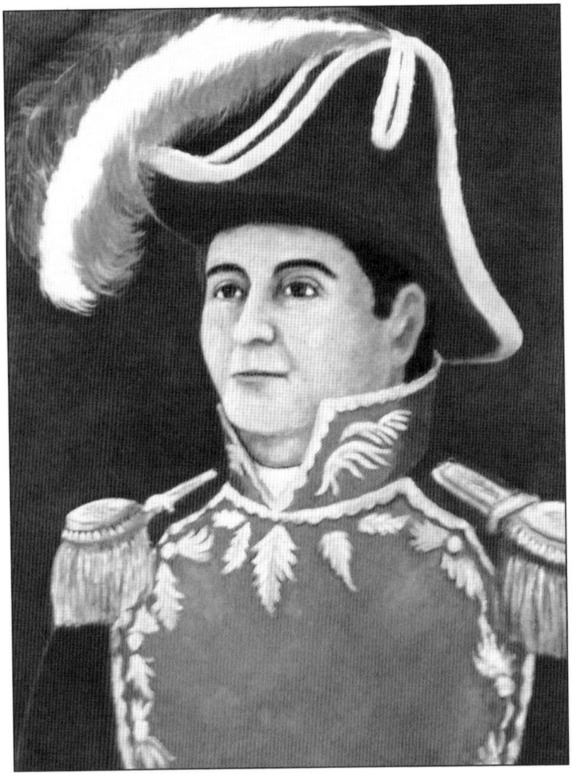

New Mexico governor and general Don Manuel Armijo was a Mexican war hero. He was maligned and disdained by American yellow journalists who sought to destroy his reputation among the people. They succeeded. Armijo in 1846 had extensive land holdings near El Camino Real, all of which he lost during the Mexican-American War and after. This 1980 painting is by Maximiliano "Max" Salazar.

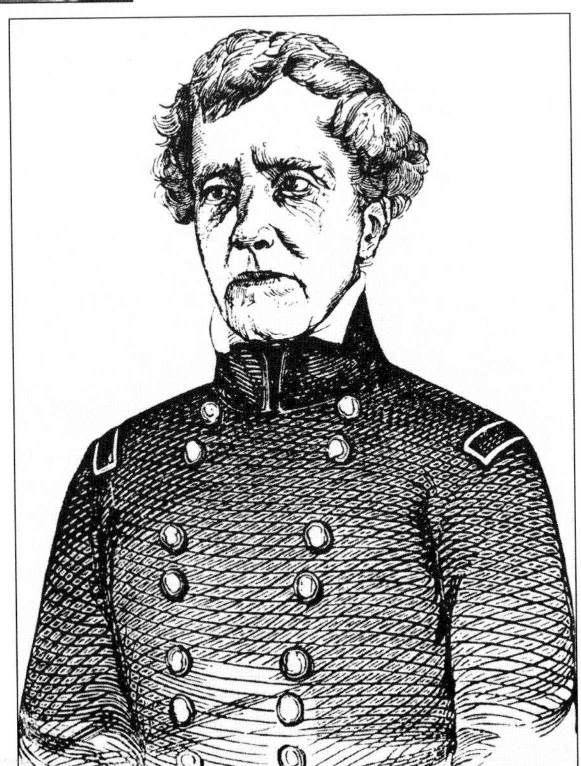

Col. Stephen Watts Kearny led Missouri troops in a conquest of New Mexico. After an apparent takeover, Kearny headed toward California on El Camino Real, feeling confident he had accomplished his goal. While in New Mexico, the colonel set up what he called the "Kearny Code," a set of rules meant to stiffly govern the region. Strict penalties would be dispensed to anyone not following the rules.

Col. Pascual Bailón Martínez led New Mexican forces along with other officers in response to the American invasion of 1846. Battles continued in New Mexico until the Treaty of Guadalupe Hidalgo was signed between Mexico and the United States, effectively ending the war in 1848. Colonel Martínez distinguished himself in battle and was highly decorated.

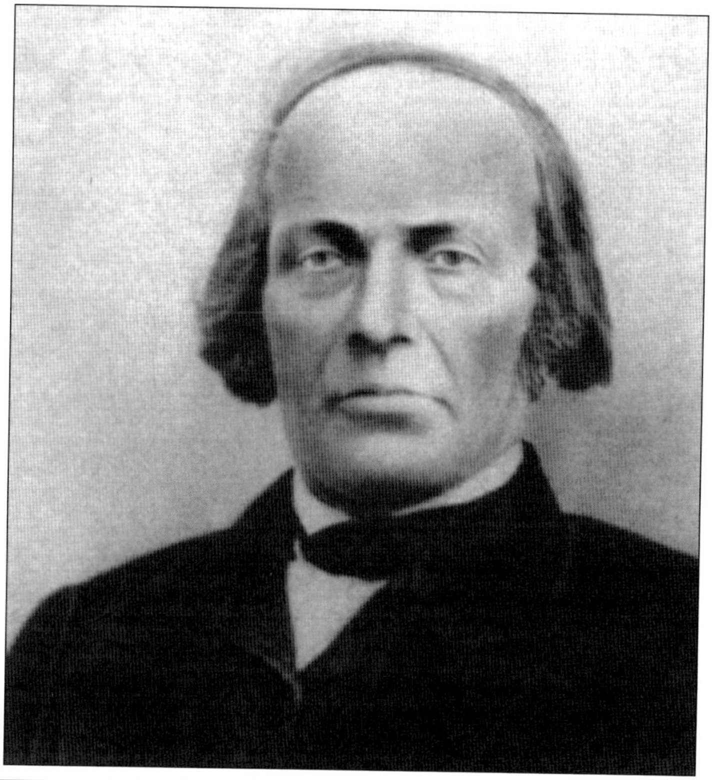

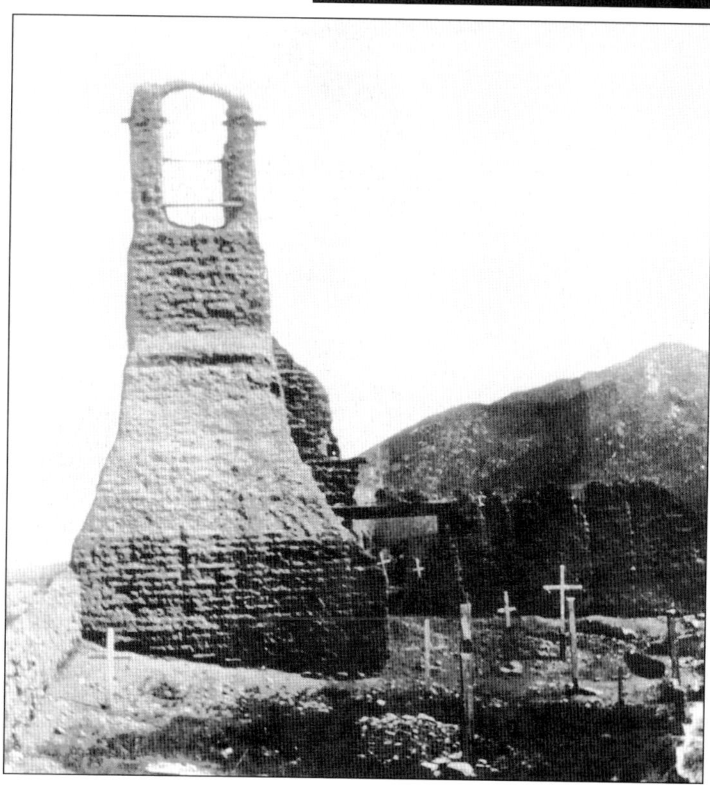

San Gerónimo de Taos Church at Taos Pueblo was destroyed by American forces during the Mexican-American War. Col. Sterling Price ordered the use of howitzers and cannons plus the blasting of the building. Fleeing Indian families who were huddled inside left the church and were shot. This was known as the Taos Massacre. Crosses mark where those killed during the attack were buried. This real-photo postcard was printed around 1907.

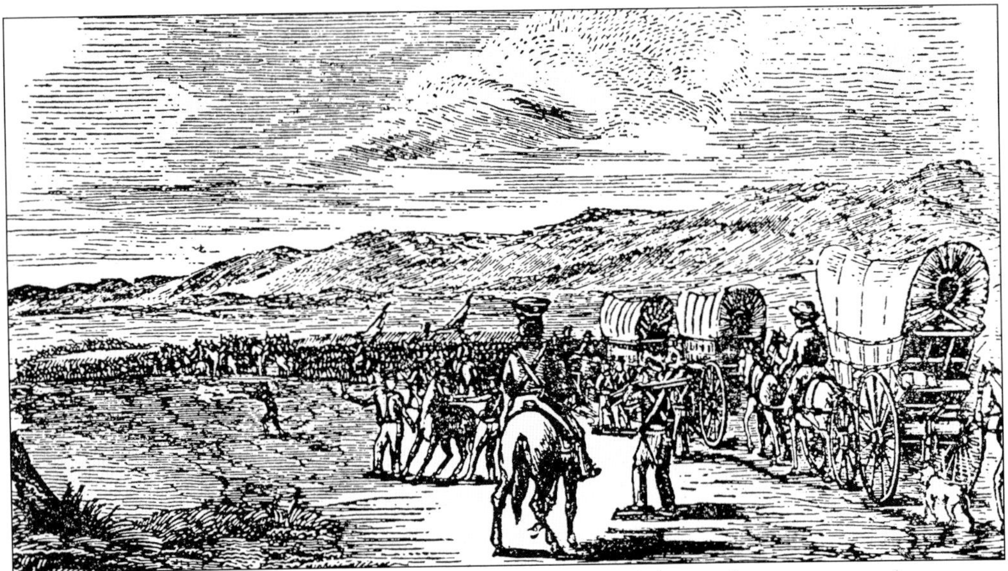

American forces are shown marching along El Camino Real during the invasion and conquest. Many of the troops were dressed in regular clothes rather than uniforms. They walked or rode mules since most of the men did not have horses. Historians of the period write that these men were undisciplined, rowdy, and abusive. They also confiscated goods and wagons. This etching is from the *Journal of William H. Richardson*, published in 1848.

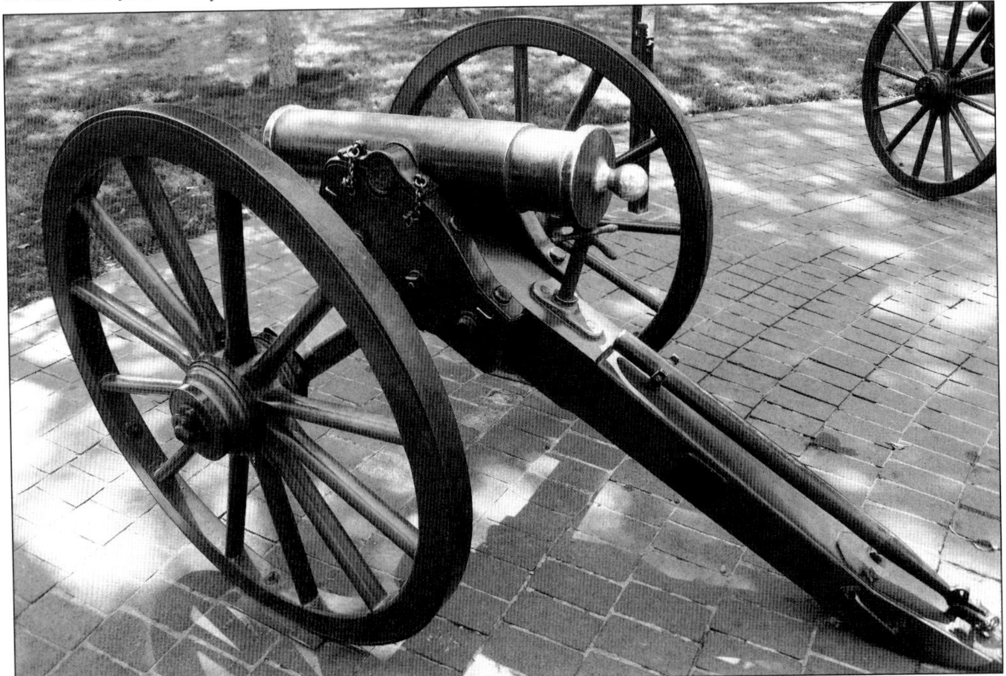

Cannons such as this M1 1841 mountain howitzer had a range of 1,000 feet. They were used during the Mexican-American War and the American Civil War. The Confederate forces retreating from New Mexico through Albuquerque buried some of their cannons in the fields to facilitate fleeing. These at the Old Town Plaza are replicas of those found. (Photograph by Ramón Juan Carlos de Aragón.)

Confederate general Henry H. Sibley's route into New Mexico in 1862 ran along El Camino Real to Santa Fe. The Confederates scored a victory in taking over the capital but suffered defeat at the hands of Lt. Col. Manuel Antonio Chávez and his troops at Glorieta Pass. The Confederates also retreated along the Royal Road and headed back toward Texas.

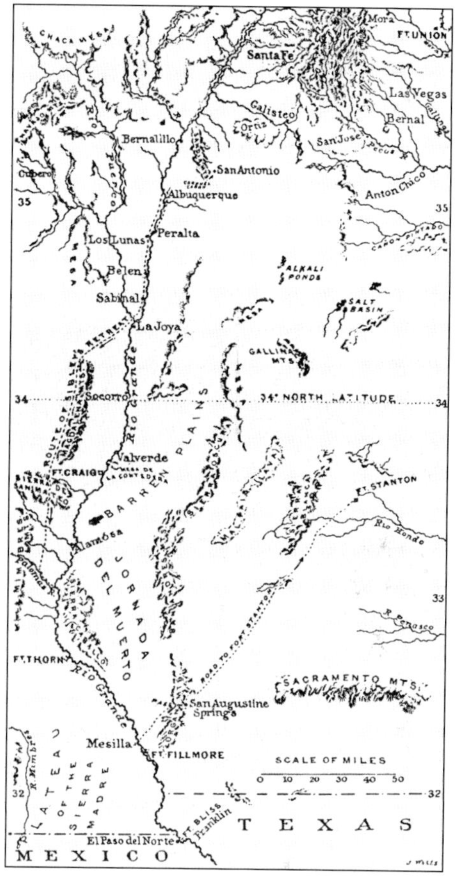

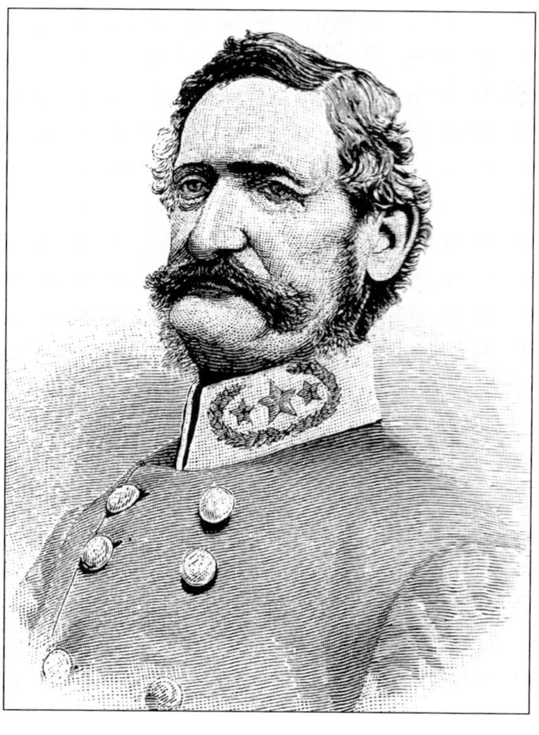

General Sibley commanded the Confederate army that invaded New Mexico in 1862. A victory would have assured that the Confederacy secured the West and vital seaports in California. However, his forces were defeated by New Mexico volunteers under Lt. Col. Manuel Antonio Chávez. This engraving is from Benson J. Lossing's *Pictorial Field Book of the Civil War in America*, published in 1876–1878.

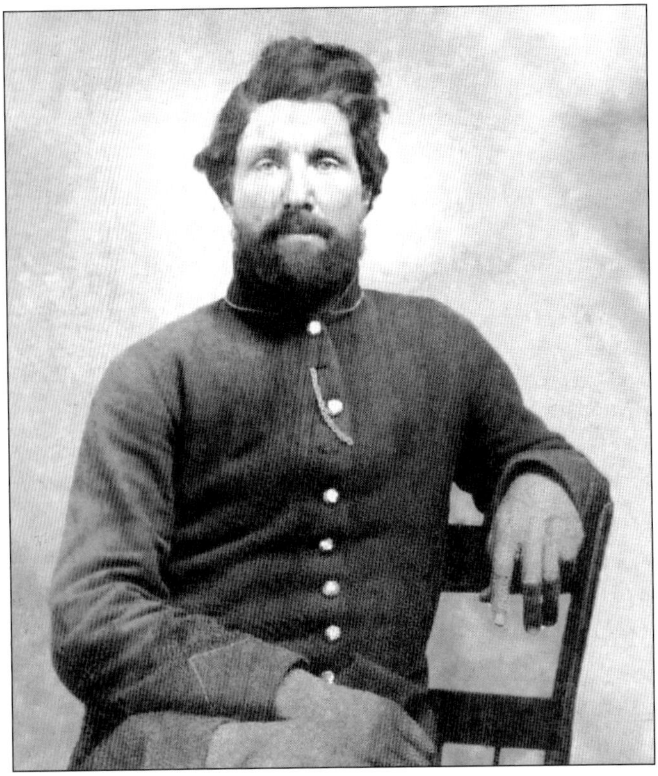

Albuquerque Union army post quartermaster and commander Capt. Herbert M. Enos ordered that supplies at the Albuquerque depot be burned on March 1, 1862. Anything his forces could not transport was destroyed. Warehouses were rented from area residents, who watched in horror as even their own goods were burned. Enos did not want anything to fall into the hands of the approaching Confederate forces.

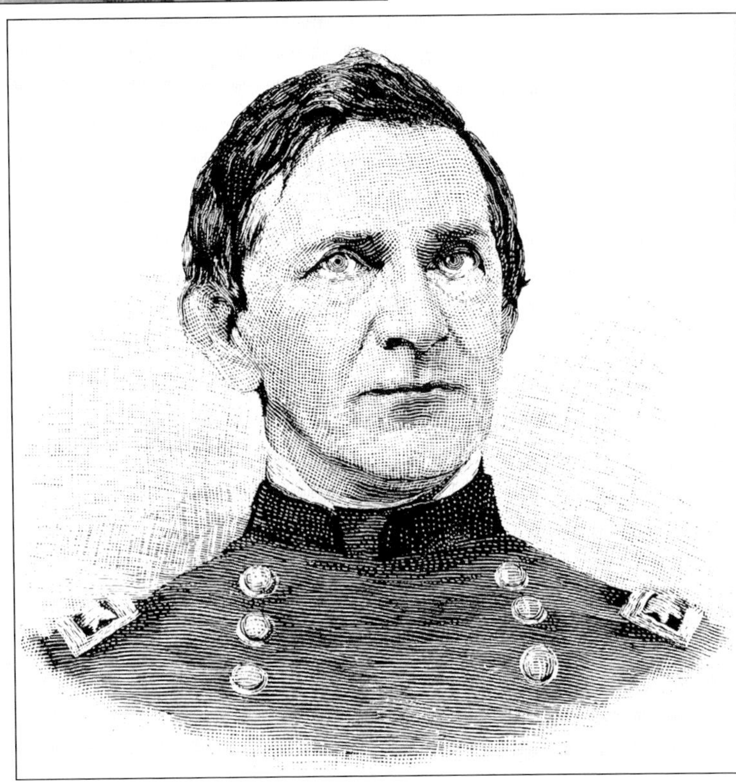

Col. Edward Sprigg Canby served as the commander of Union forces in New Mexico during the Civil War. His regiments were composed of primarily Hispanic volunteers, since regular troops had left New Mexico to fight for the Union and Confederacy. His troops provided their own arms and supplies. Two major battles were fought at Valverde and Glorieta.

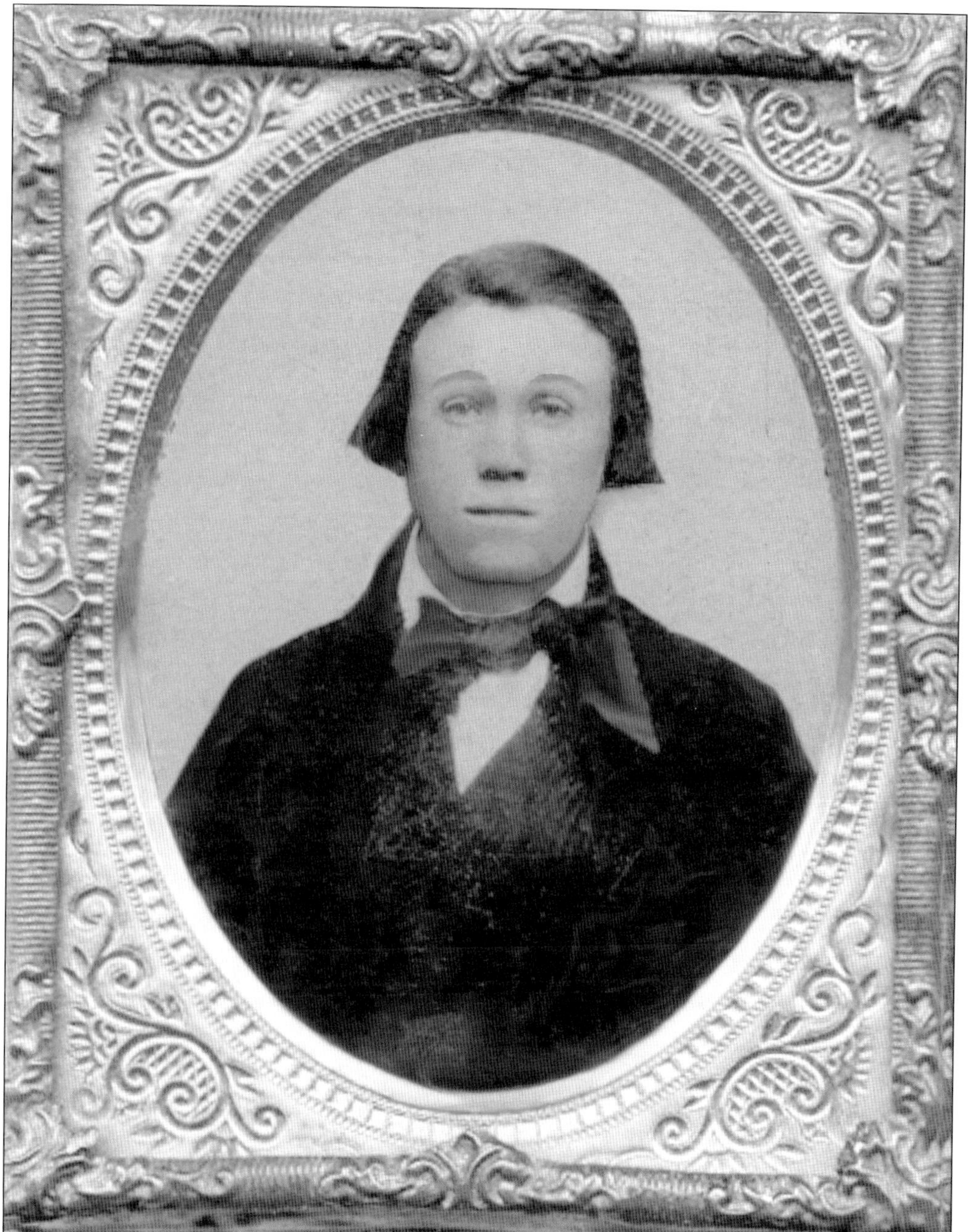

Lt. Col. Manuel Antonio Chávez was called "Savior of the Union at the Battle of Glorieta." Without Chávez's heroic tactics, the Confederacy might have won the West in 1862, thereby changing the course of history in the United States. Chávez, with 200 of his unit, scaled the cliffs at Glorieta. They caught the Confederate rear guard by surprise by lowering themselves with ropes on the other side of the furious battle. They killed those guarding the supply trains and burned the wagons. They also destroyed munitions and cannons and drove off the Confederates' horses and mules. It was a devastating blow for the Confederates, who were winning the hand-to-hand combat. They withdrew and retreated. A loss turned into a victory for the Union volunteers.

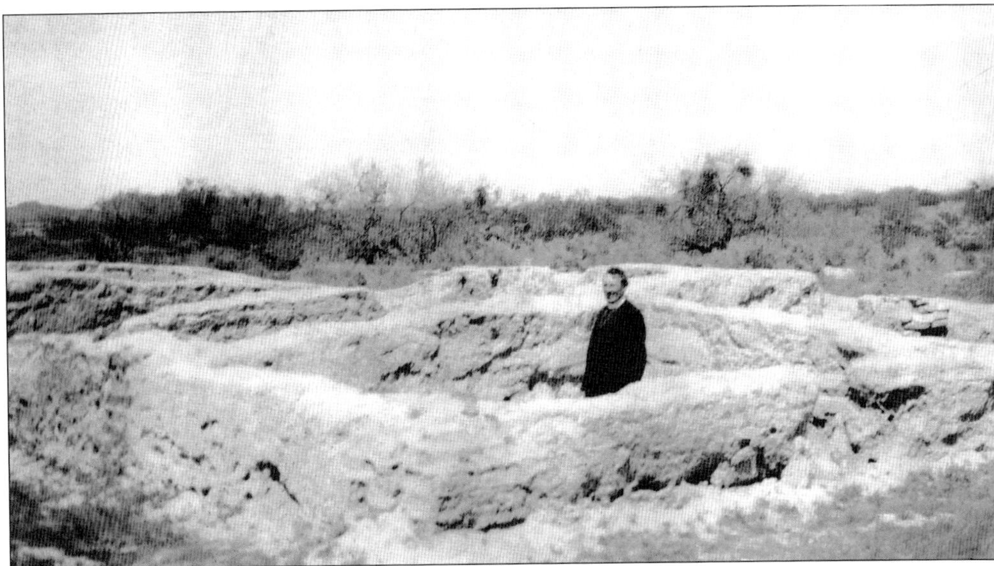

This man is surveying the hacienda ruins of Lt. Col. Manuel Antonio Chávez at Los Ojuelos in 1930. Chávez was the hero of the Battle of Glorieta. He had an extensive ranch and bought and sold products on El Camino Real. Chávez and his ranch hands were often called upon to track Indians.

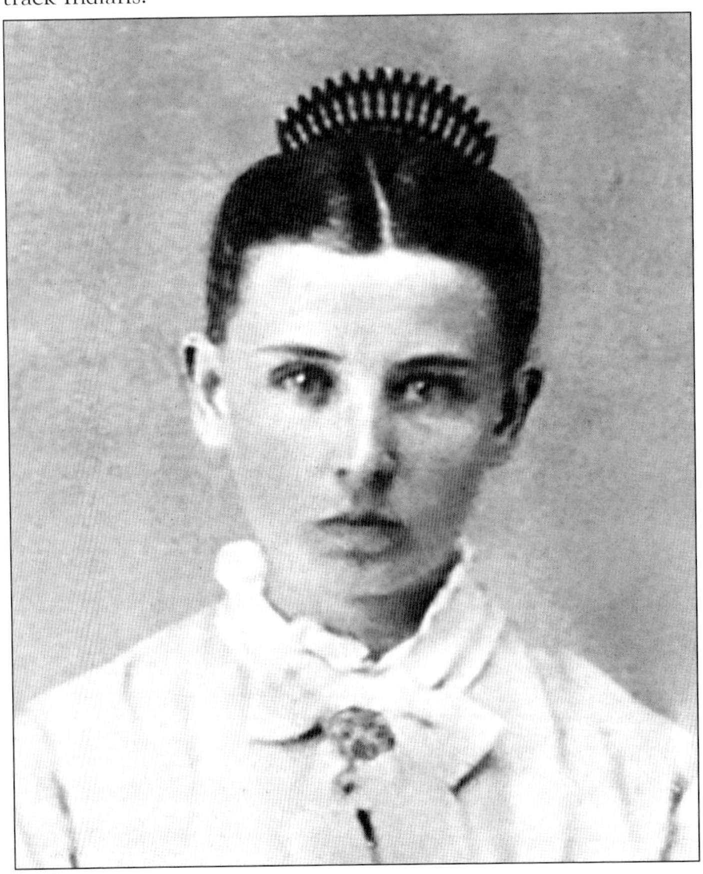

Vicenta Labadie de Chávez, wife of Lt. Col. Manuel Antonio Chávez, is shown wearing a *peineta*. This was a popular headpiece made of tortoiseshell worn by New Mexican women and girls. Peinetas were most often produced and imported from Mexico. Vicenta and other women furnished the troops with meals during the Civil War.

These typical c. 1882 cavalry soldiers from New Mexico were actively involved in the Indian campaigns after the Civil War. Soldiers were stationed at Fort Union near Las Vegas, New Mexico, or at any number of forts in the territory. Their terms of enlistment varied from a few months to a few years. Officers served longer.

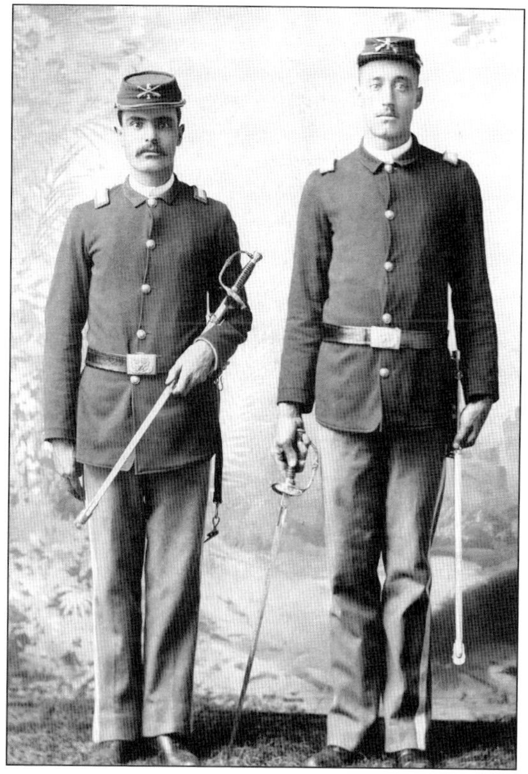

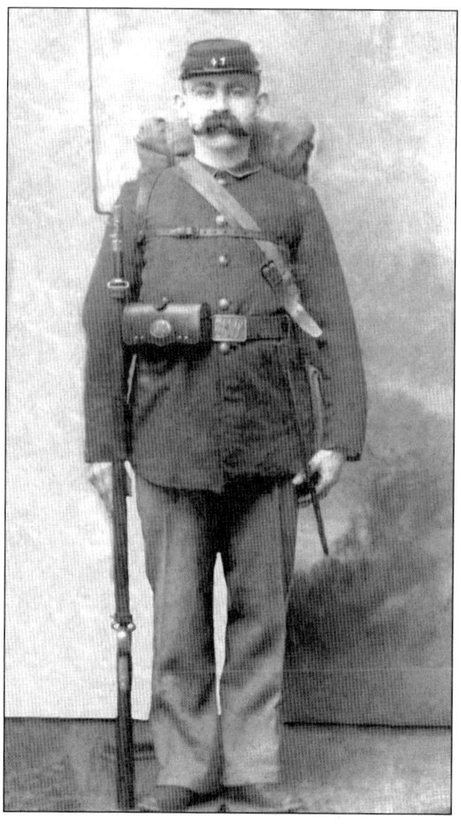

This fully equipped soldier serves as an example of how well prepared some troops were to fight in battle during the latter part of the 19th century. Soldiers such as this were often seen coming and going on El Camino Real either marching toward battle or returning to a fort after fighting.

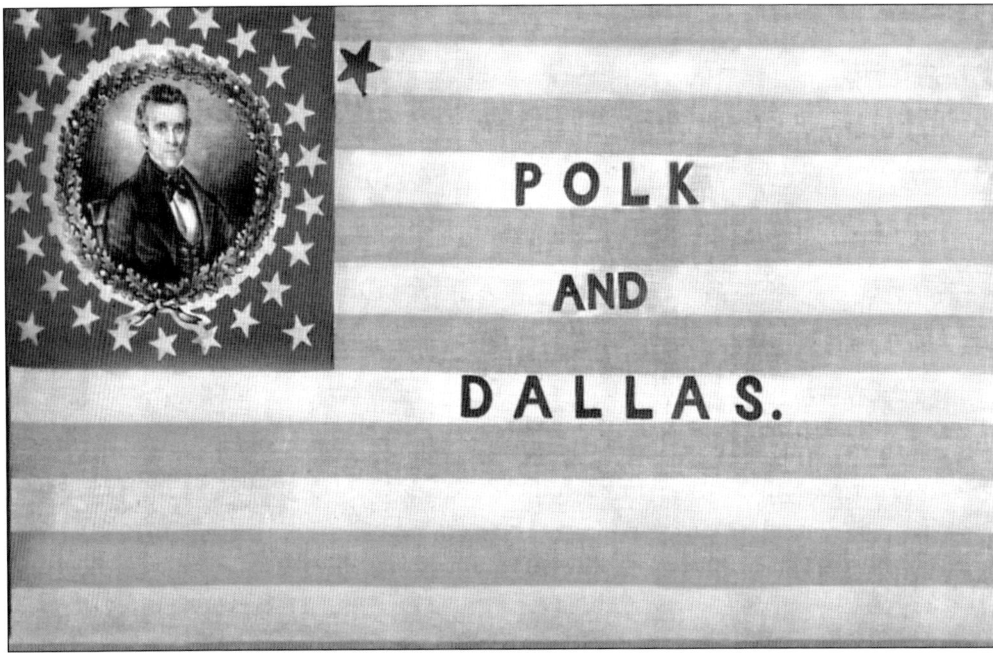

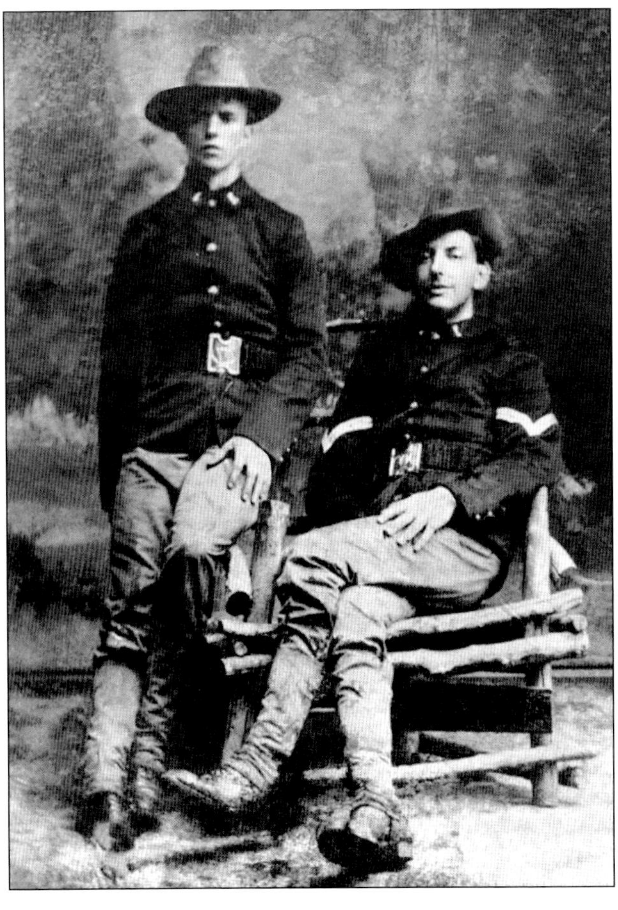

This political ribbon was for presidential candidate James K. Polk and his running mate, George Mifflin Dallas. President Polk declared war on Mexico and sent troops into New Mexico in 1846. He believed in the doctrine of Manifest Destiny, which stated that it was ordained by God that the United States would extend its borders from the Atlantic to the Pacific.

American cavalrymen such as those pictured on this c. 1870 tintype patrolled and fought in Indian country. They distinguished themselves as Indian fighters and at times were highly decorated. At the same time, the cavalry protected miners and squatters who were defying treaties and encroaching on Indian properties.

Five

Trials and Tribulations of a Road

After over 200 years, changes were in store for New Mexico and its special El Camino Real de Tierra Adentro. During its early history, it can be said that El Camino Real was a pathway to hardship, understanding, compassion, and history in the making. During peaceful times, Native Americans in New Mexico traded and shared religious philosophies and ideas among the Indians. Solar eclipses, moon phases, and other natural phenomena featured prominently in Indian ideologies. Into this mix was cast drought, diseases and epidemics, intertribal wars, and suffering both before and after the arrival of Europeans, plus the decline of wildlife for food and the decrease in religious rituals. El Camino Real certainly did not escape the endless story of world history. The old road had its ups and downs. The upside was trade and commerce that benefited everyone. The downside was battles and warfare plus unexpected heart-wrenching deaths along this sorrowful, eventful, and very important world journey that touched the lives of many. For American adventurers at the beginning, profit was the rule of the day.

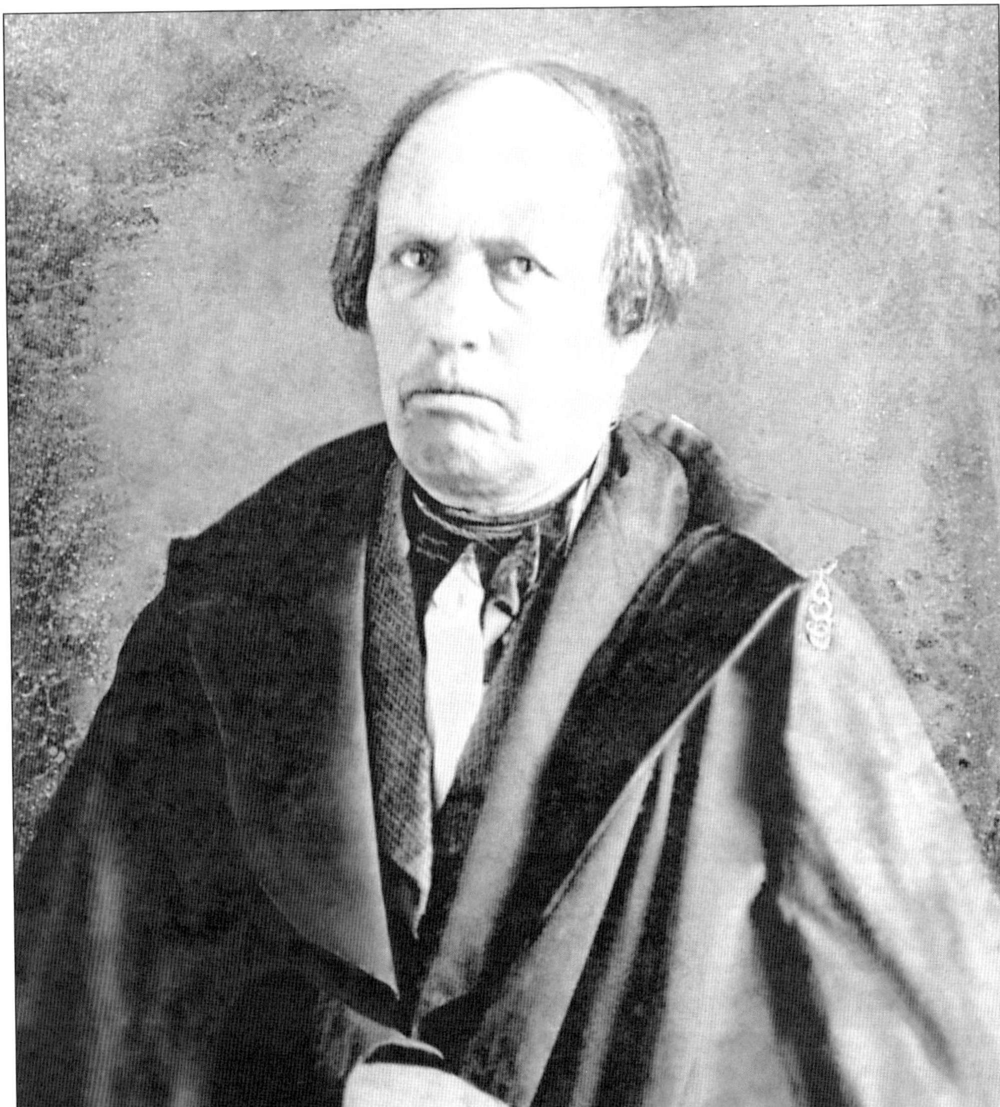

Presbítero Don Antonio José Martínez is considered New Mexico's folk hero priest. He fought against injustices in the church and in society. He championed Native American rights, protection of the environment, conservation of wildlife, and civil rights as a major proponent who spearheaded the movement of equality in the United States during the 19th century. It is acknowledged that he was ahead of his time. Martínez was outraged by the near extermination of the bison and its terrible impact on hunger. He and his family were frequent travelers on the Royal Road and he was popular throughout New Mexico. His father, Don Severino Martínez, purchased goods and merchandise that were transported on the road.

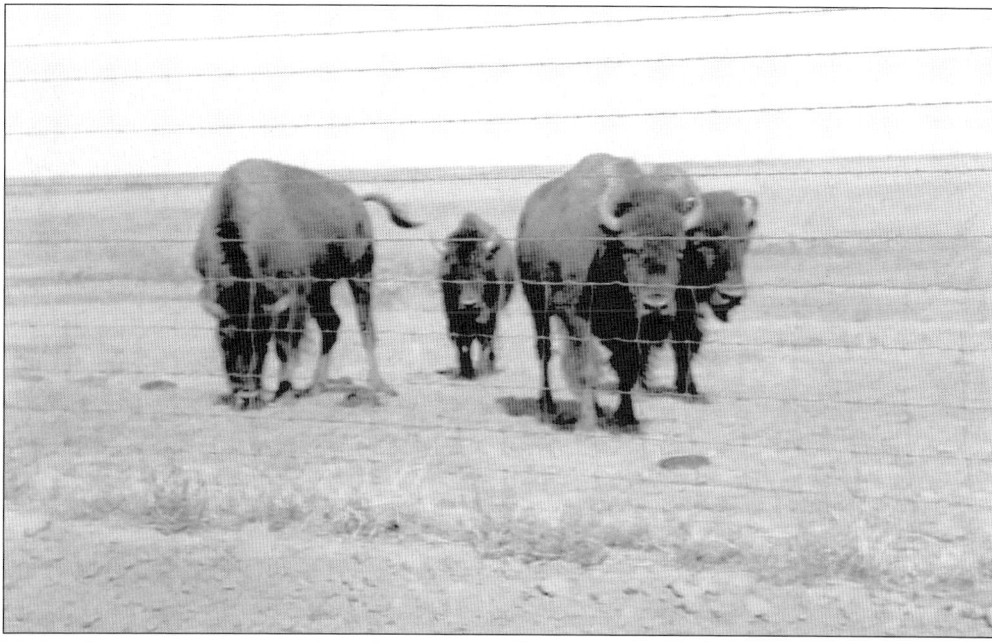

Native Americans were not allowed to enter and hunt in restricted US federal lands that were formerly Indian lands. Barbed wire was strewn across vast areas of New Mexico. Fenced-off areas included forests, wildlife ranges, regions with rivers and streams, and spaces where bison had roamed freely for thousands of years. American fur traders and hunters nearly caused the extinction of the bison, often called the American buffalo.

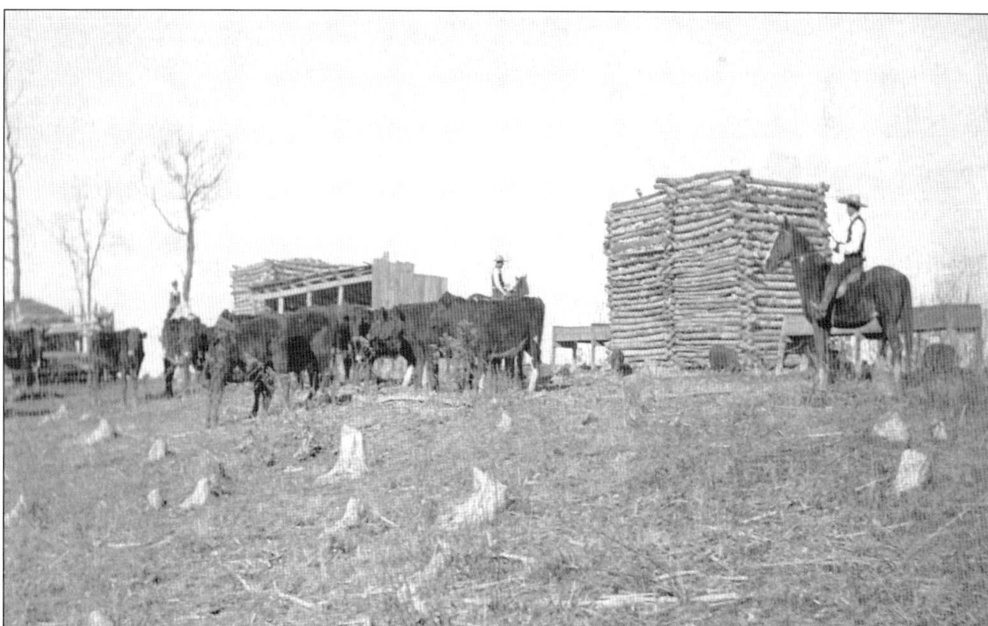

Extensive lumber was used in the construction of buildings and ranches by Americans after New Mexico became a part of the United States. Many stumps can be seen in this photograph of the large Anderson Ranch from trees that were cut. The purpose of the high log piles is unknown.

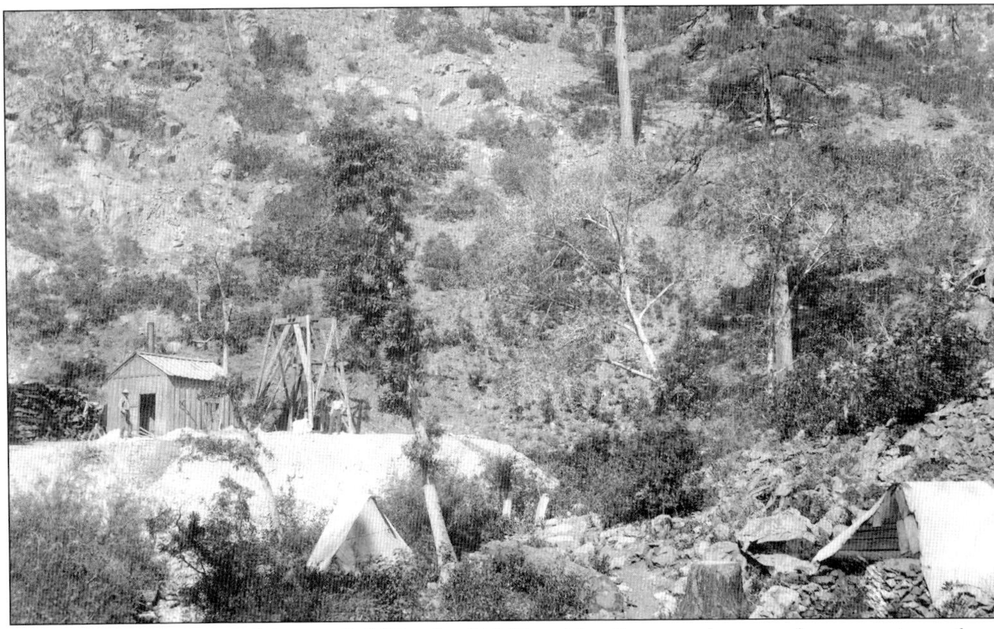

Before the infamous California Gold Rush of 1849, gold-, silver-, and copper-hungry miners from the East swarmed into New Mexico. They set up camps indiscriminately in Indian territory and Spanish private and community properties. This spurred Indian wars and an ageless struggle over Spanish and Mexican land grants.

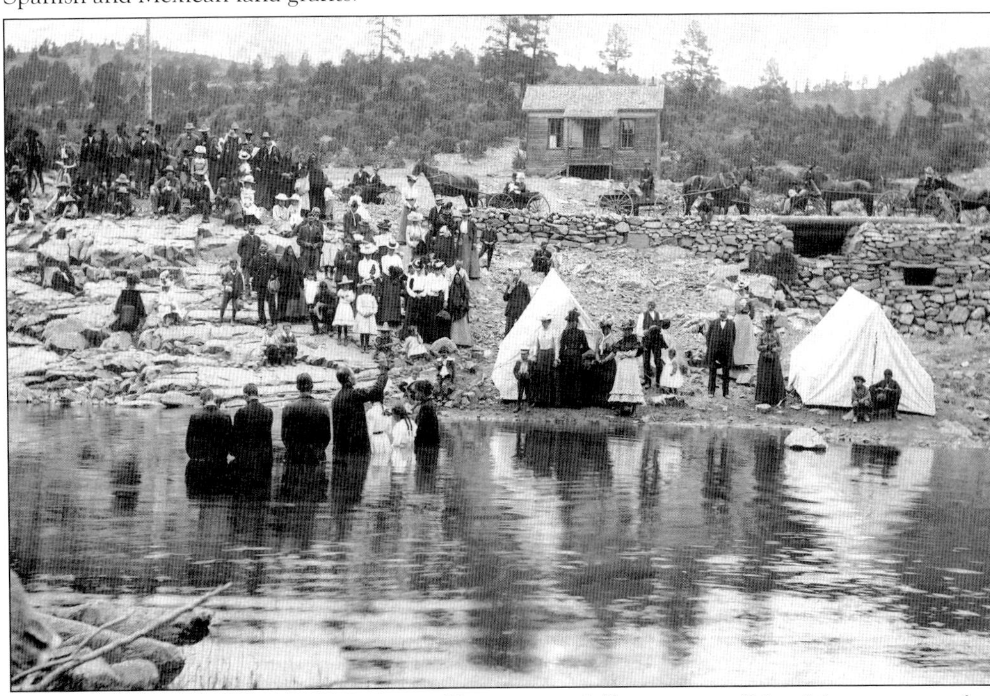

American Presbyterian ministers performed baptisms in different areas of New Mexico, most often along El Camino Real in southern New Mexico, which had been taken over by Confederates. The Catholic Church under the new bishop Jean-Baptiste Lamy left the area vulnerable to indoctrination by other faiths. (Courtesy of Lawrence O. Ealy.)

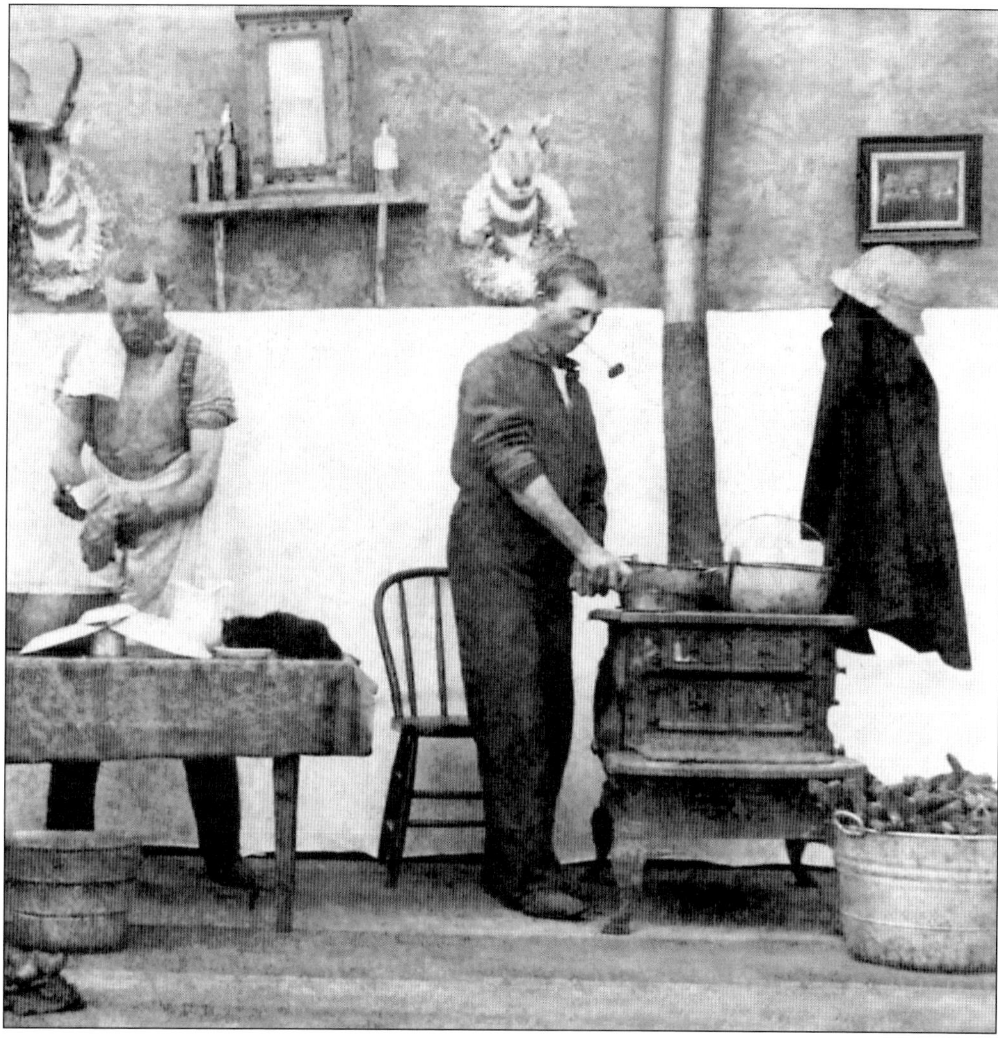

Copper ore was found in southern New Mexico by Lt. Col. Manuel Carrasco in 1800. This became known as the Santa Rita del Cobre Mine, begun in 1803. In time, approximately 20,000 mule teams loaded with copper annually transported the ore from here to Mexico City along El Camino Real. A Spanish military presidio was established to protect the area, along with a very large, thriving community of miners and their families. Once New Mexico was taken over by the United States, American miners swarmed in by the hundreds. They set up their tents anywhere and everywhere while seeking riches. Millions of dollars in gold, silver, and copper ores were exported to the East. This was a boon for the country after the Indians were dispossessed of their lands.

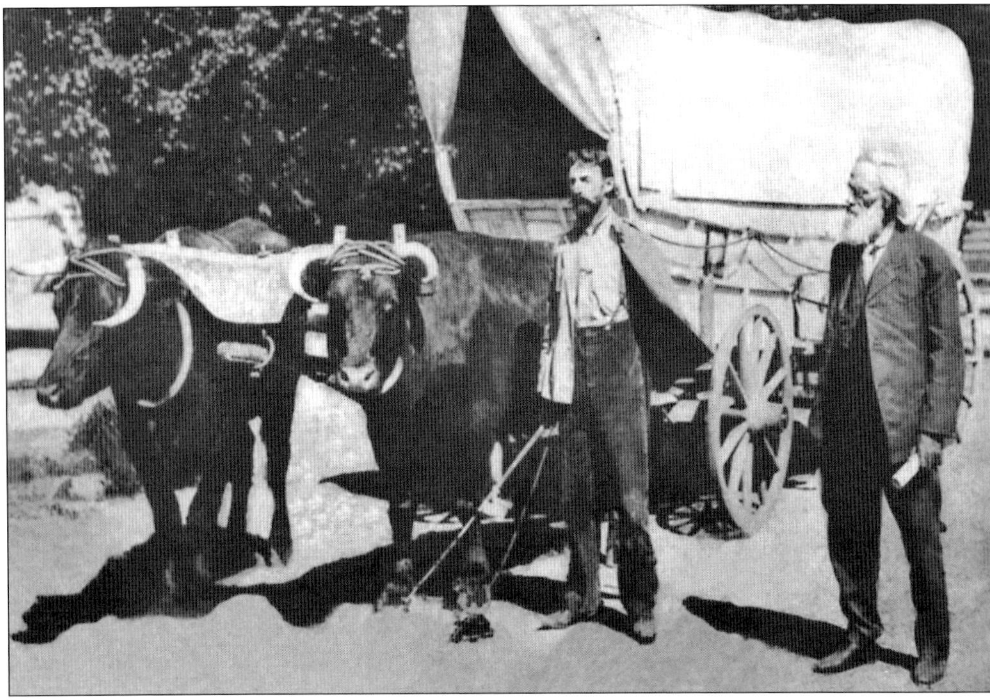

American merchants, traders, bankers, and lawyers flocked to New Mexico on the Santa Fe Trail, which ran from Missouri to Santa Fe. Some unscrupulous American opportunists seeking land and wealth enjoyed immense profits through land theft and high prices for merchandise and goods. Some of these men traveled on El Camino Real checking out areas along the ancient trail.

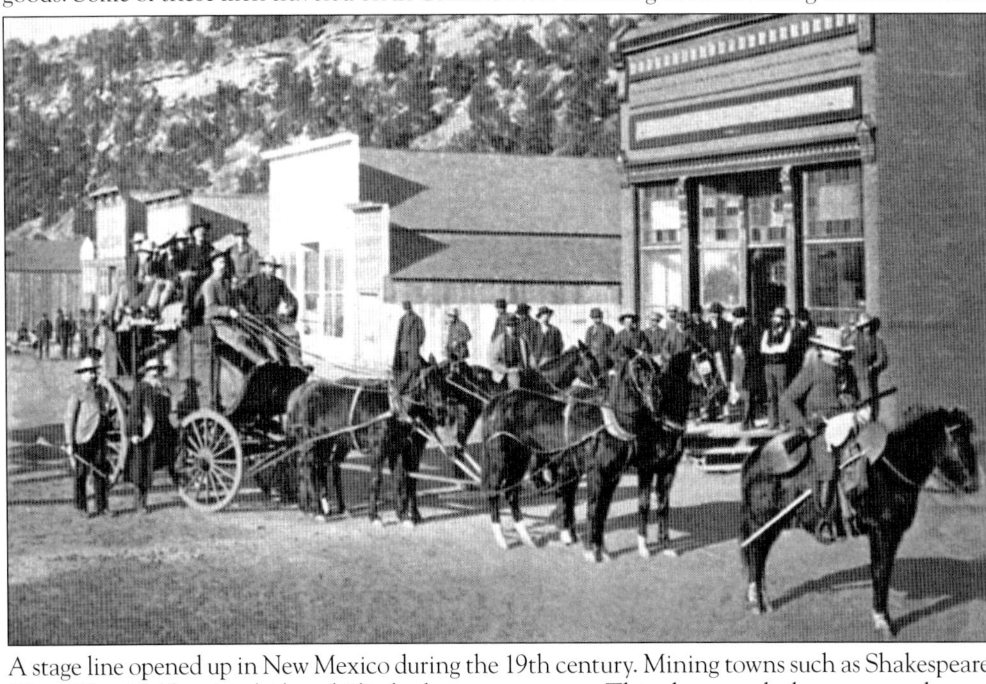

A stage line opened up in New Mexico during the 19th century. Mining towns such as Shakespeare, Silver City, Golden, Madrid, and Elizabethtown sprang up. This photograph shows one such town full of miners. Men with rifles are apparently guarding the ore that is being taken out.

Confederate renegades, outlaws, and cowboy rebels from the town of Seven Rivers, New Mexico, added much to the turmoil on El Camino Real. This ruckus town no longer exists, but while it did, Texas cowmen from there rustled cattle and shot up towns and villages in the late 1800s.

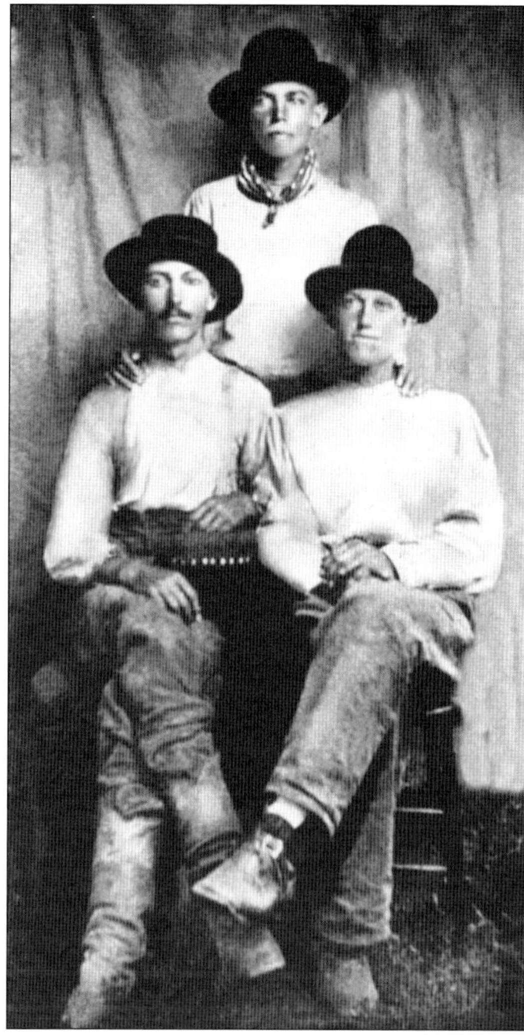

The advancing society encroached even in isolated areas, as seen in this turn-of-the-century photograph. This old house with a surrey wagon in front has railroad equipment nearby. Those working on the railroad set up camp and placed their equipment and railroad ties on private properties along the railroad lines.

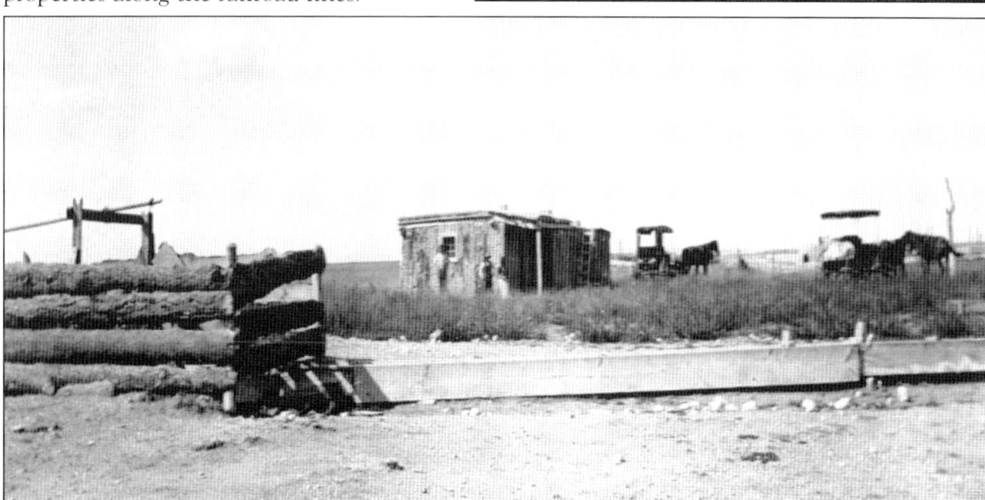

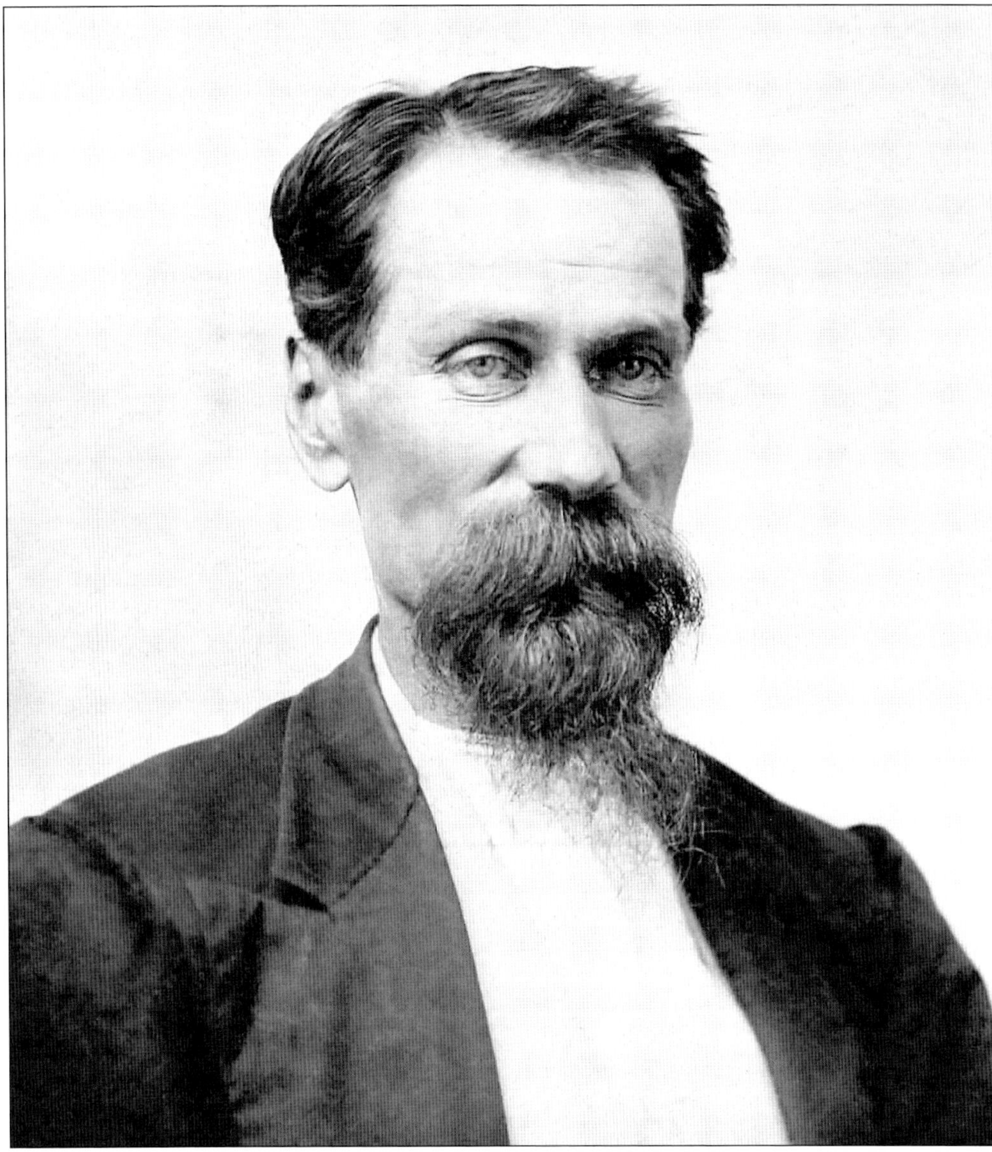

Leander H. McNelly served as a private in Company F of the 5th Regiment of Texas Mounted Volunteers, which invaded New Mexico under Confederate general Thomas Green. The Confederates took over Mesilla in southern New Mexico in 1862 and proclaimed it the capital of Arizona Territory. Two battles were fought there. McNelly fought in the Battle of Valverde against Union Hispanic volunteers near El Camino Real. There were many casualties, and Capt. Saturnino Baca wrote, "The Rio Grande ran red from the blood of those who died." McNelly served as an aide to Gen. Henry H. Sibley on his retreat and later as a captain of a murderous quasi-military force of Southern sympathizers among the Texas Rangers. They were financed by Texan cattle ranchers and fought against Mexicans who tried to regain their stolen lands, livestock, and other possessions.

This stunning *carte de visite* photograph of William H. Bonney, also known as Billy the Kid, was taken by itinerant Silver City photographer Harry Lucas in 1880. Lucas was associated with Alfred S. Addis, who photographed the Kid's boyhood home in Silver City in 1879. The striking similarity between this pose and the famous tintype photograph of Bonney may provide a clue as to the tintype photographer.

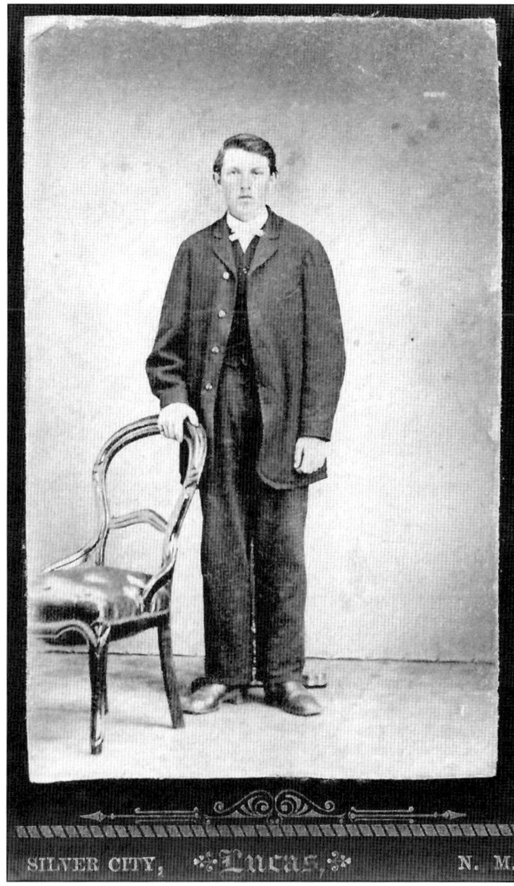

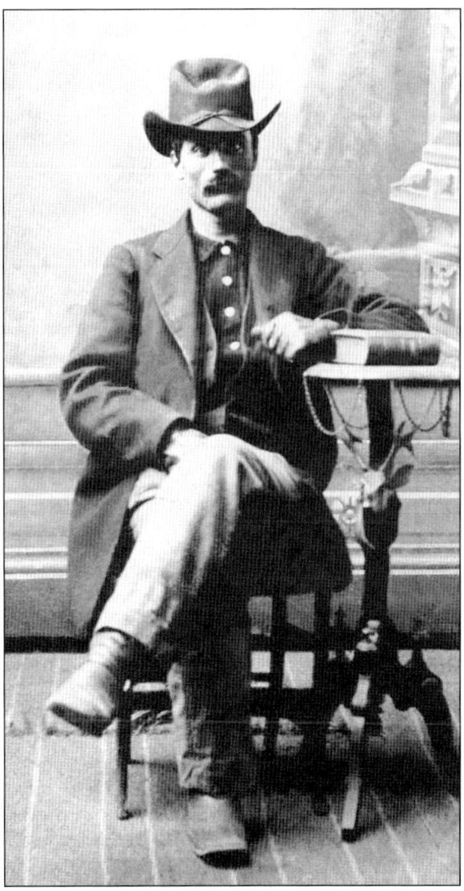

This tintype photograph of Sheriff Patrick Floyd Garrett, taken by James N. Furlong in Las Vegas, New Mexico, around 1881, may show the sheriff after killing William H. Bonney. The famous sheriff owned a ranch nearby and spent a great deal of time in Las Cruces and Mesilla. He was mysteriously murdered while traveling on El Camino Real in 1907.

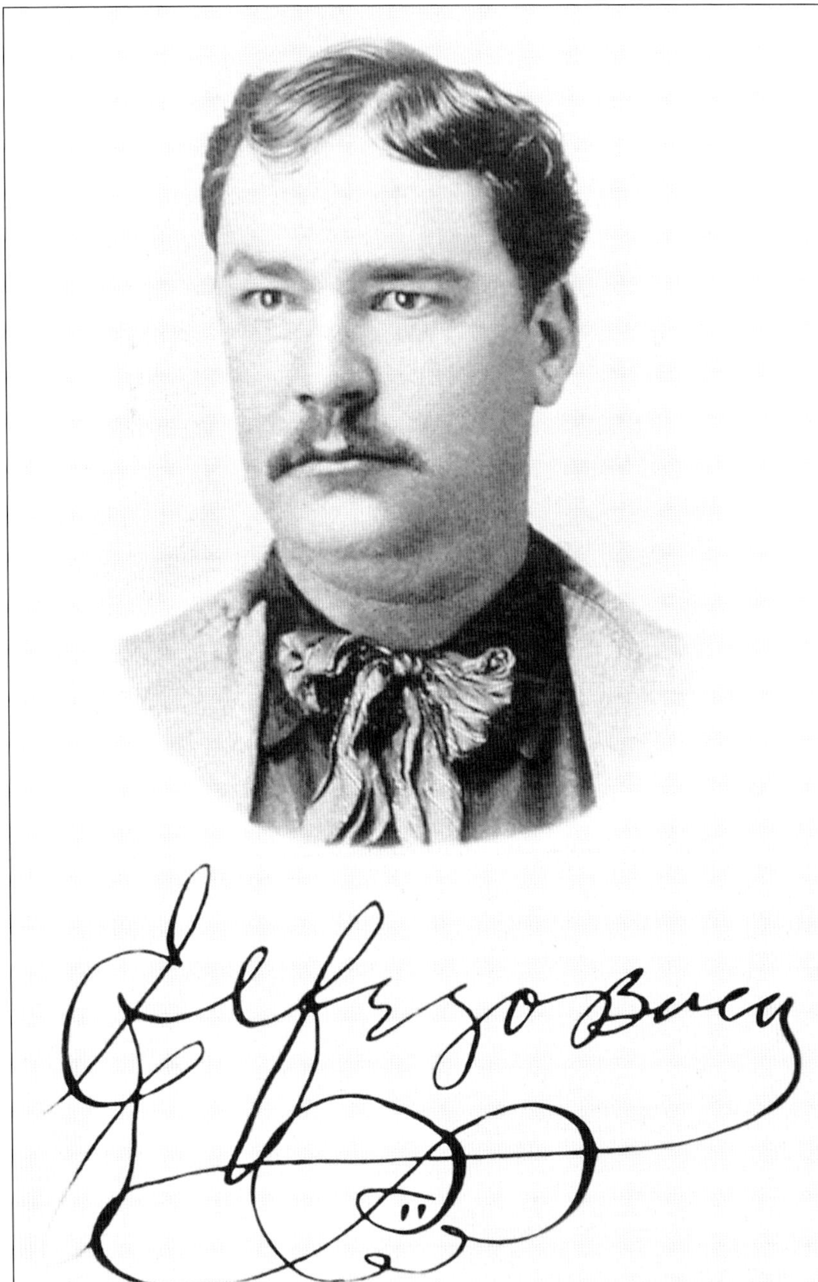

The most iconic figure associated with El Camino Real was Sheriff Elfego Baca. He was a legend in his own time. In 1884, at the age of 19, Elfego took a famous stand against 40 to 80 rowdy cowboys of the John Slaughter outfit who were shooting up the town of San Francisco (now Reserve). The drunken cowboys pinned Baca down in an old adobe building, where the young lawman held them off. This was known as the "Frisco Shootout." After 33 hours and 4,000 bullets fired, Elfego was unharmed when he was rescued. By 1888, he was a US marshal. Walt Disney produced a TV series about him in the 1950s called *The Nine Lives of Elfego Baca*. He was also the subject of the film *Elfego Baca: Six Gun Law* as well as comic books and other related merchandise.

Thomas Benton Catron led the notorious Santa Fe Ring. This was a powerful group of corrupt American attorneys, judges, lawmen, and politicians. These men were speculators who dealt in fraudulent land deals, mining, cattle, and railroad ventures throughout New Mexico, including areas along El Camino Real.

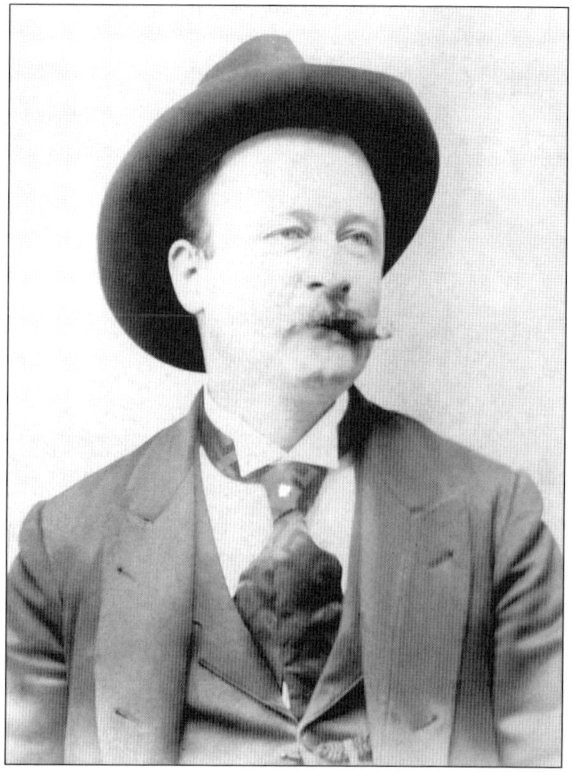

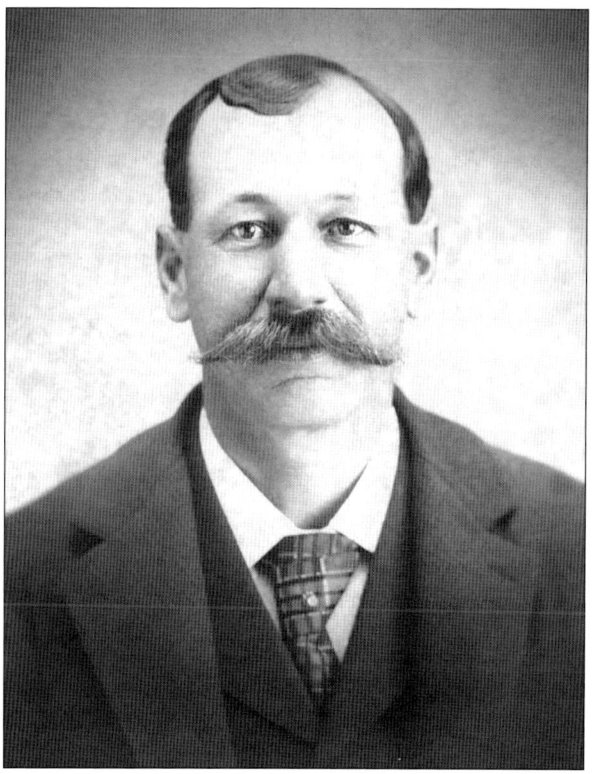

A 19th-century murder mystery on El Camino Real involved the deaths of Col. Albert Jennings Fountain and his young son. His buckboard was recovered on the way to Lincoln, New Mexico, but their bodies were never found. Those investigating the murders continued to search for clues along trails that branched out from El Camino Real.

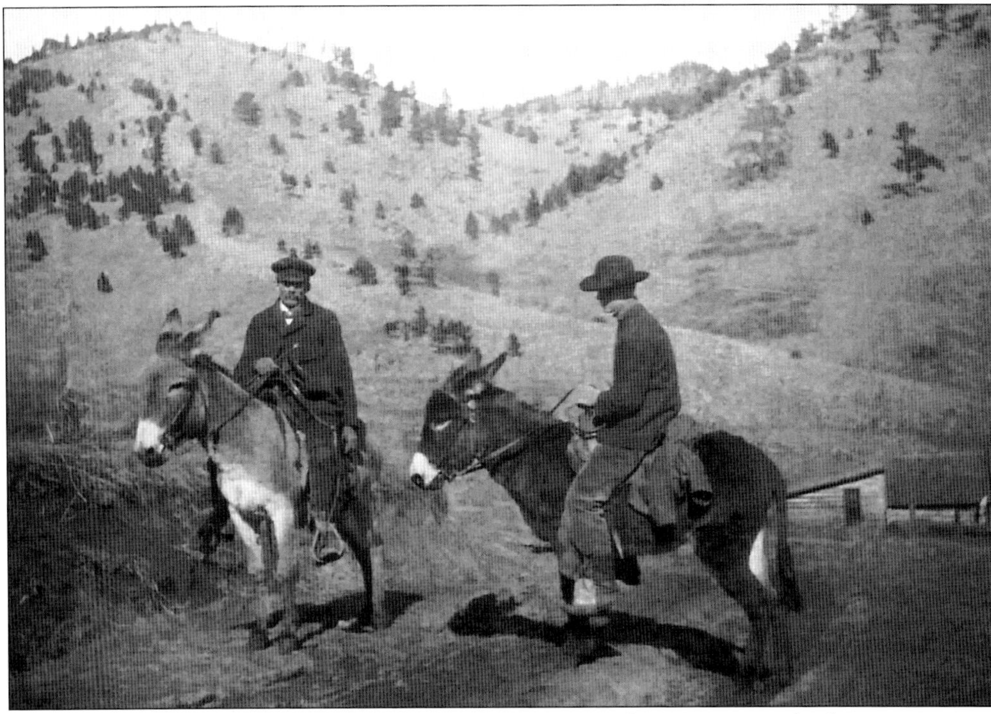

Some Americans arriving in New Mexico had to rely on mules to get around. These two in 1899 went out exploring near the trail. So many unprepared people were coming into the territory that some enterprising individuals rented mules at high prices. For example, during the 1890s, tourists rented mules to get around.

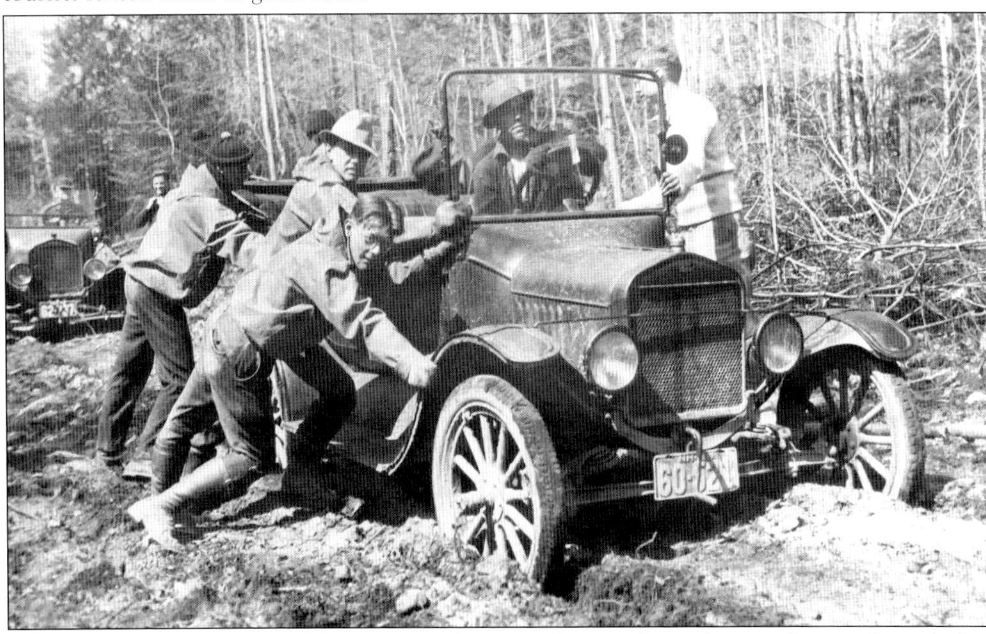

Once automobiles came into New Mexico, they were frequently stuck in mud on roads, including El Camino Real, as shown here. There were times when people who were stuck sought help from nearby farms and ranches. They had to use horses to pull them out of the mud.

Six

Flourishing and Decline

El Camino Real de Tierra Adentro most certainly experienced a great deal of success and had a great impact during its long history. This changed both politically and religiously with the American takeover in 1846. Massive flocks of sheep and goats were introduced into New Mexico by the Spanish. This became a dominant industry in the territory. The Navajo readily adapted to both the goats for meat and milk and the Merino sheep for their long fleece, and the looms introduced by the Spanish helped them to produce their famous rugs. All of this stimulated cultural exchange between the Indians and the Spanish.

An influx of Easterners from the United States sought new opportunities. The Santa Fe Trail steadily replaced commerce and trade on El Camino Real. New Mexico was adversely affected in several ways, including the Catholic faith of the Spanish and Indians. Ironically, this came from the appointment of a French American bishop.

Bishop Jean-Baptiste Lamy invoked the powers of censorship over the native clergy and wholesale excommunication by casting out from the church any person or community not providing "owed" tithes. He sought collections through the courts to enforce his rule. Lamy seized properties for unpaid tithes. He demolished the 18th-century Spanish colonial adobe church of St. Francis, perhaps holding the remains of Gov. Don Diego de Vargas, to build his Romanesque French Revival cathedral as a personal monument as an enforcer of his doctrine of "right versus wrong" in New Mexico. This was the norm of the period. Another event was the wholesale slaughter of sheep by the US military and cattle barons who wanted to take over the land for their empires. This struggle created cattle and sheep wars that were devastating not only to the land but also to the people.

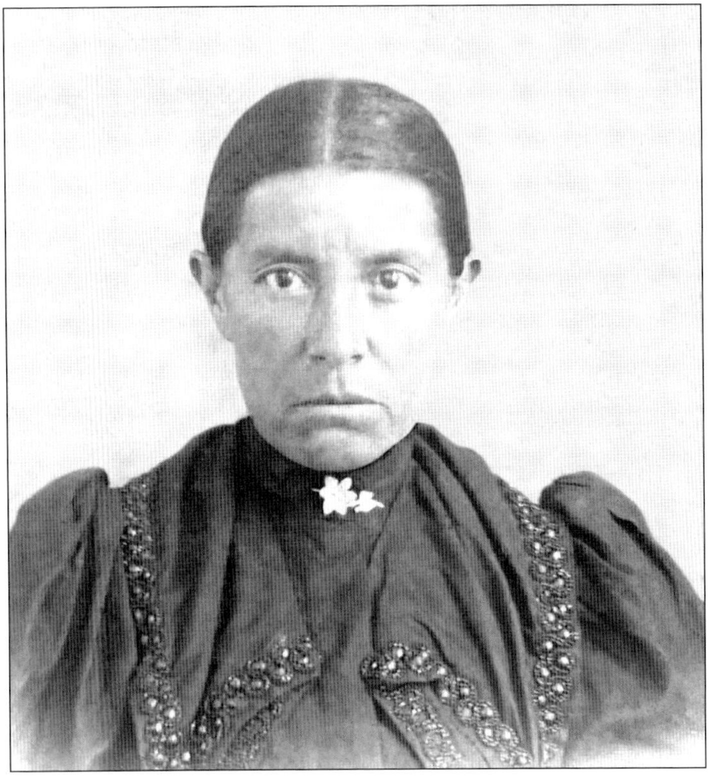

Juana María Martínez, the sister of famed New Mexico folk hero priest Padre Don Antonio José Martínez, often traveled with her older brother on trips to and from Mexico. Padre Martínez served as a consul for American immigrants entering into the territory. He was often aided by his family, who helped new settlers establish roots.

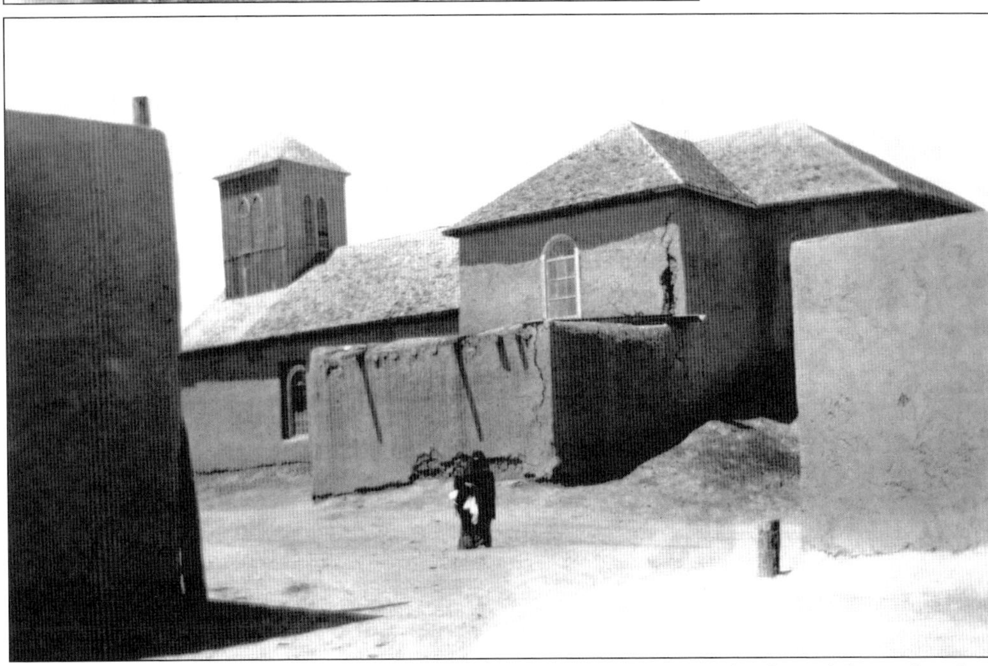

Iglesia de la Nuestra Señora de Guadalupe, the no-longer-extant Our lady of Guadalupe Church in Taos, was built in the 18th century. This was the parish church of Padre Antonio José Martínez. It was from the pulpit here that the famous minister preached against injustice and for civil rights during the mid-19th century.

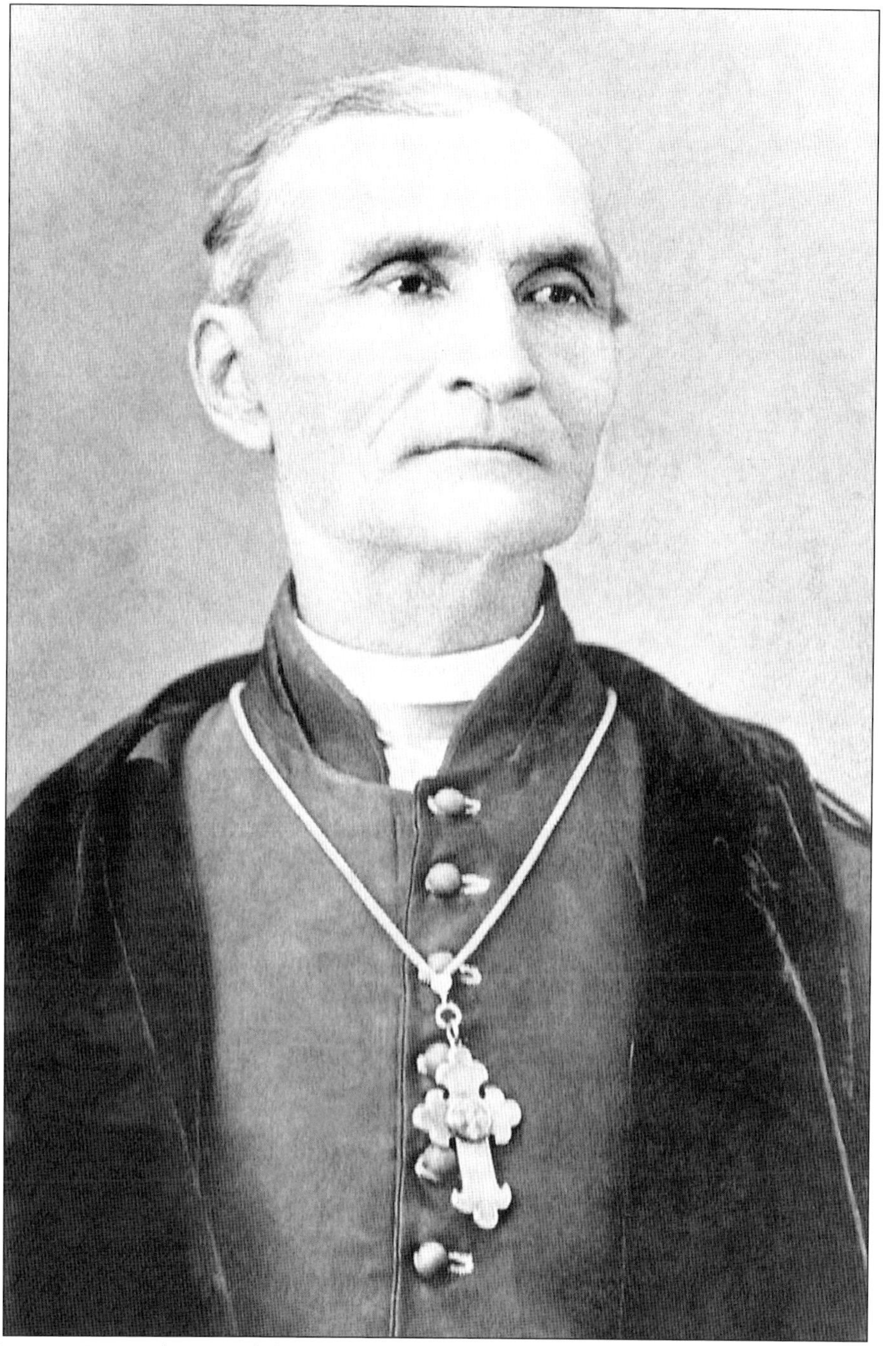

Jean-Baptiste Lamy, the French bishop and later archbishop of New Mexico, was assigned by a French pope in 1850. This controversial Catholic bishop was memorialized in Willa Cather's book *Death Comes for the Archbishop*. Having no knowledge of the Spanish language or the ageless customs of the people, Lamy bitterly clashed with the descendants of the original Spanish settlers and the Native Americans alike. He censored or removed dozens of Mexican clergy who opposed him. The new bishop wielded a heavy hand with the aid of Joseph Projectus Machebeuf, his vicar general.

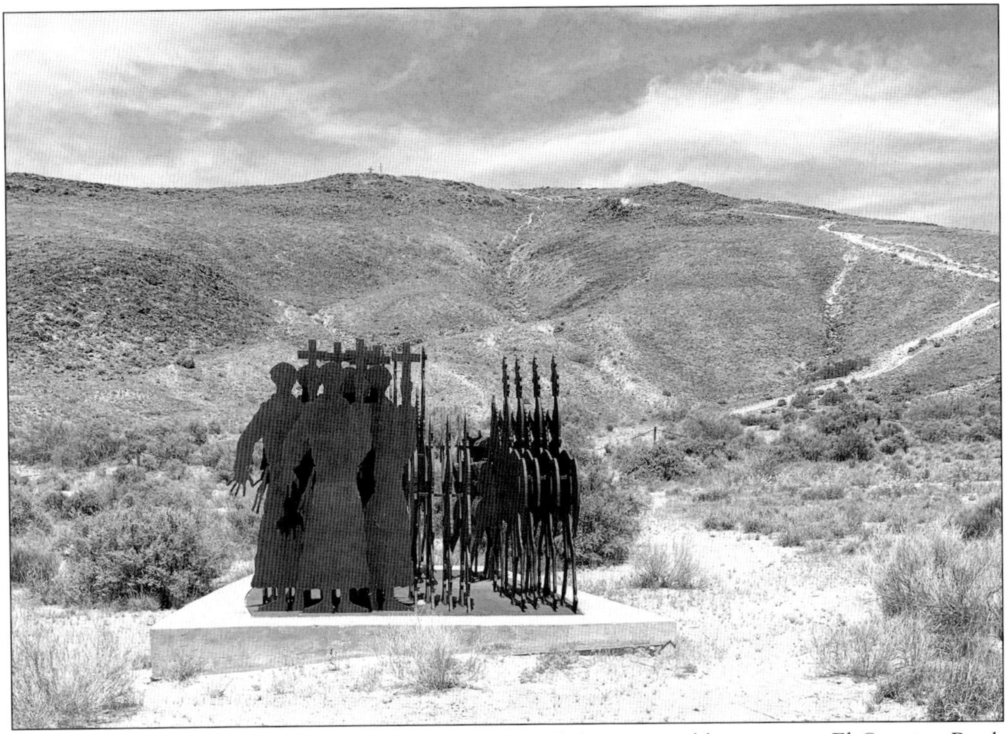

This sculpture at the base of El Cerro honors Spanish history and heritage on El Camino Real. Noted sculptor Armando Álvarez created a piece in iron at the site called *La Puerta del Sol*, the Pathway of the Sun. This sculpture graphically depicts the intrigue and adventure of El Camino Real.

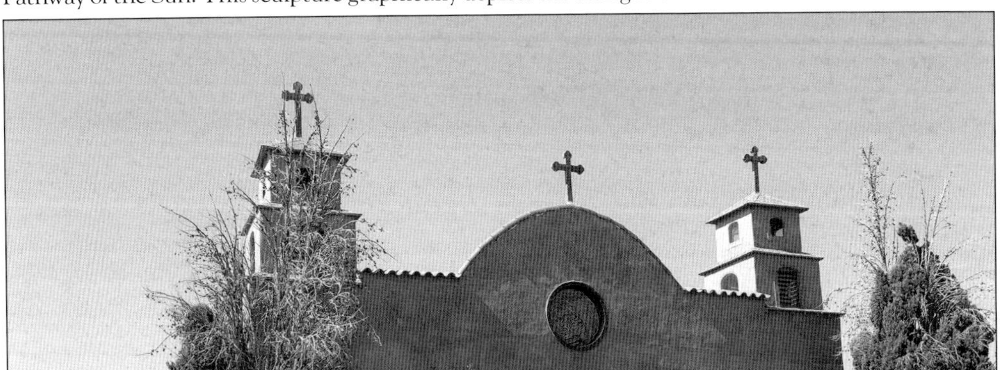

San Antonio was a farming community established in the 18th century near Socorro, New Mexico, on El Camino Real. Pictured is the San Antonio church, which is no longer in use. The small town now has two restaurants and a gas station to serve residents and passing tourists who stop by to photograph the historic church.

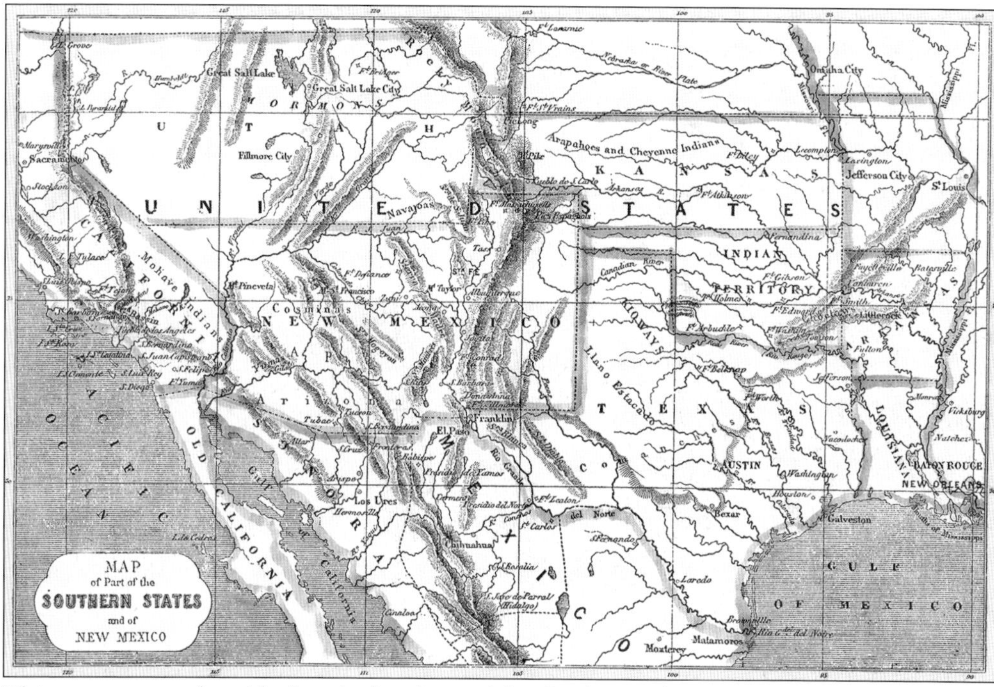

This rare map produced before the breakout of the Civil War shows part of the Southern states and New Mexico. The boundaries of New Mexico Territory are delineated as stretching from Colorado and Kansas through Arizona, Nevada, and up to California. Extensive Indian territories at the time are also shown.

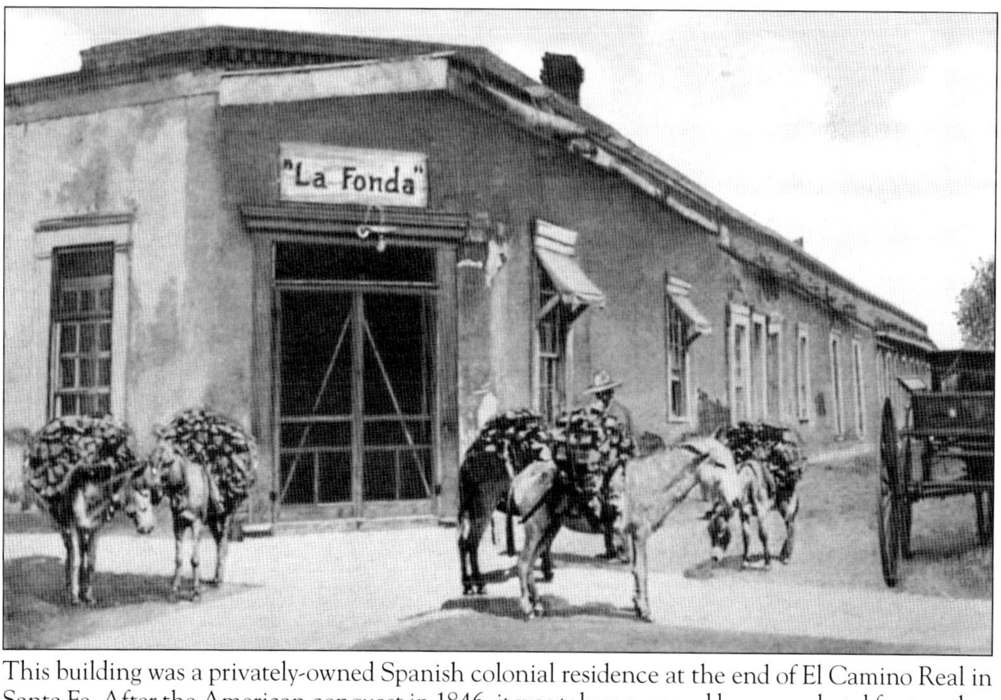

This building was a privately-owned Spanish colonial residence at the end of El Camino Real in Santa Fe. After the American conquest in 1846, it was taken over and became a hotel for travelers on the Royal Road and the Santa Fe Trail.

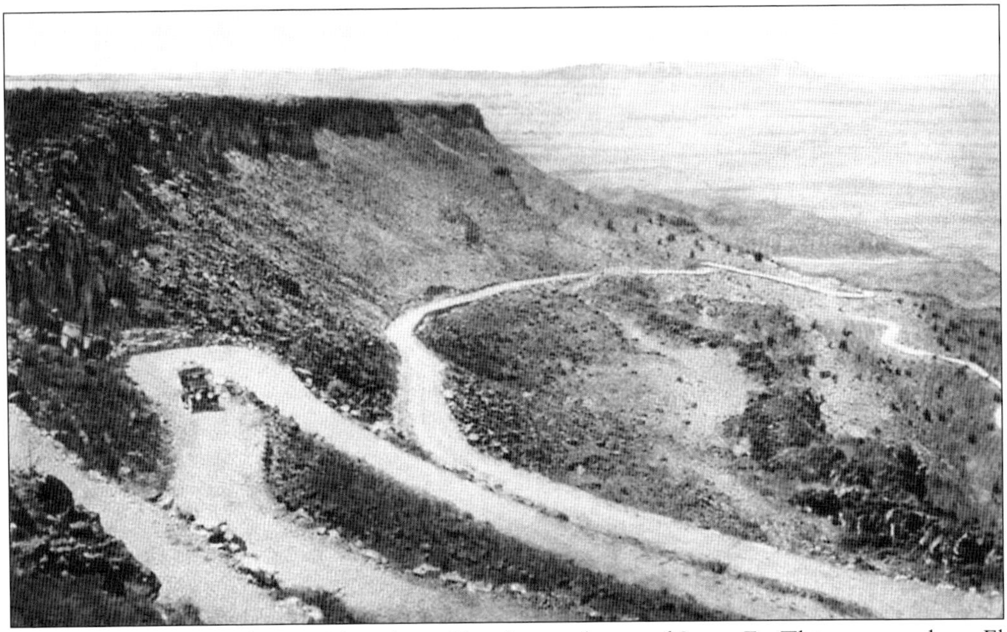

La Bajada Mesa, "the descent," lies about 10 miles southwest of Santa Fe. This steep path on El Camino Real was the main route to enter and depart from the capital city. During the advent of the age of the automobile, there were 23 hairpin turns on the road. A Spanish village also called La Bajada at the bottom of the hill served travelers. This postcard was published by Curt Teich & Co. of Chicago in 1908.

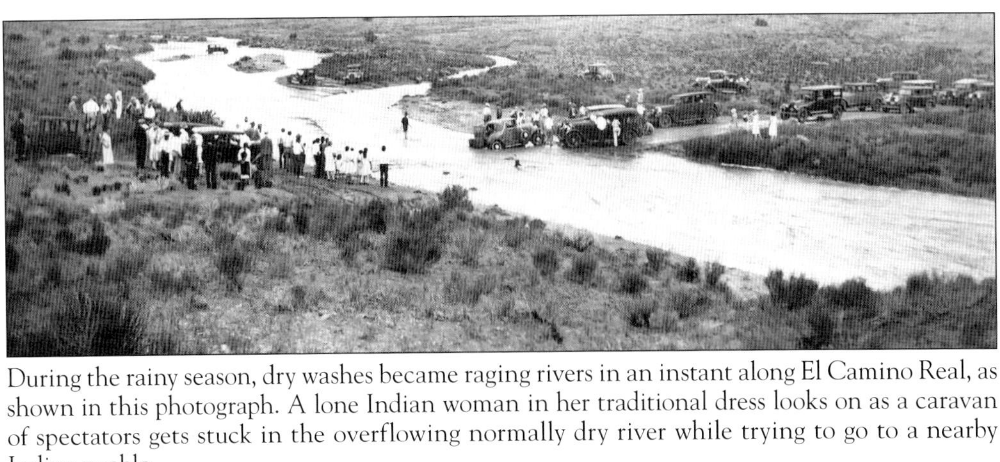

During the rainy season, dry washes became raging rivers in an instant along El Camino Real, as shown in this photograph. A lone Indian woman in her traditional dress looks on as a caravan of spectators gets stuck in the overflowing normally dry river while trying to go to a nearby Indian pueblo.

John Teitlebaum was one of several Jewish immigrants who arrived in New Mexico to set up stores for goods they purchased from many sources. These individuals became extremely successful and wealthy. Several of these merchants built lavish homes in Santa Fe to entertain guests. Some of them still stand.

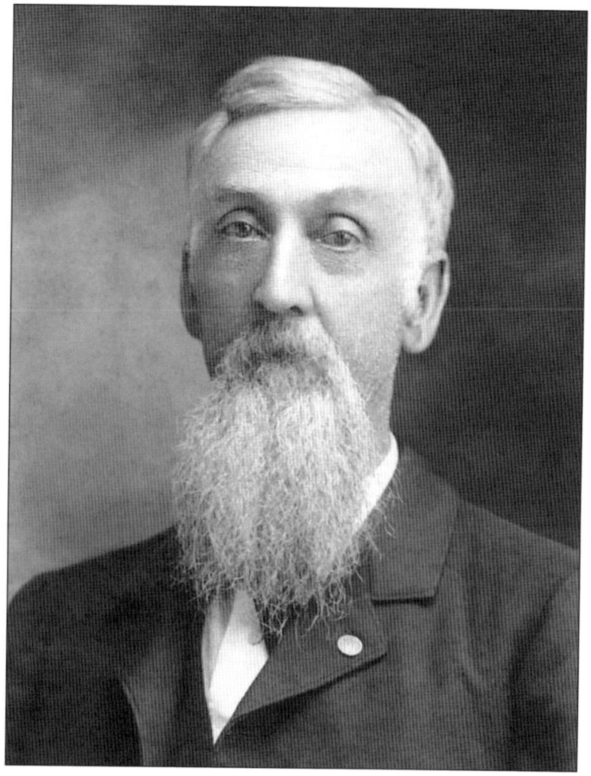

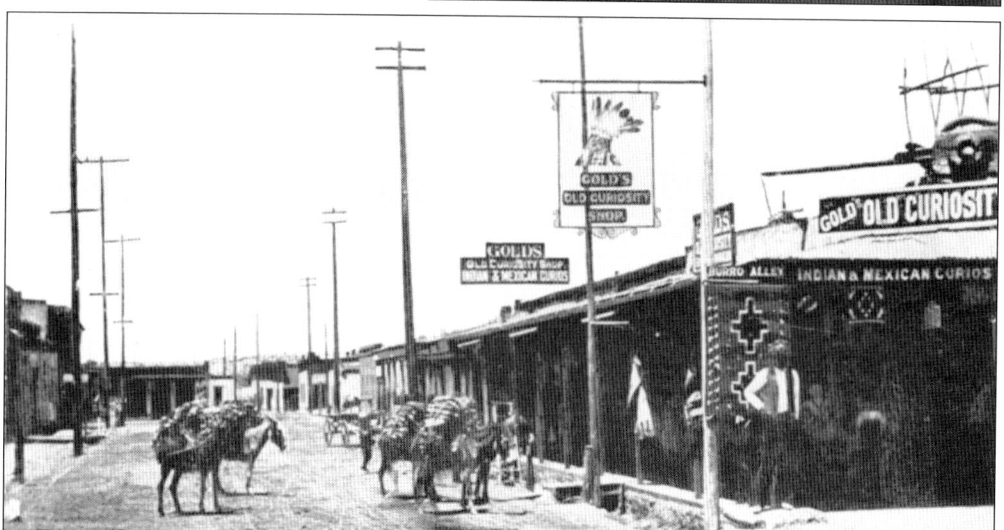

This is a c. 1906 real-photo postcard of El Camino Real in Santa Fe showing shops. Gold's Old Curiosity Store survived well into the 20th century. A 17th-century Spanish carreta was placed on the roof. This was a landmark that was photographed often.

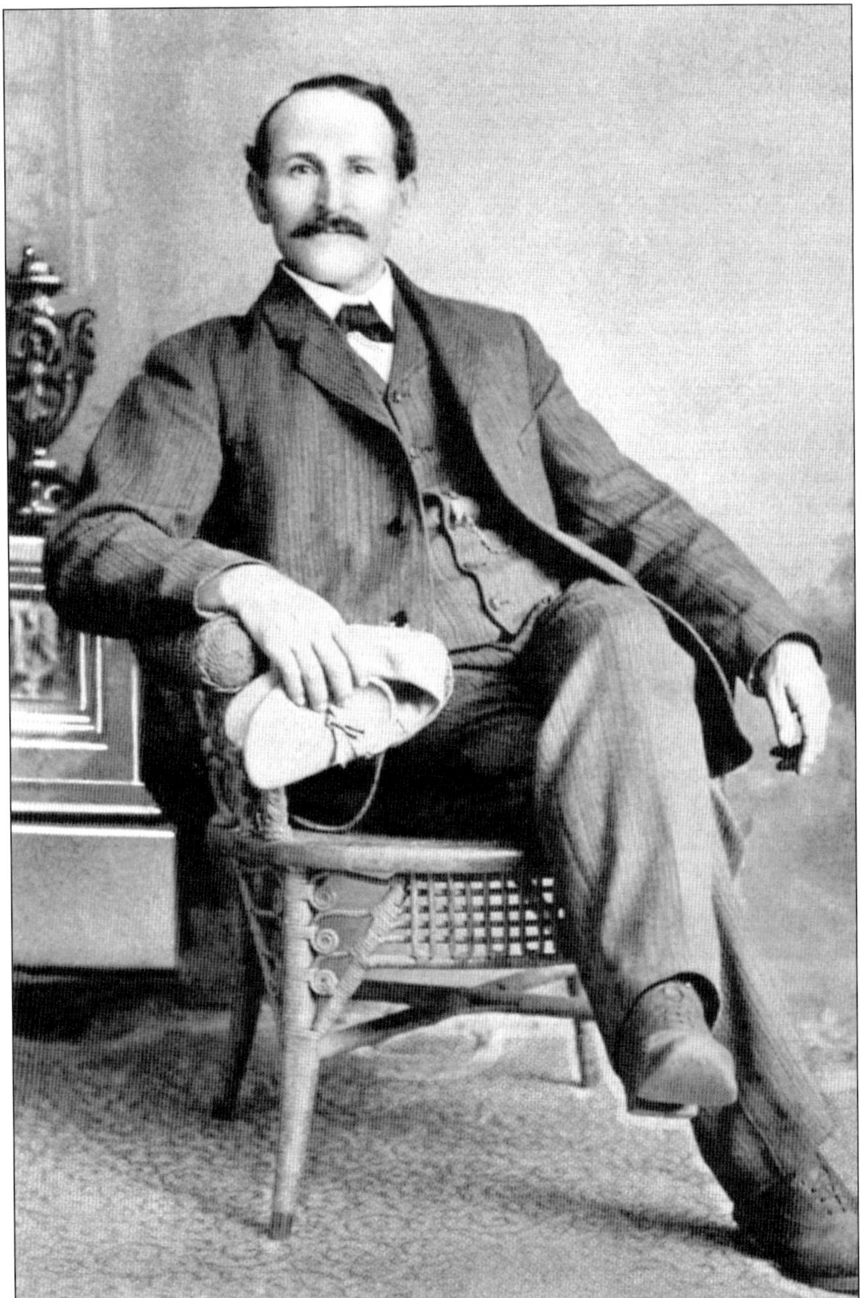

Jesús S. Candelario, in this photograph from about 1908, was a well-known merchant in Santa Fe. He was called "the Curio Man." His father, Antonio José Candelario, had a lucrative business as a trader on the Royal Road. His establishment was near the end of the trail on the Santa Fe Plaza. The senior Candelario exported goods produced in New Mexico and imported merchandise from Mexico. Jesús learned the business at a young age. As an adult, he operated the Old Curio Store on West San Francisco Street. He often claimed the site of his business had served as a general store since the 17th century. Candelario is recognized for personally preserving many of the Spanish arts and crafts that were rapidly disappearing during his time in New Mexico.

This little girl is giggling and playing with her dog, which lies at her feet on a Conestoga wagon around 1900. This is unusual for the time, since children were seldom shown having a good time and playing in early photographs. This picture illustrates kids enjoying themselves on the trail.

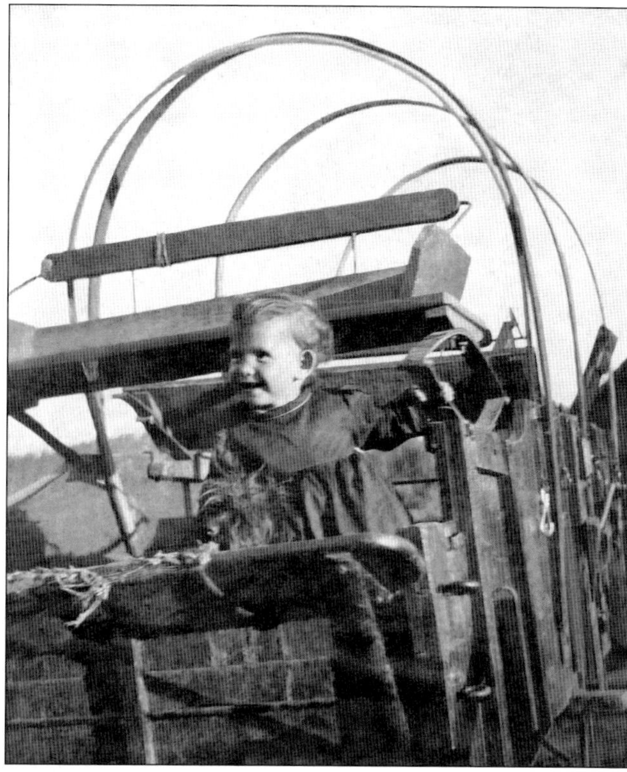

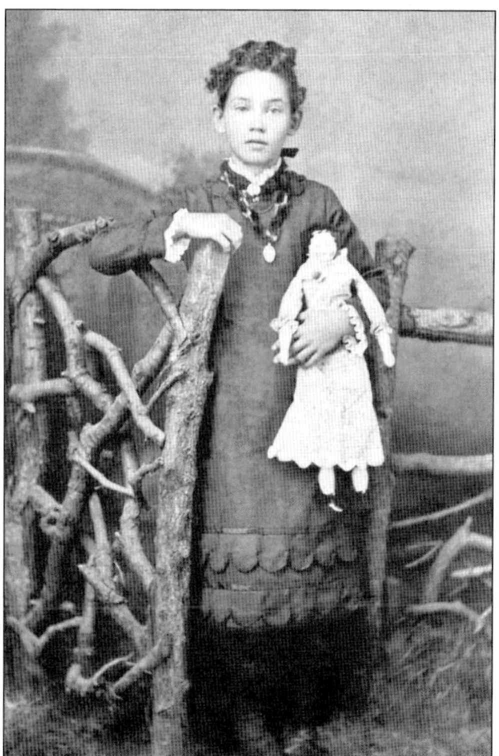

When thinking of early trade, children rarely come to mind. But as might be expected, children would wait for a new toy. Little girls would wait for a shipment of dolls. In this carte de visite taken around 1870, a New Mexican girl poses with her prized new doll.

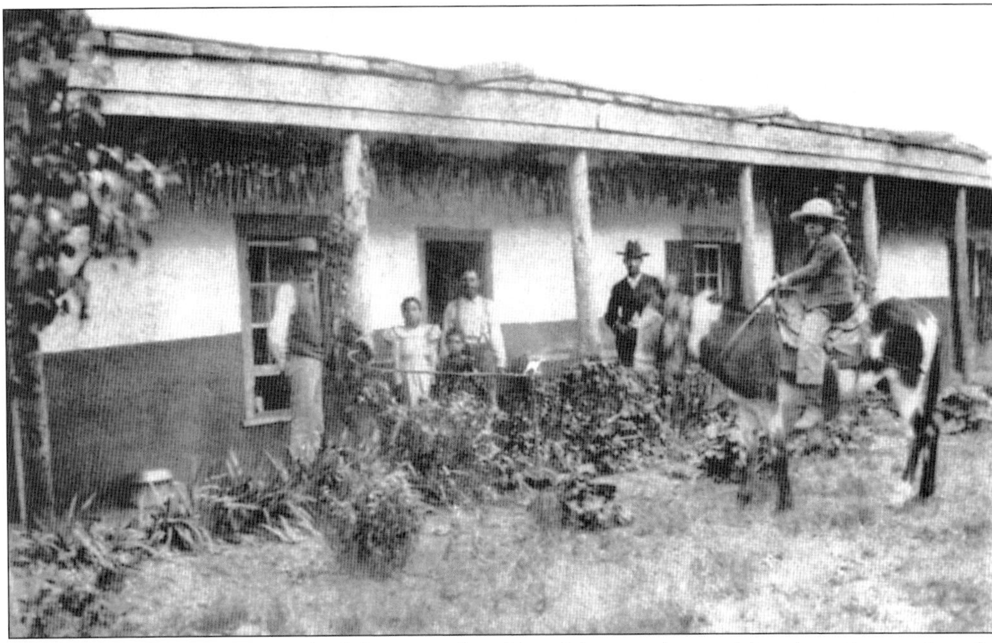

Texas merchant May Hays, far left, arrived in New Mexico along with others inspecting the land for new opportunities. He visited this Spanish hacienda in a place called Ojo del Apache, or Apache Springs. This large, sprawling ranch house served an extensive area of farming and cattle ranges in an old Spanish community. Note the drying ears of corn hanging from the rafters. (Courtesy of Gloria Hays Martínez.)

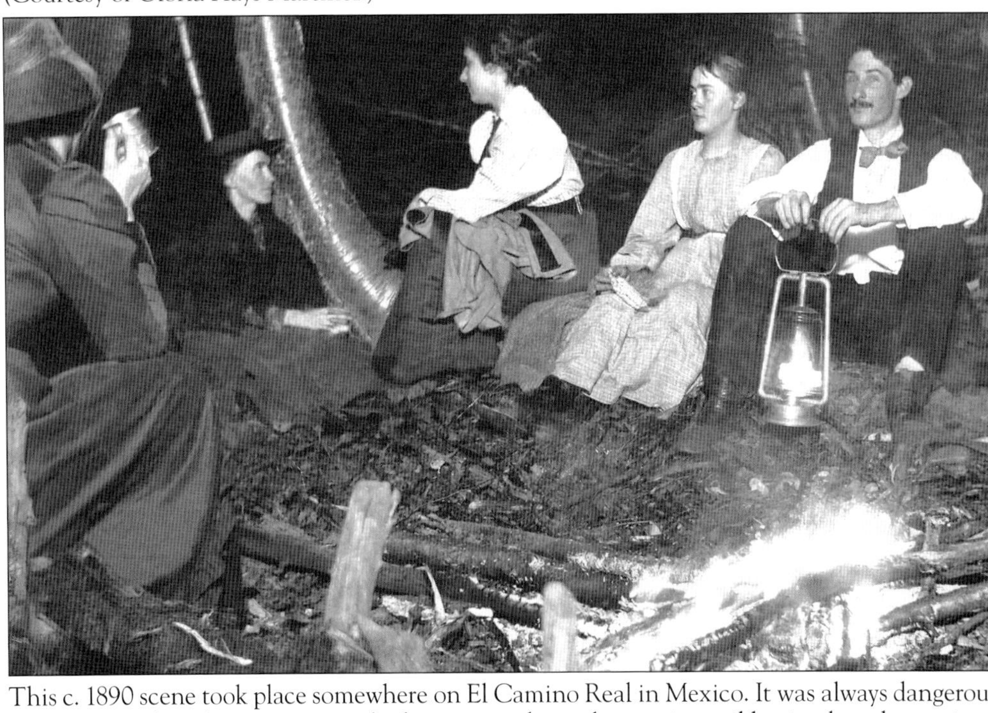

This c. 1890 scene took place somewhere on El Camino Real in Mexico. It was always dangerous to travel at night. Those journeying had to protect themselves against wild animals and sometimes against threatening bandits.

Doña Rosalía Castellano de Mondragón, center, is pictured with daughters Luz, left, and Margarita. Rosalía was the wife of Capt. Don Pedro Mondragón of the Santa Fe Presidio militia. These soldiers were assigned to protect travelers and traders on both El Camino Real and the Santa Fe Trail.

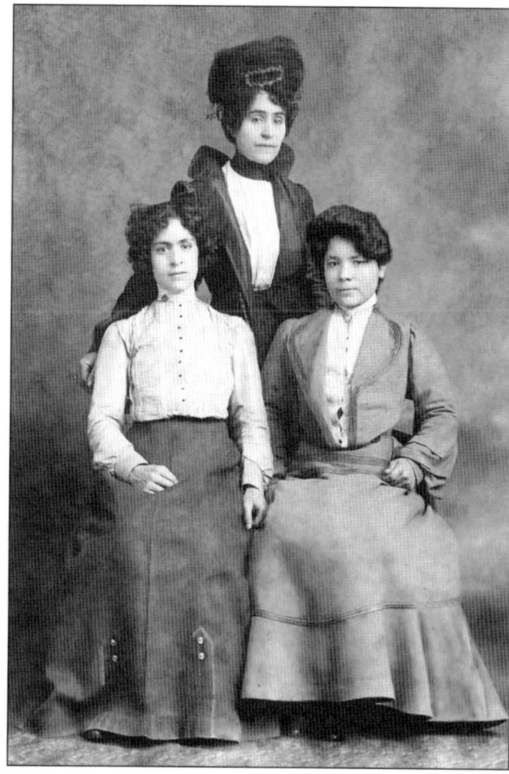

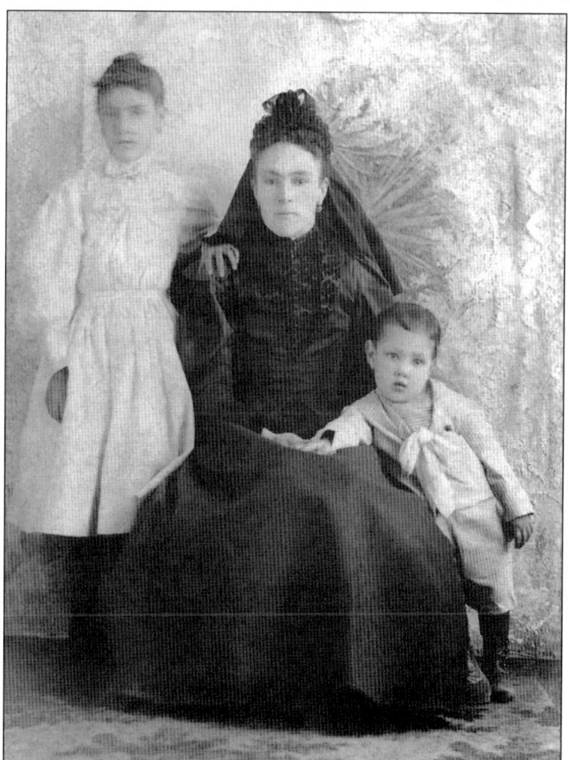

Doña Catalina Mondragón de Valdez is at center with daughter Virginia, left, and Pedro Mondragón. She was a well-known *curandera*, a medicine woman, who continued the long Spanish colonial tradition of healers. The earliest Spanish women healers had an ingrained knowledge of medicinal plants and roots used to heal various illnesses and injuries. They were indispensable for travelers on the long journeys on El Camino Real.

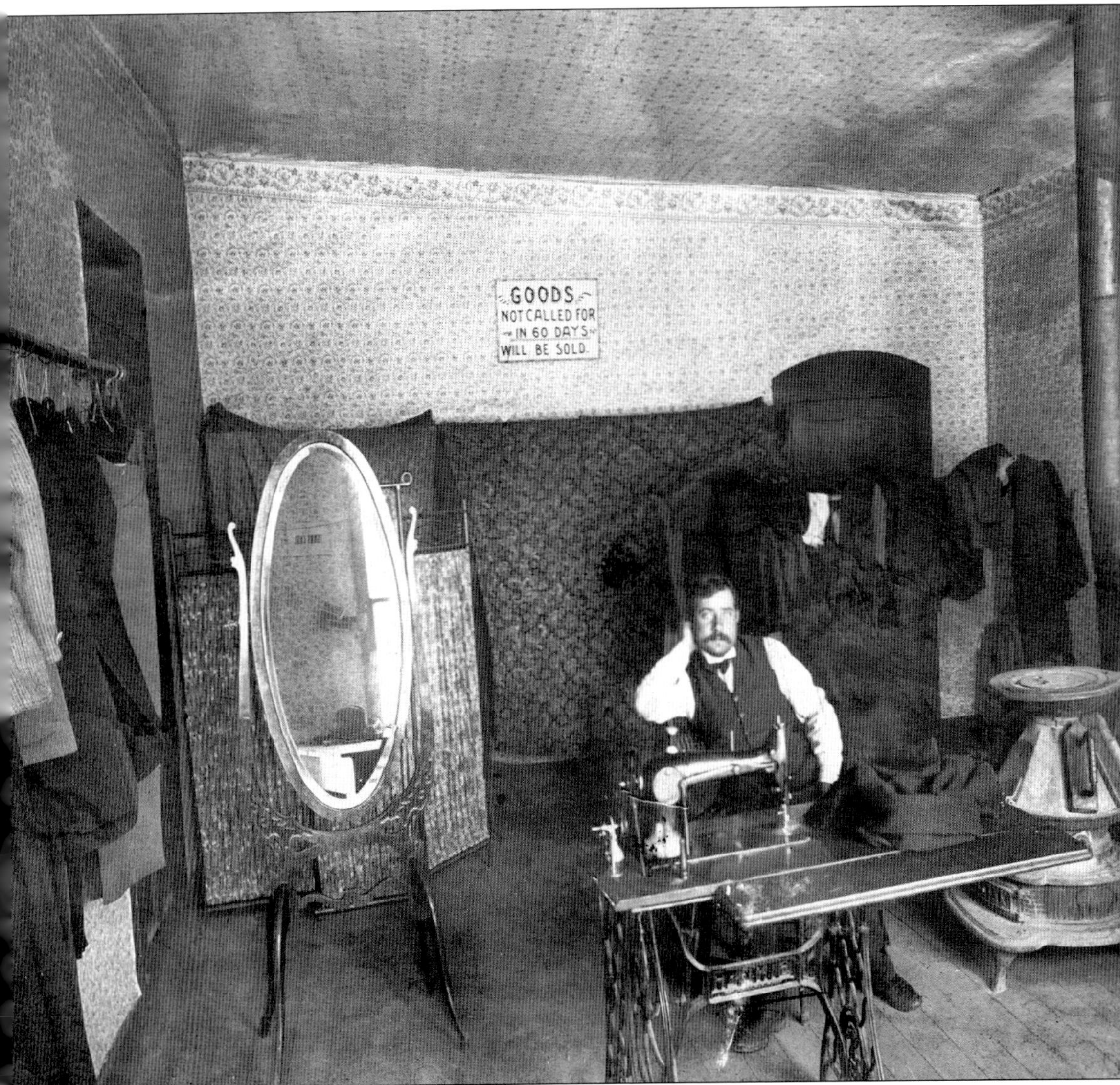

Tailors and women who sewed clothing for locals and travelers had a long history in the area. Hand-sewn clothes were traded and sold. Late in the 19th century, sewing machines arrived in the territory. The clothing industry that developed has been virtually unnoticed in history books, but this, of course, was vital to the success of the colony. Those fashioning clothes anxiously waited for popular fabrics to arrive from Mexico. Here, tailor Pedro Ciddio waits patiently in his shop for customers. Tailors in Santa Fe and other major cities of the time were expert at fashioning clothes. In fact, some were trained in the East before resettling in New Mexico and setting up shop. Ciddio was an Italian immigrant. Many Italians opened up businesses in the territory.

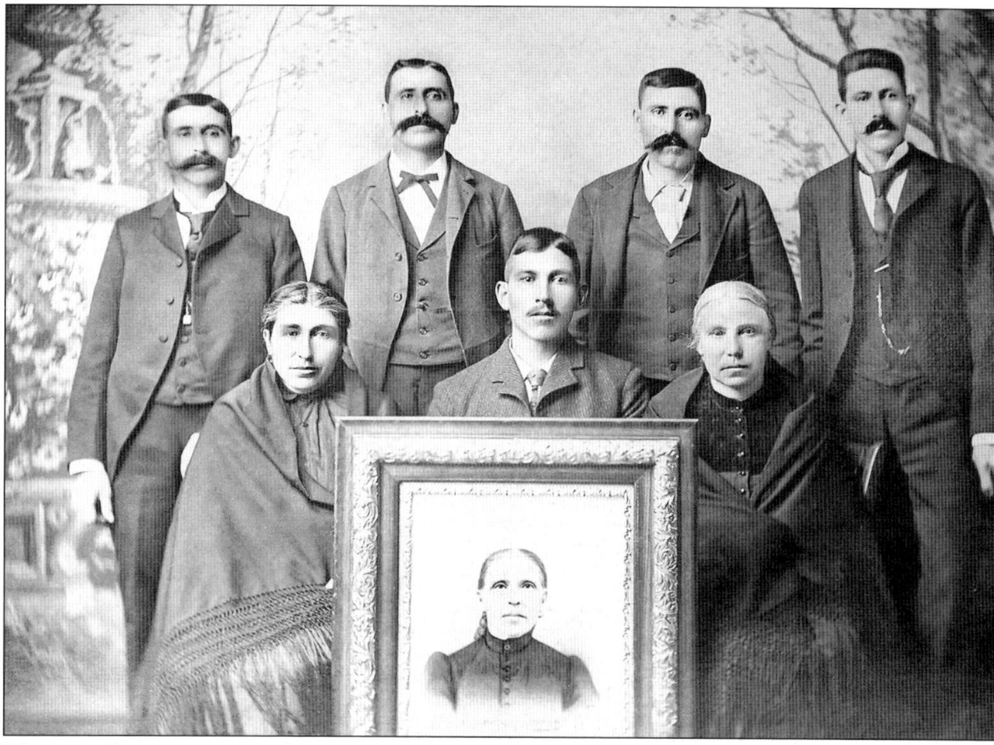

This proud group poses with a portrait of the matriarch of their family. The two seated women are dressed with the traditional rebozos (shawls) of the period. Shawls arrived with the caravans from other places such as Mexico. Many of the women preferred black shawls.

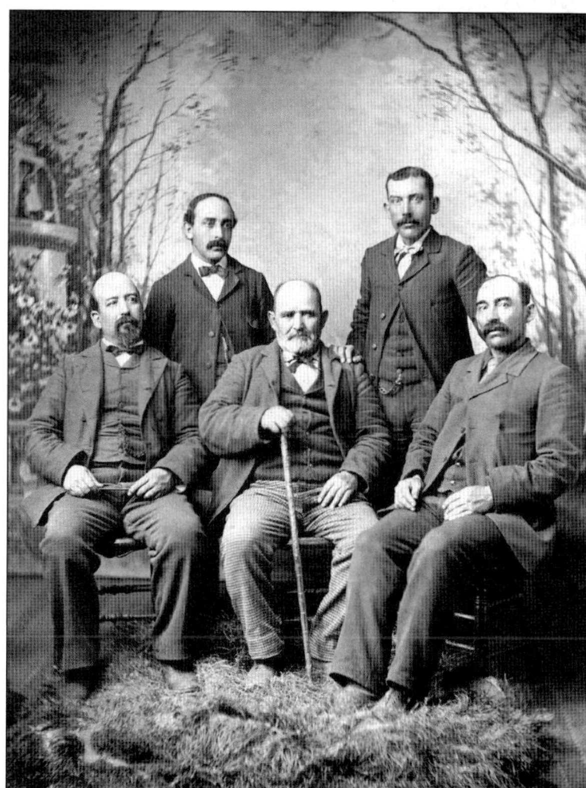

El Camino Real merchant and trader Manuel Gonzales, center, is pictured with sons (from left to right) Porfirio, Patricio, Cruz, and Anselmo, with a traditional trade fur on the floor. Don Manuel was one of a large group of teamsters who journeyed on the road in his early years transporting goods to customers.

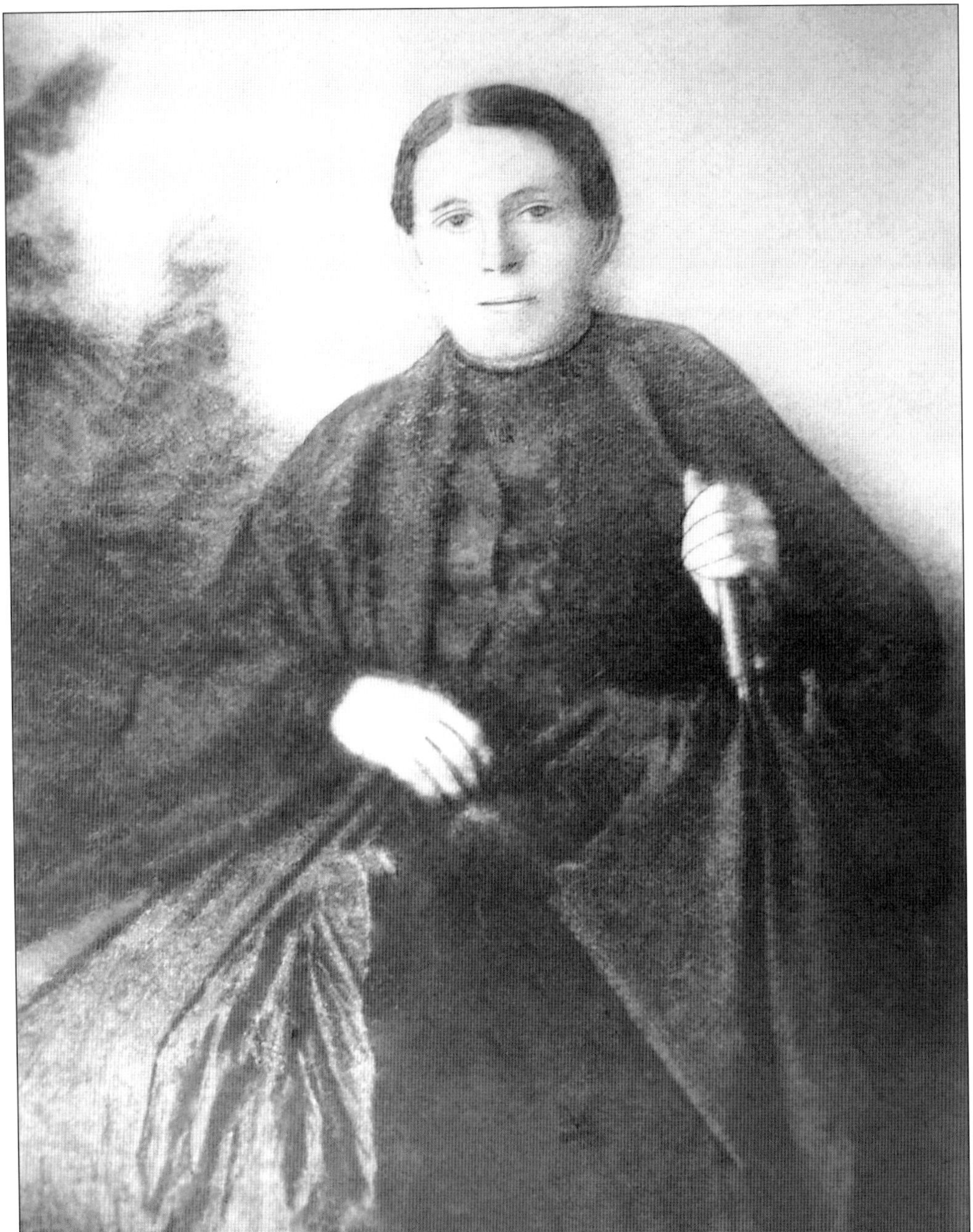

Doña Bárbara Chávez de Sánchez is shown at a young age in her black mourning clothes. She was married to Charles Overman, an Indian agent and delegate to the constitutional convention of 1850 for New Mexico statehood. He was killed during an Apache attack in which they stole livestock and horses. Her second husband, Don Desiderio Sánchez y Luna, a merchant, was also killed by Indians. Bárbara was the niece of Gen. Don Manuel Armijo, the last Mexican governor of New Mexico. His sister Isidora was her mother. Doña Bárbara is best remembered for being the matriarch of the settlement of Los Chavez near Los Lunas. She owned the property that would become a community and that would carry her maiden surname.

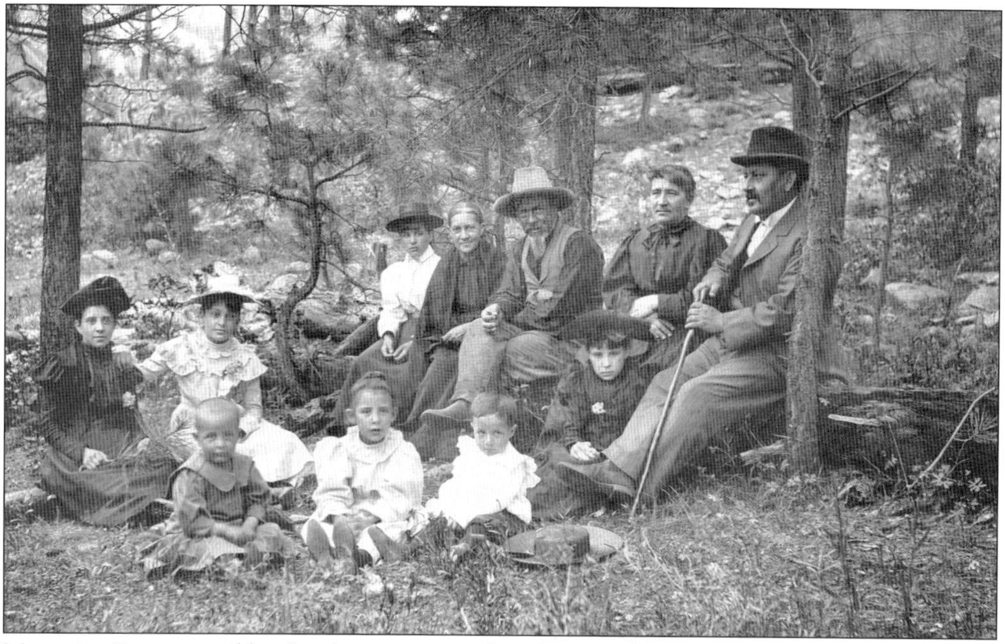

Margarito Romero and his family are seen in this photograph camping on their extensive land. Romero and his brothers were well-known merchants who ran successful businesses. His enterprise extended throughout the territory. He ventured into medicinal remedies he bottled and packaged. Romero hired salesmen who sold his products.

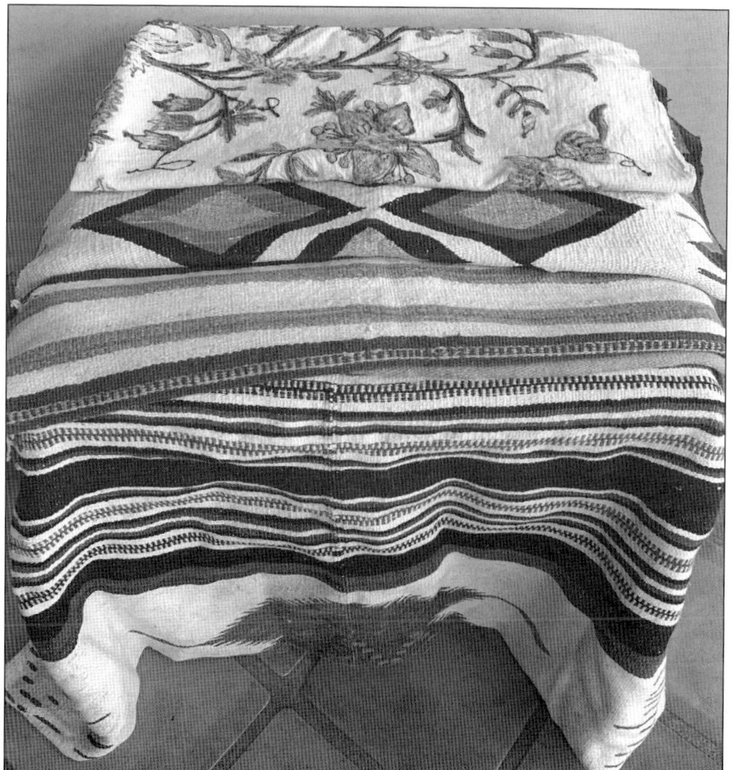

Pictured here are a c. 1870–1880 Rio Grande blanket with serrate patterns, a c. 1890 Rio Grande blanket with a bands-and-stripes pattern and three-color beading, and an undated *colcha* with wool colored with natural dyes on two-ply tightly woven cotton twill fabric with geometric and floral motifs in elaborate patterns. These New Mexican types of weavings were often sold in Mexico.

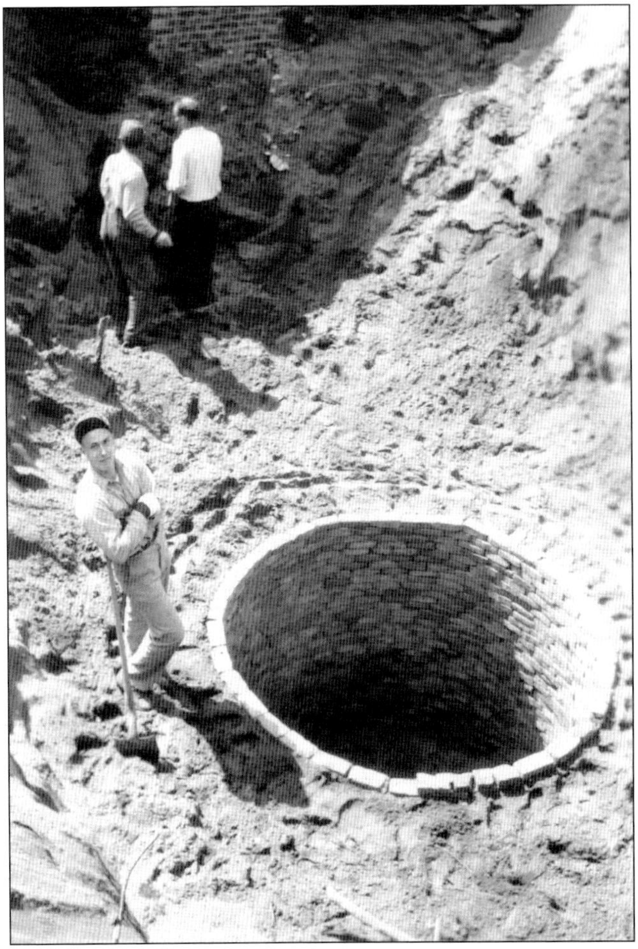

Archaeologists continuously make new discoveries in New Mexico. This group uncovered an ancient buried well near the Royal Road in the 1940s. During this period, many people were out exploring and digging. Some Native American artifacts were dug up and sold at shops in Santa Fe.

Things were rapidly changing for Native Americans in New Mexico. These two Pueblo Indian girls look out by their more modern homes as a photographer catches them from a distance. Since this was a regular occurrence, Native Americans prohibited photography at the pueblos. Earlier photographs are still purchased and collected.

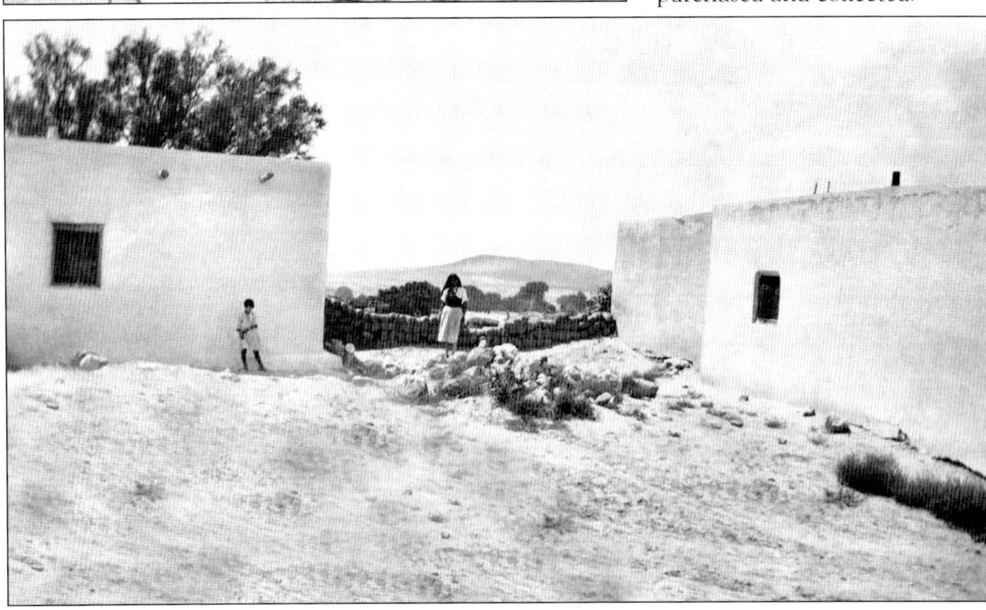

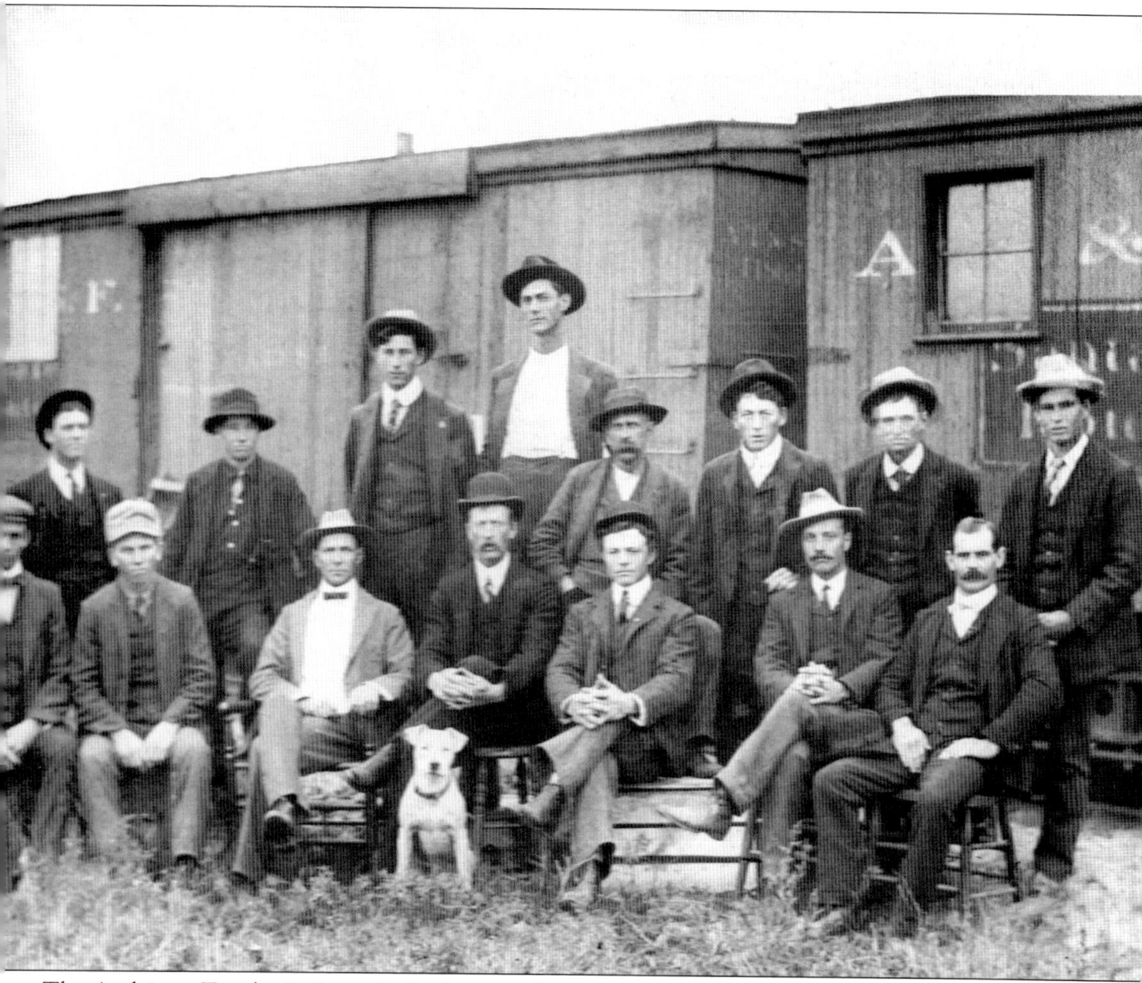

The Atchison, Topeka & Santa Fe Railway ran by or near El Camino Real through New Mexico Territory. These railmen and officials pose for a formal picture around 1879 to celebrate the arrival of the railroad. It would signal a boon for immigration into the Southwest, but it unfortunately displaced Indians, old Spanish communities, land grants, and descendants of the original settlers from their lands and homes. In time, the old Spanish road also died out. Some of the men seen in this photograph were politicians and individuals who either owned stock in the railroad or had other interests.

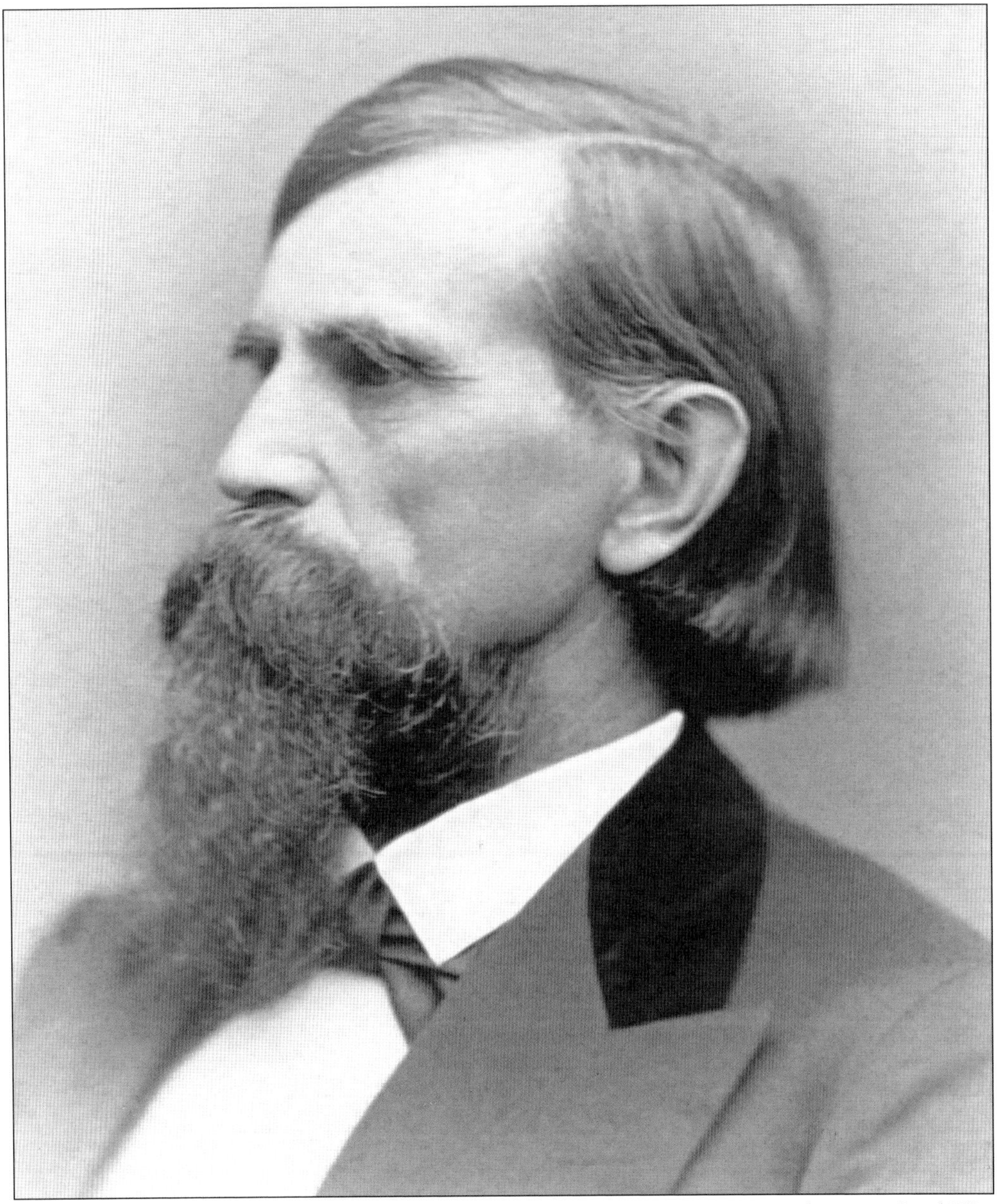

Lewis "Lew" Wallace was a legendary territorial governor of New Mexico and Union Civil War general. He wrote the famous novel *Ben Hur* while in office at Santa Fe. He frequently traveled along El Camino Real south of Santa Fe, exploring the territory and possible mining interests. A famous episode of his career was dealing with Billy the Kid, and the Lincoln County War. It is written that Wallace promised amnesty to the Kid but reneged. This is still disputed by historians, but they do credit Wallace with helping to stop lawlessness in New Mexico. The photograph is from the Boston studio of C.F. Conly.

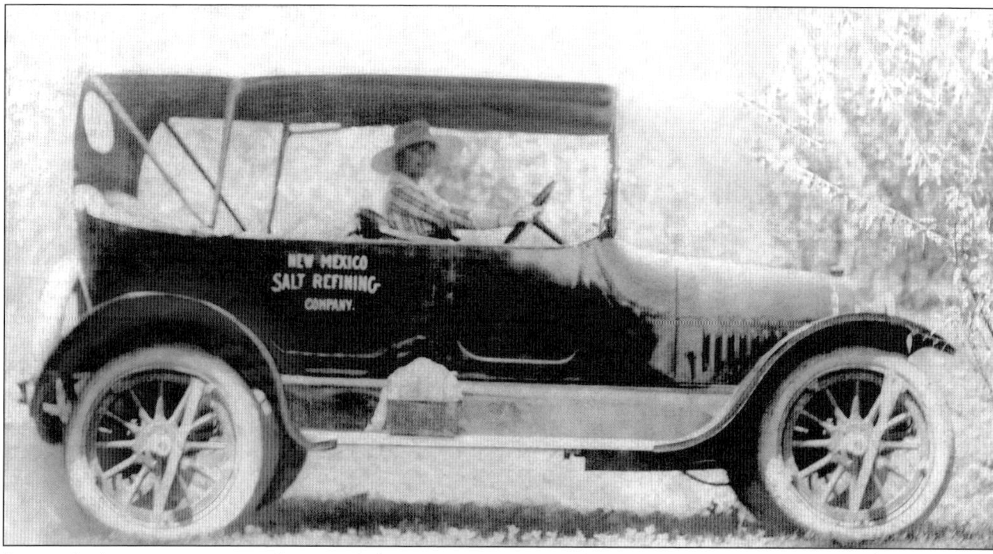

Lucia de Aragón poses in the Las Salinas company car about 1923. She became the owner of the largest salt company in New Mexico. The La Salina Grant, which she owned, had a long history of salt trading dating back centuries. At one time, the New Mexico Salt Refining Company sold stock and had $250,000 in assets.

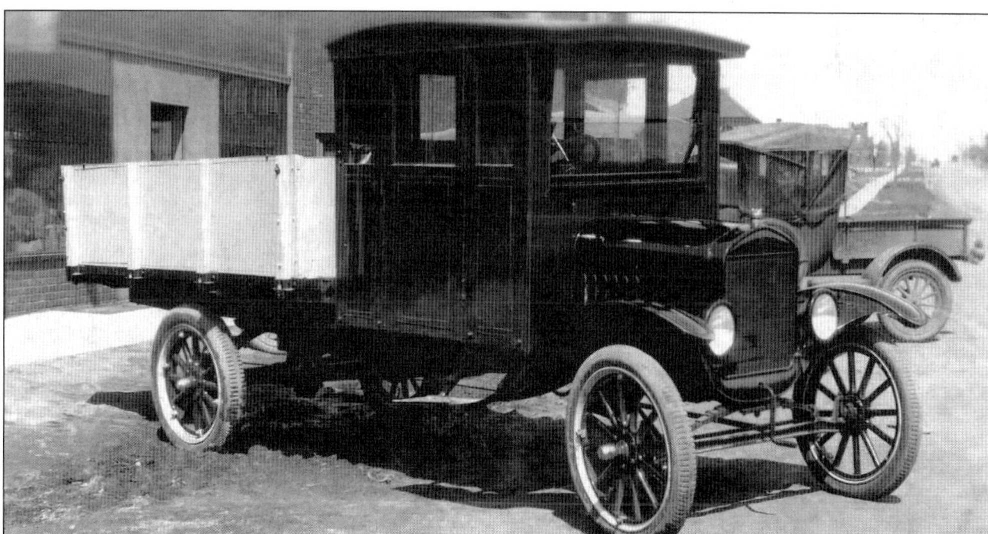

Trucks are loading merchandise at a warehouse in Albuquerque in the early 1920s. They were ready to roll out to sales outlets around New Mexico, including south along the Royal Road. There were many stores in towns and villages along the trail.

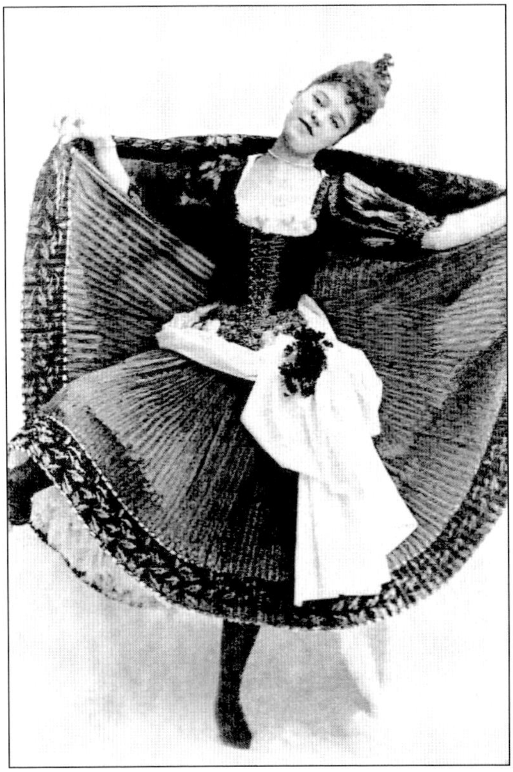

This dancer in an 1850s carte de visite photograph displays her skills. Entertainers such as musicians, dancers, and singers traveled throughout New Mexico. Some of them had a widespread reputation when they performed for weddings and other celebrations. Many were considered celebrities.

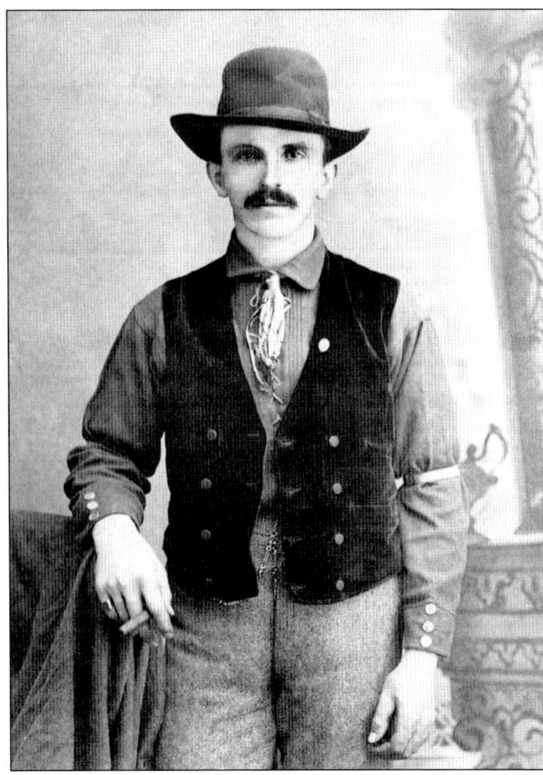

Professional gamblers such as the one shown here plied their trade in towns and villages on the Royal Road. Card players would set up games and entice the vulnerable throughout the territory. In larger cities, they frequented saloons. Many of their victims lost their money and sometimes their property.

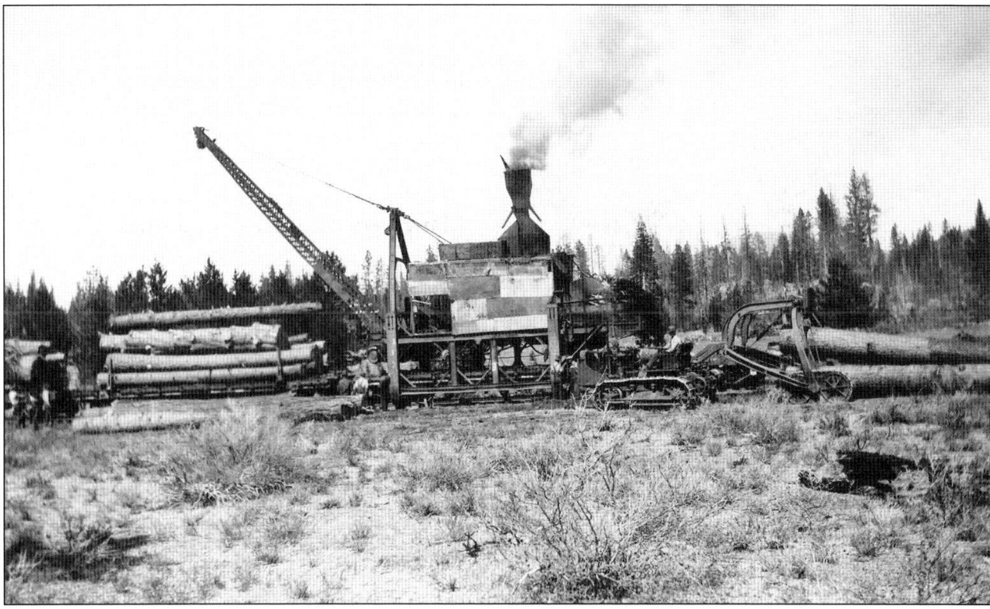

After New Mexico Territory became an integral part of the United States, deforestation was uncontrolled. This logging machinery was photographed in northern New Mexico at an unknown date. The logging industry spread through the thick New Mexico forests, which also adversely affected wildlife.

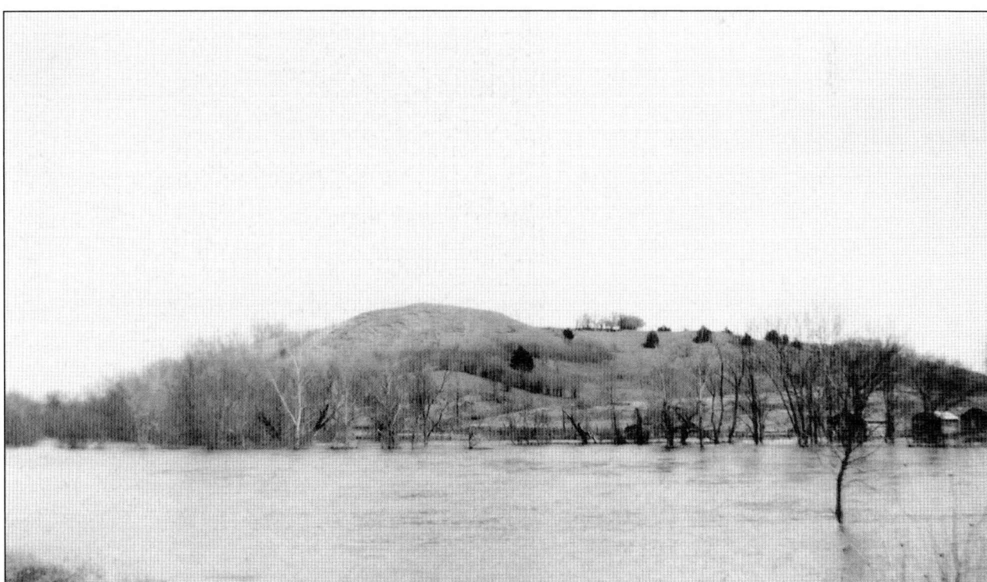

Throughout the long history of El Camino Real, the Rio Grande and its tributaries would suddenly flood. Rushing waters caused loss of lives, livestock, goods, and possessions. Riverbanks overflowed and inundated nearby buildings, as seen in this photograph taken on March 23, 1948.

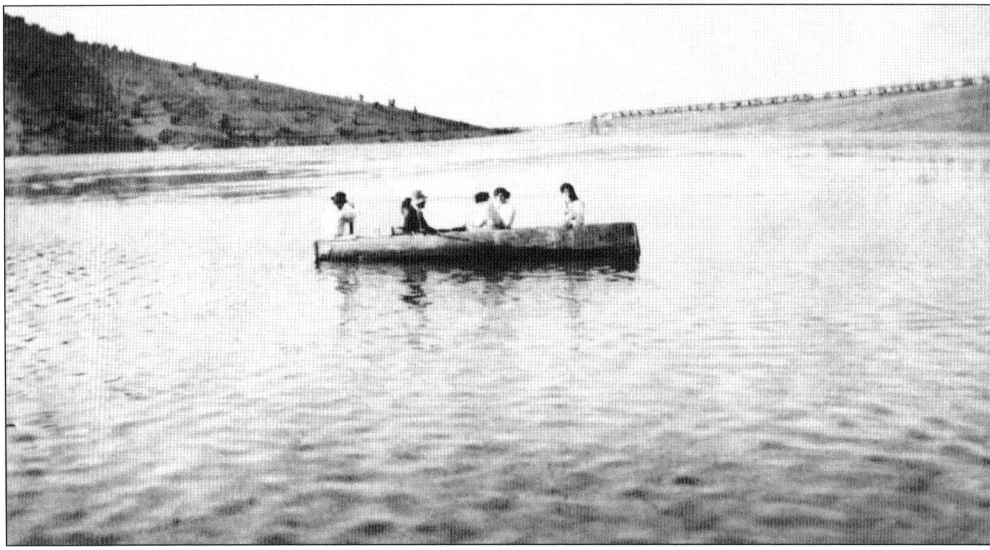

A group takes a canoe ride on the Las Salinas lakes around 1930. The large lakes had provided salt to New Mexico and the Southwest for centuries. The salts drawn from these lakes were traded and sold by the Indians. When the Spanish took over, salts were removed on a much larger scale and traded on El Camino Real.

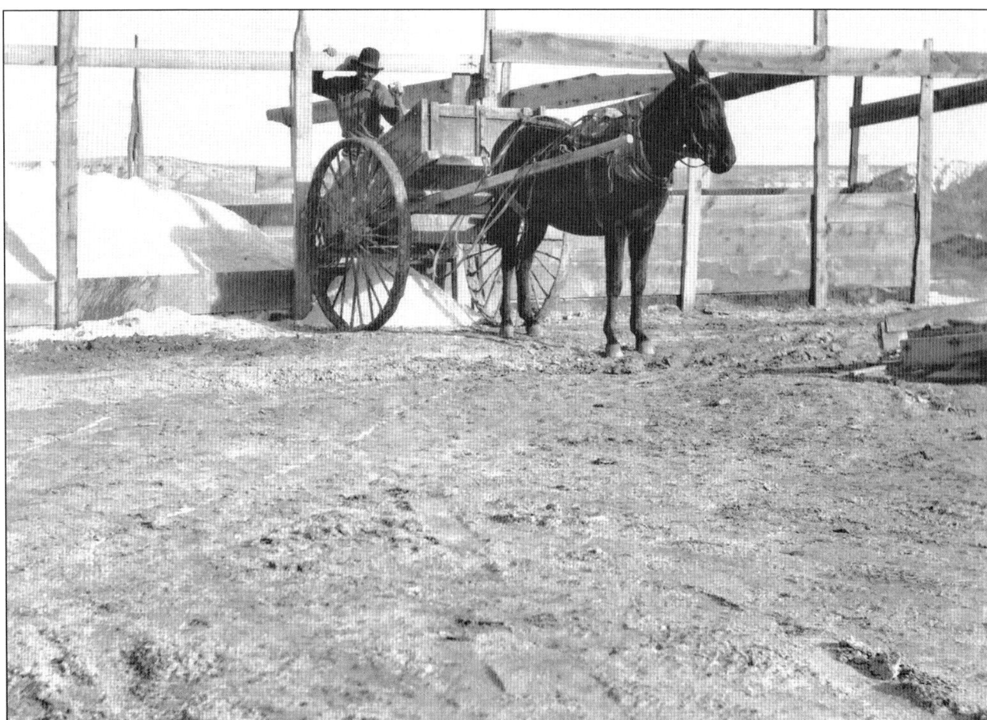

Salt was mined and traded for hundreds of years from lakes near Moriarty, New Mexico. A group of Pueblo Indians called Los Salineros maintained a lucrative business of salt trading for generations. Spanish merchants continued to mine salt, which they transported on El Camino Real into Mexico and other parts of New Mexico.

A portion of the original El Camino Real in Tome, New Mexico, is still used today. It lies in an area where visitors can park and walk in the footsteps of history. Sunken tracks, which were left by the heavy supply wagons of the past, can still be found in some isolated areas of New Mexico. For the most part, however, these ancient ruts have faded away.

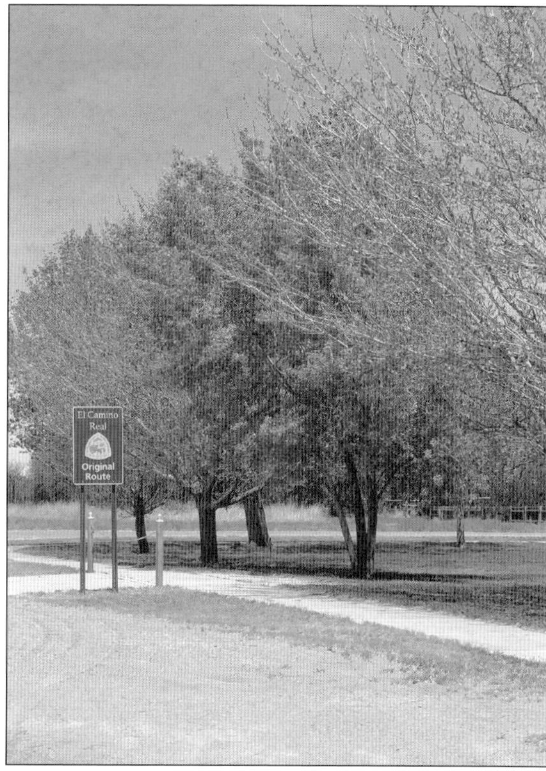

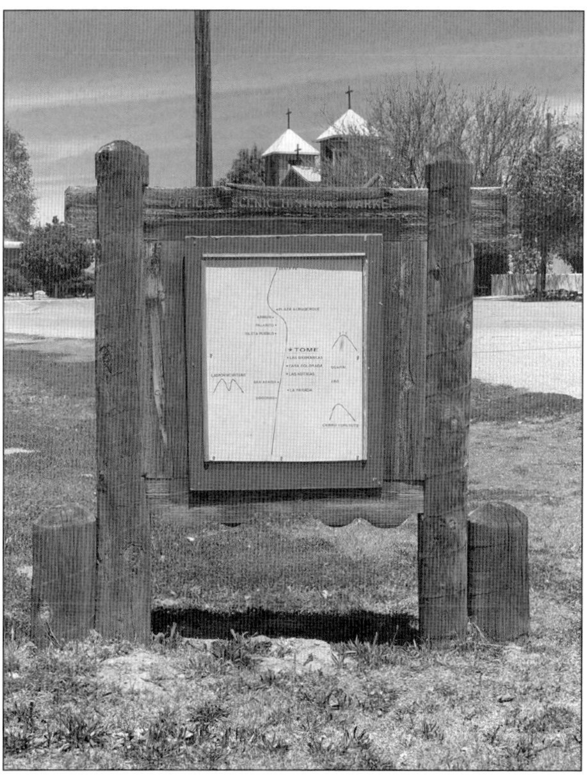

The New Mexico Historic Preservation Division began recognizing important and highly significant landmarks and sites in 1935. Striking brown log-hewn markers holding prominent positions at accessible locations began to appear throughout the state. Residents and visitors alike were readily informed about historic places, routes, and events in New Mexico's history. Recognized towns and villages that dotted El Camino Real were acknowledged.

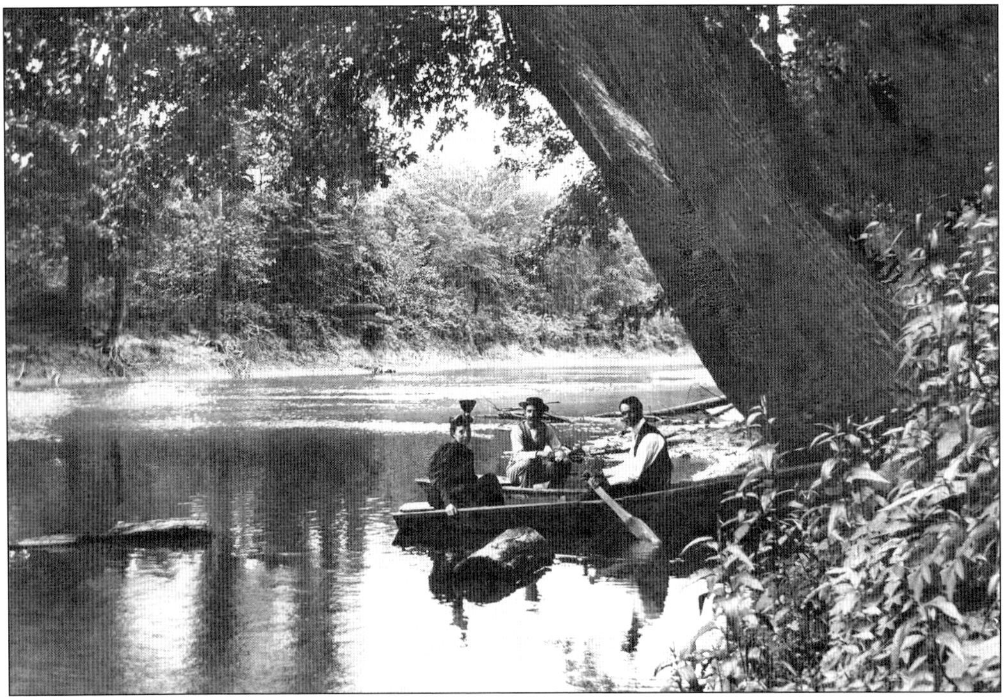

These people decided to take a boat ride on a calm stretch of the Rio Grande. The often-raging river had areas where the water channeled off and formed ponds, and others that could be used for recreation. Canyoneering up and down the Rio Grande became a popular sport.

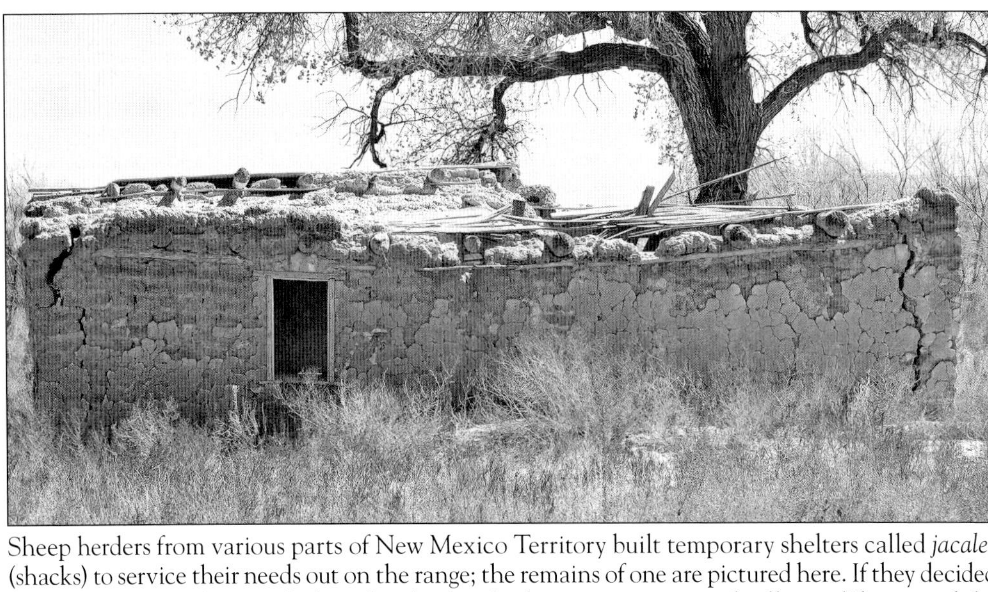

Sheep herders from various parts of New Mexico Territory built temporary shelters called *jacales* (shacks) to service their needs out on the range; the remains of one are pictured here. If they decided to live someplace along with their family, they built more permanent dwellings. (Photograph by Santiago Pacheco.)

Seven

The Lasting Legacy of El Camino Real

On June 15, 1999, US senator Pete V. Domenici of New Mexico wrote,

> New Mexico is a unique place in the sense that it is the only state in the union where several languages and cultures make up a diverse population mosaic. It is also the only state where the Spanish language has been used continuously since the early Spanish settlements were established in 1598, by Don Juan de Onate and the persevering colonists. Our New Mexican heritage including our tolerance for different cultures and languages, is part of what makes New Mexico so special . . . the 400th anniversary commemoration of the first permanent Spanish settlement in New Mexico, predating the English settlement of Jamestown in 1610 by twelve years is an event memorializing that distinct heritage.

In 1940, the US Exposition Commission commemorated the 1540 exploration of New Mexico by Don Francisco Vasquez de Coronado. In 1991 and 1992, the city of Albuquerque and the state of New Mexico celebrated the 500th anniversary of the Spanish discovery of the Americas by Christopher Columbus. Programs and celebrations were funded by the City of Albuquerque Columbus Quincentenary Committee, the City of Albuquerque Urban Enhancement Trust Fund, the Hispanic Culture Foundation, and various other state agencies and local governments. They were interested in commemorating and honoring the highly significant contributions of the Spanish and their descendants to New Mexico in particular and the United States in general.

What was handed down from the past by El Camino Real de Tierra Adentro is still felt today and will continue to be passed down for many generations to come.

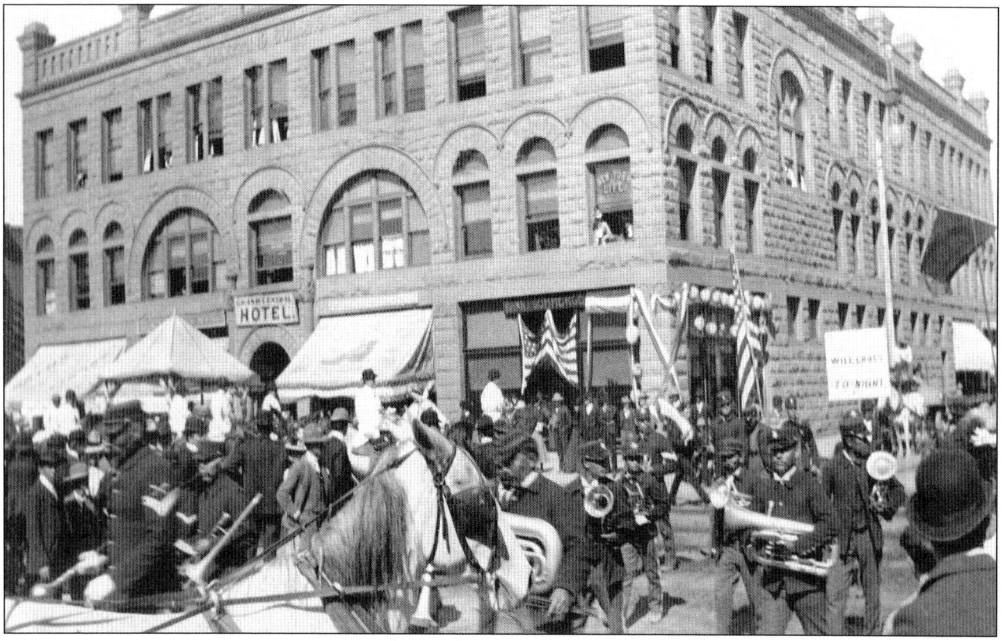

In January 1912, New Mexico was admitted as the 47th state after the vast territory had been split up by the government to also form Arizona. A grand celebration was held in Albuquerque, pictured here. People traveled from other towns to Albuquerque and the capital city of Santa Fe to celebrate.

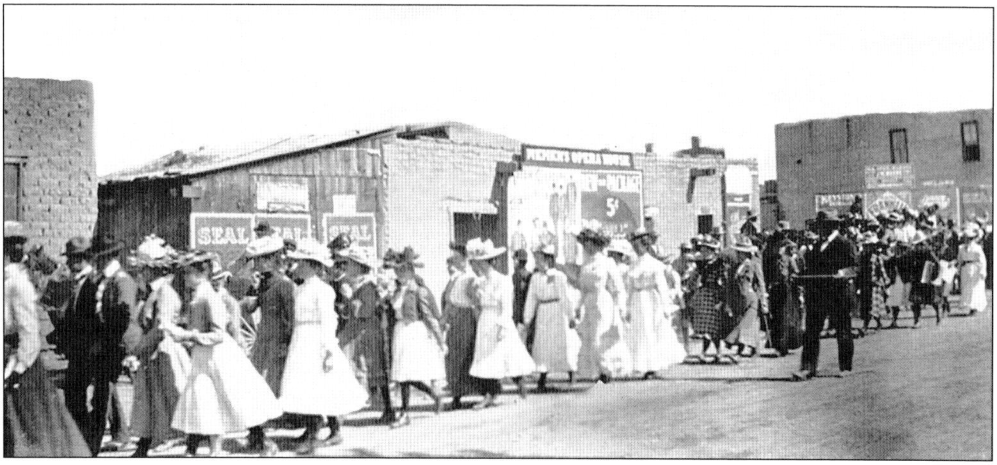

Suffragettes took to the dirt road of El Camino Real in Albuquerque demonstrating for the right to vote around 1910. Under both the previous Spanish and Mexican governments, women were provided with many rights that were not enjoyed by American women in the East, including land ownership.

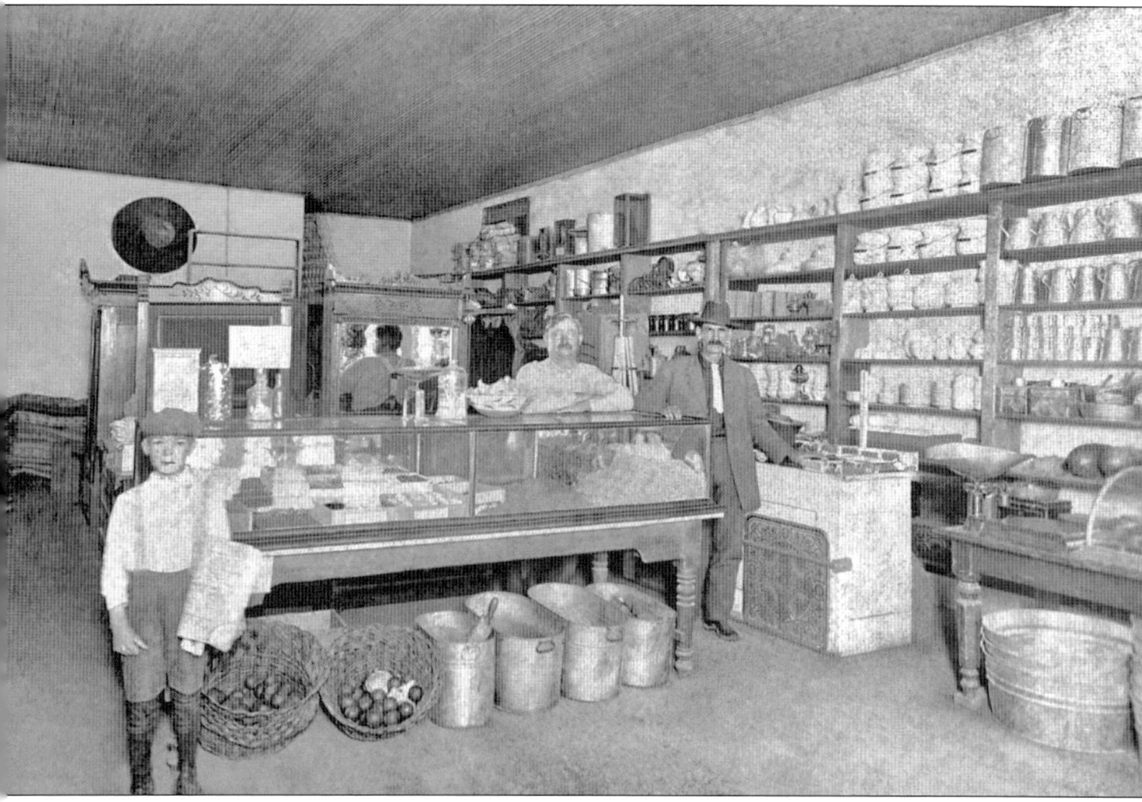

In 1912, when New Mexico became the 47th state, newspaper boy Maximiliano "Maximo" de Aragón sold newspapers announcing the event. He is pictured with storeowner Juan Vigil, center, and customer Benedito Peralta. This photograph appeared on the front page of *El Independiente* (the Independent). All three traveled on the Royal Road, which was a dusty dirt road in most parts well into the second decade of the 20th century. The newsboy's career highlights included selling newspapers to former sheriff Elfego Baca and meeting Buffalo Bill Cody at his show in Albuquerque near the old trail in 1914.

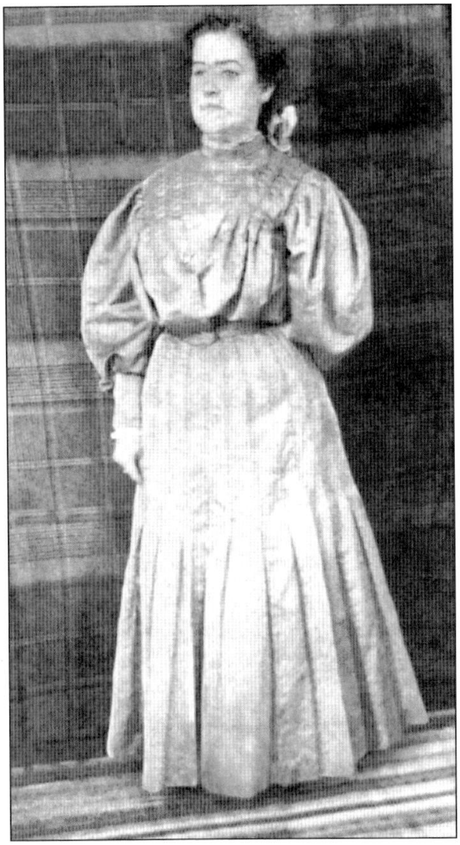

This New Mexico weaver proudly poses with rugs she made around 1890. Spanish women seldom took credit for the things they made, such as wool blankets and wool rugs. They became expert at this trade on El Camino Real. Navajo women still produce world-renowned rugs through the techniques and upright looms they were furnished by the Spanish during the colonial period.

This is a dance during the Santa Fe Fiesta around 1939. People have gathered to view the dance and have a good time. Fiestas were meaningful celebrations both for Indians and Spanish settlers. This deeply ingrained heritage dates back several centuries.

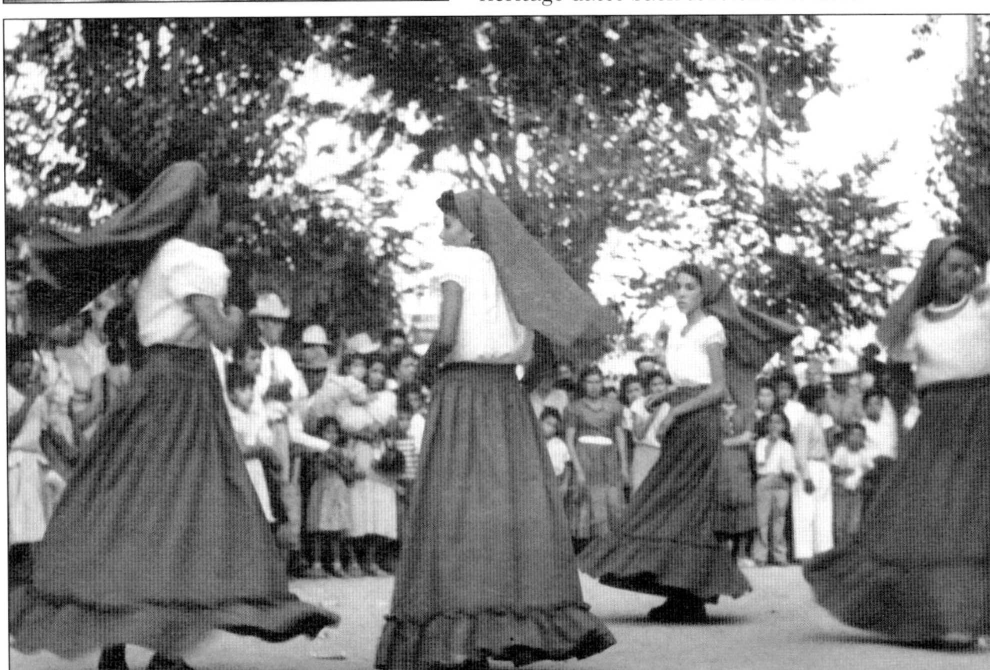

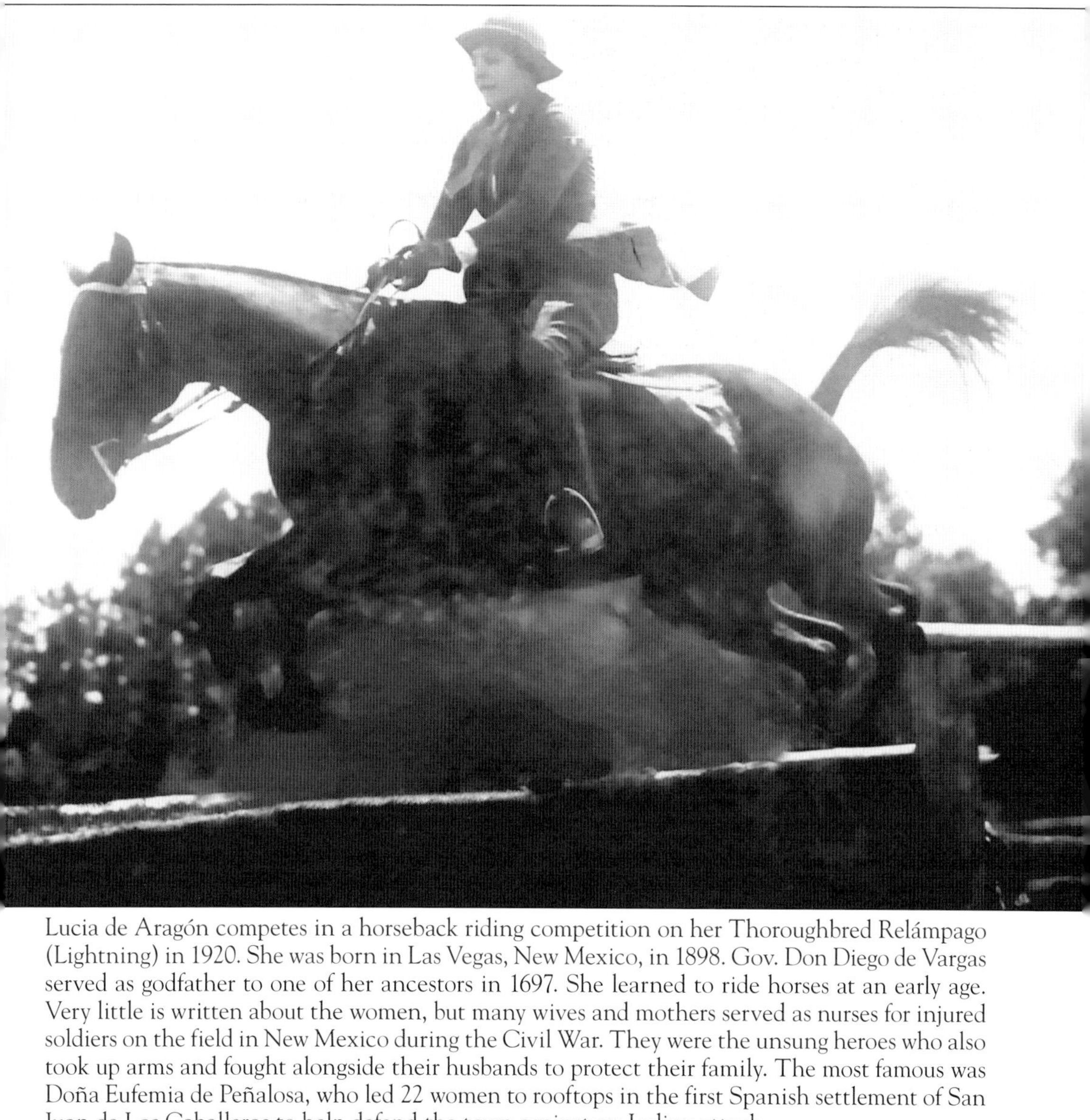

Lucia de Aragón competes in a horseback riding competition on her Thoroughbred Relámpago (Lightning) in 1920. She was born in Las Vegas, New Mexico, in 1898. Gov. Don Diego de Vargas served as godfather to one of her ancestors in 1697. She learned to ride horses at an early age. Very little is written about the women, but many wives and mothers served as nurses for injured soldiers on the field in New Mexico during the Civil War. They were the unsung heroes who also took up arms and fought alongside their husbands to protect their family. The most famous was Doña Eufemia de Peñalosa, who led 22 women to rooftops in the first Spanish settlement of San Juan de Los Caballeros to help defend the town against an Indian attack.

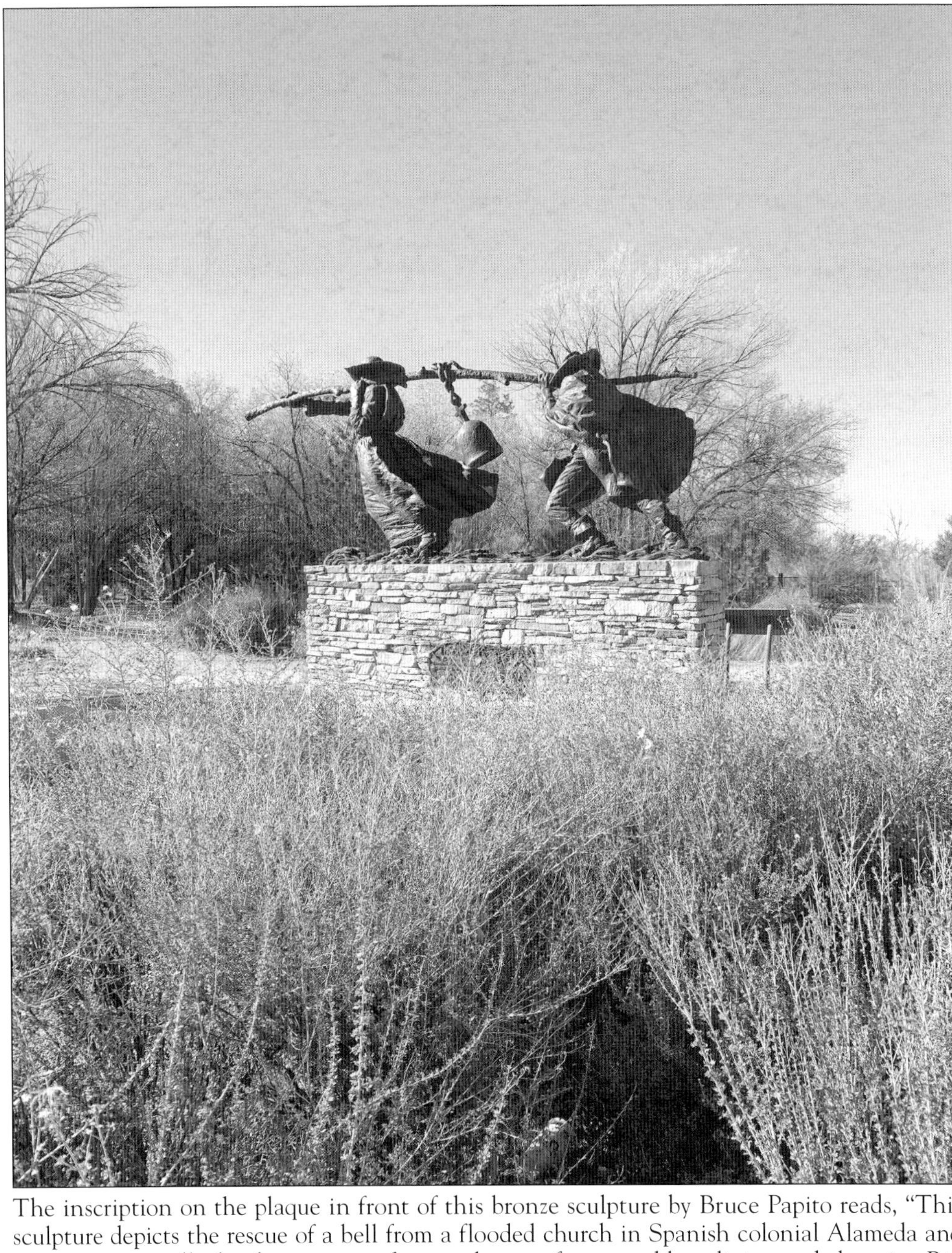

The inscription on the plaque in front of this bronze sculpture by Bruce Papito reads, "This sculpture depicts the rescue of a bell from a flooded church in Spanish colonial Alameda and commemorates all who drew support from and were often tested by a living and changing Rio Grande." Sections of the ancient El Camino Real run from the eastern border with Texas to San Juan Indian Pueblo, north of the city of Española. This route is drivable and is a part of former US Route 85 designated El Camino Real Scenic Byway.

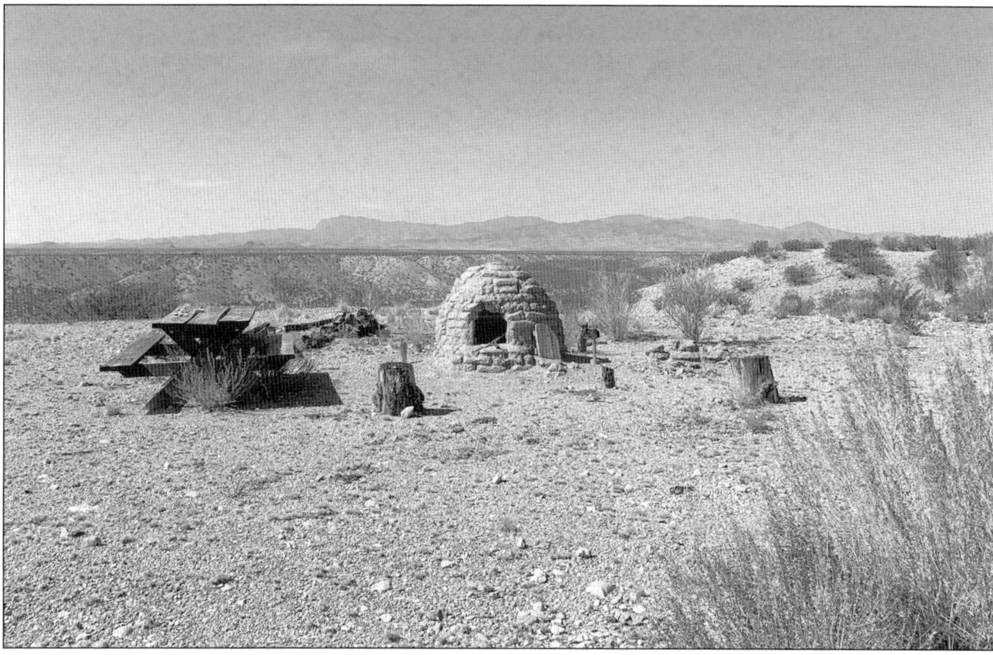

Many treasures of trade and travel can be found at El Camino Real de Tierra Adentro International Heritage Center near Socorro. This *horno* (beehive oven) is typical of those that were made in New Mexico by the Spanish during the colonial period. Native Americans readily adapted to these hornos, as well as sopaipillas and *buñuelos* (fried bread). (Photograph by Rosa María Calles.)

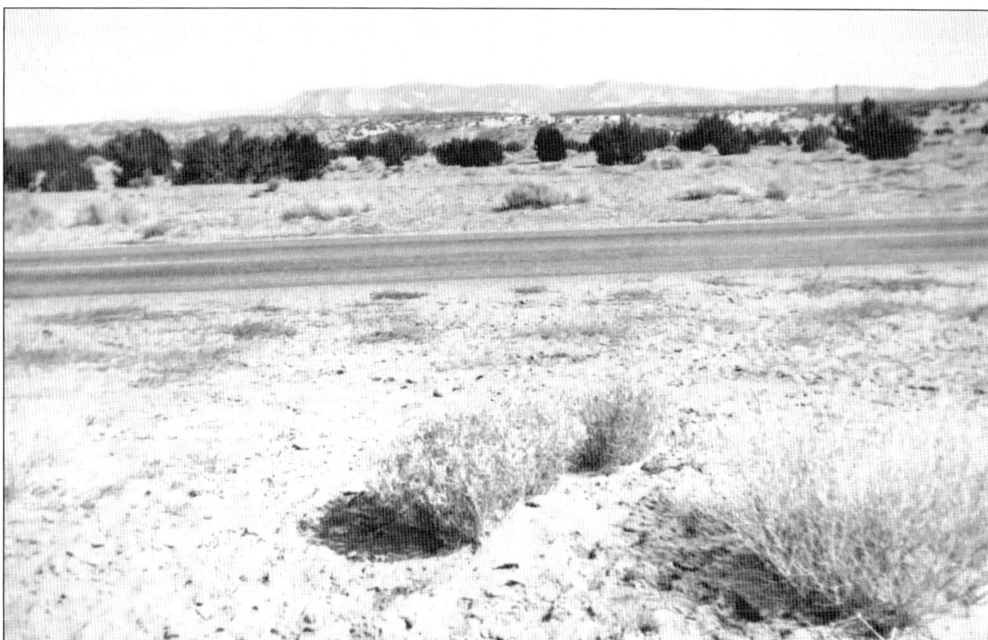

The dirt road of El Camino Real west of the Manzano Mountains, pictured here around 1940, was replaced in many areas with asphalt. In fact, many parts of El Camino Real were incorporated into modern highways. In some isolated places, the former trail still exists as a passable dirt road with cars still traveling along it.

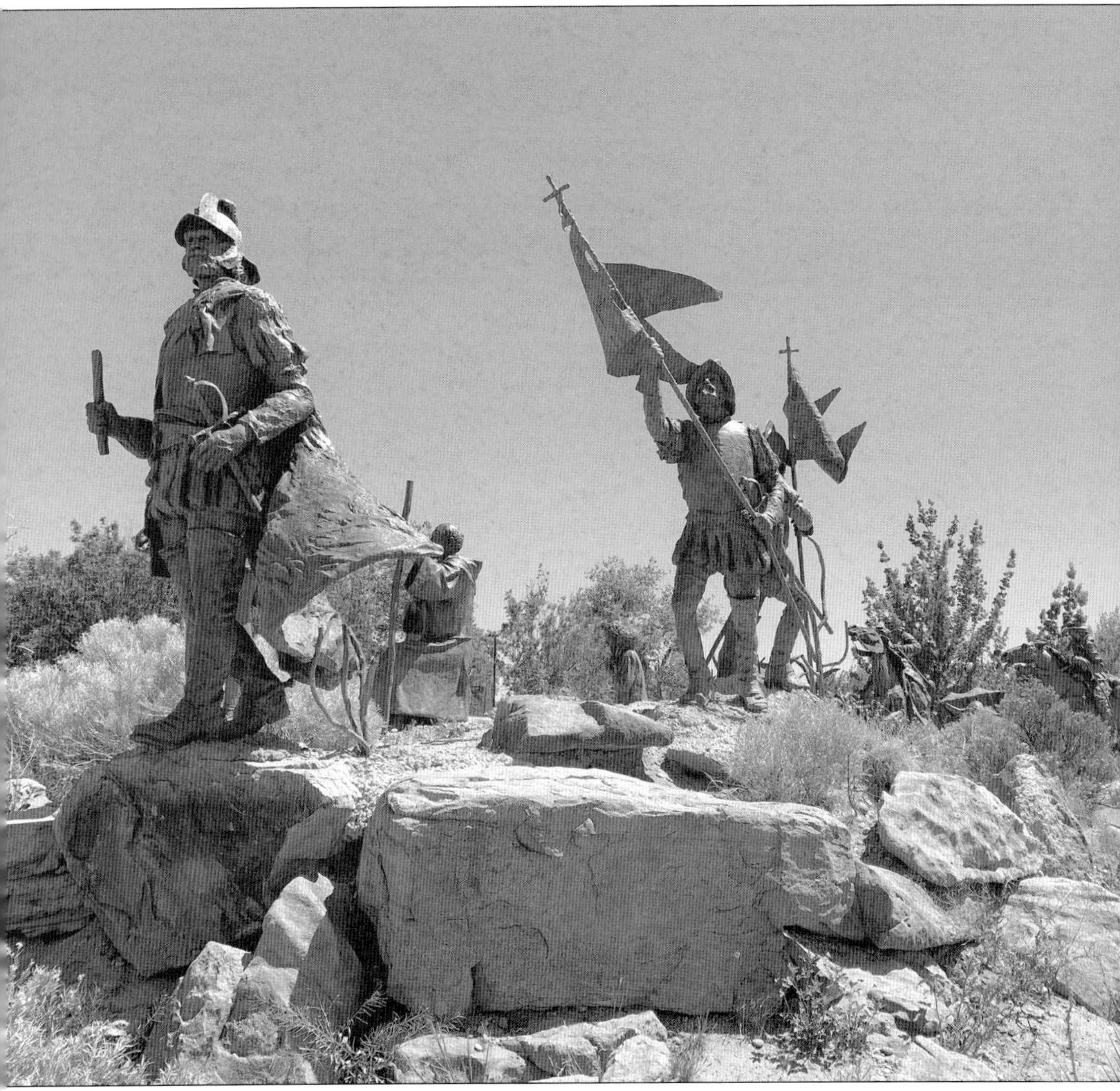

In 2005, the City of Albuquerque and the Albuquerque Museum of Art sponsored a large celebration honoring the 400th anniversary of El Camino Real. Monumental bronze sculptures were permanently installed at the front of the museum. The pieces, called *La Jornada* (the Journey), depict the conquistadores, Franciscan friars, and Spanish settlers, including the original 400 men, many of whom brought their families to New Mexico in 1598. This journey into New Mexico was treacherous, and many lost their lives along the way. These sculptures were the collaborative tricultural creations of artists Sonny Rivera, Native American Nora Naranjo Morse, and Betty Sabo.

This sculpture at the base of El Cerro honors Native American history and heritage on El Camino Real. Noted sculptor Armando Alvarez created the piece in iron at the site. It is called *La Puerta del Sol* (the Pathway of the Sun). The sculpture graphically depicts the intrigue and adventure of El Camino Real.

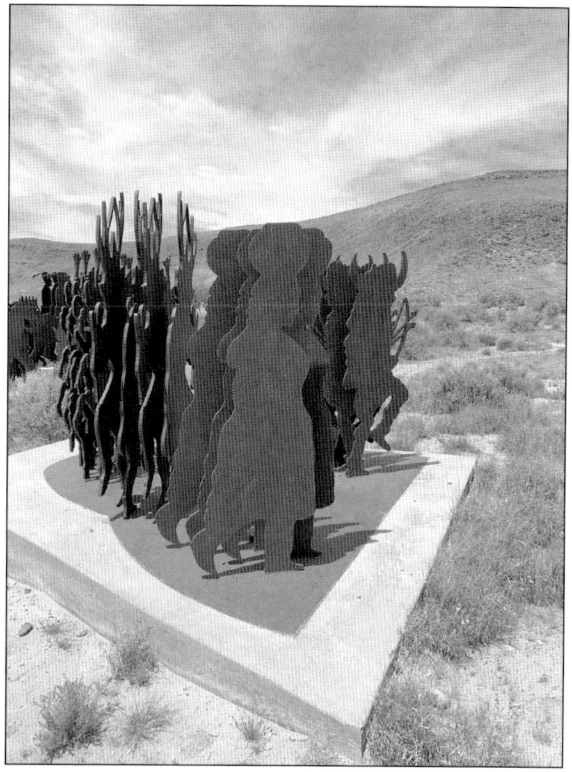

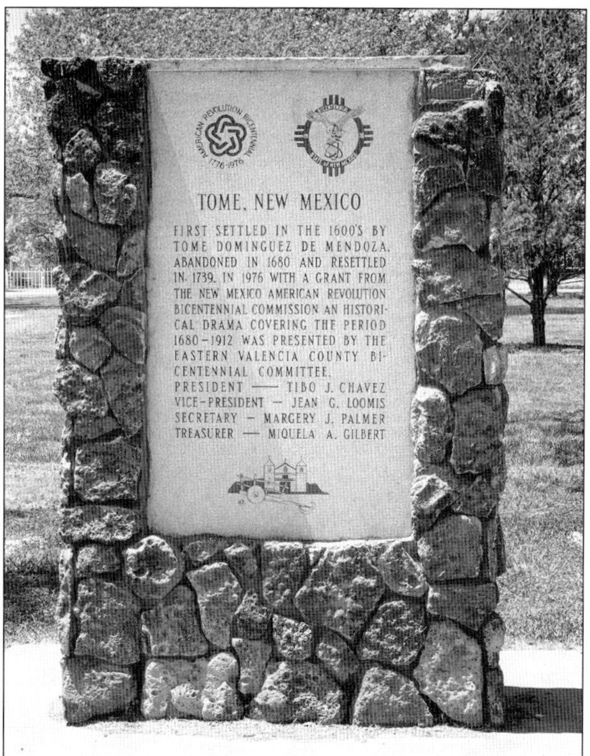

This historical marker celebrating El Camino Real and Spanish heritage is typical of those found throughout New Mexico. Officials of the New Mexico Department of Transportation long ago decided that Spanish heritage should be recognized for future generations.

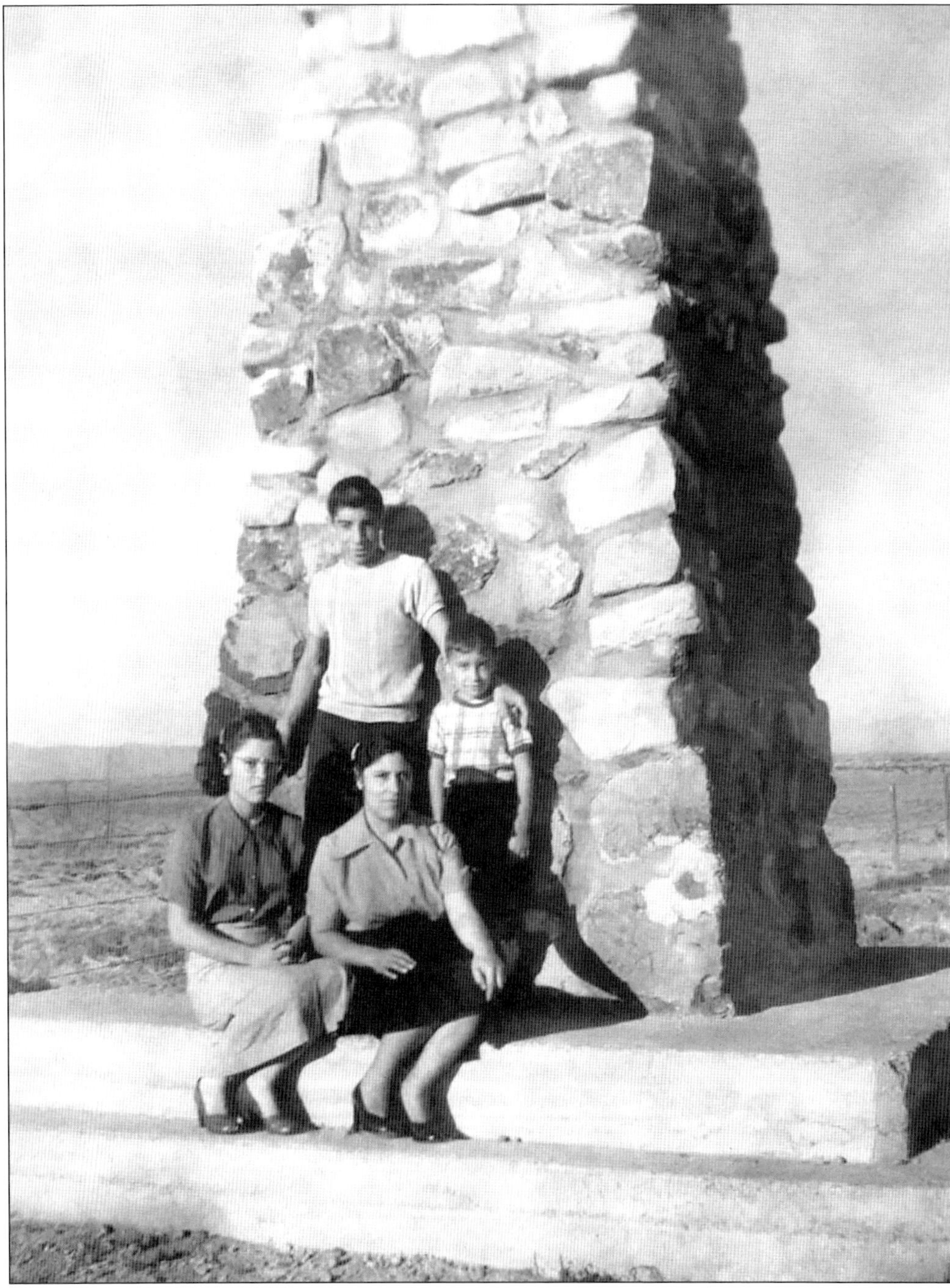

A historic obelisk was erected on El Camino Real near Santa Fe in June 1940 memorializing the "Mormon Battalion," Mormon volunteers who fought heroically against the Mexicans during the Mexican-American War. In reality, the *Batallón* was a group of Mormon families escaping the horrors perpetrated against them in Missouri and other parts of the United States and seeking refuge in Mexican territory. Col. Stephen Watts Kearny and his Missouri forces used the Mormons as a ploy to invade New Mexico. At right is the author with his mother, Cleofas Sánchez de Aragón; his sister Esperanza Virginia (left); and older brother Max.

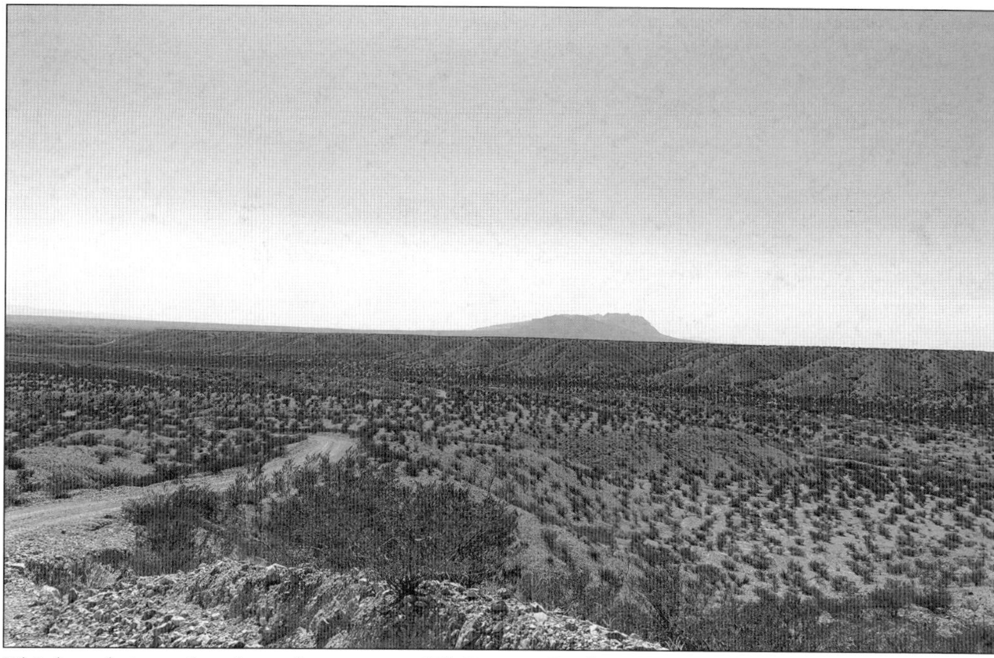

This broad view taken from the summit of El Camino Real International Heritage Center provides a good perspective of what travelers would have seen from different vantage points along the road. Some of the difficulties and hardships they experienced can be imagined. (Photograph by Rosa María Calles.)

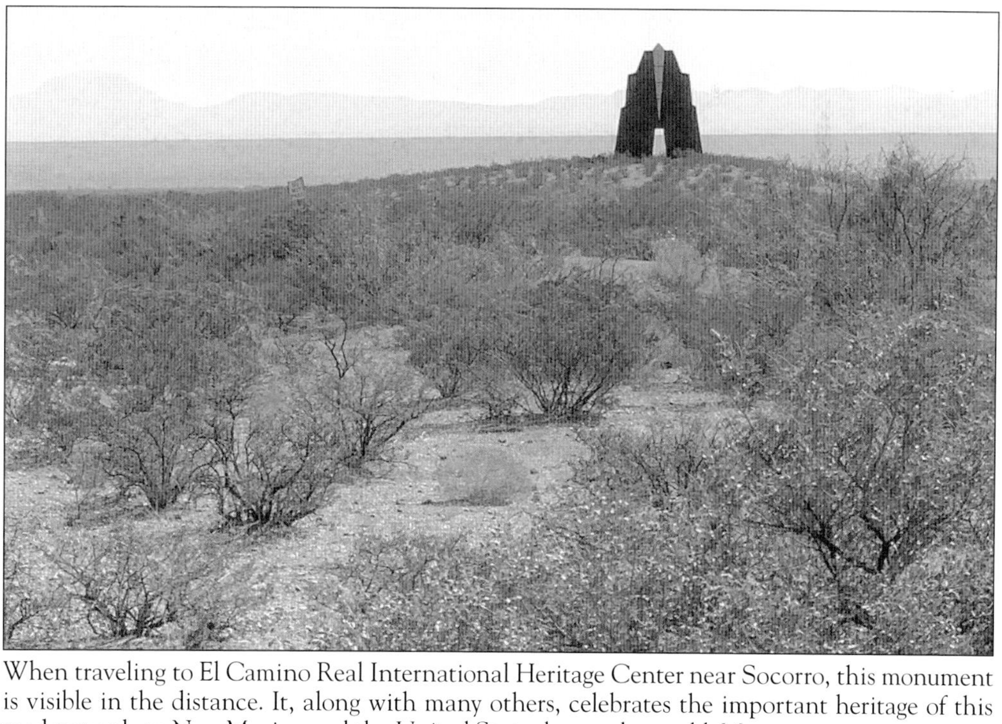

When traveling to El Camino Real International Heritage Center near Socorro, this monument is visible in the distance. It, along with many others, celebrates the important heritage of this road not only to New Mexico and the United States but to the world. Many more monuments to the Spanish cultural heritage stand throughout the state.

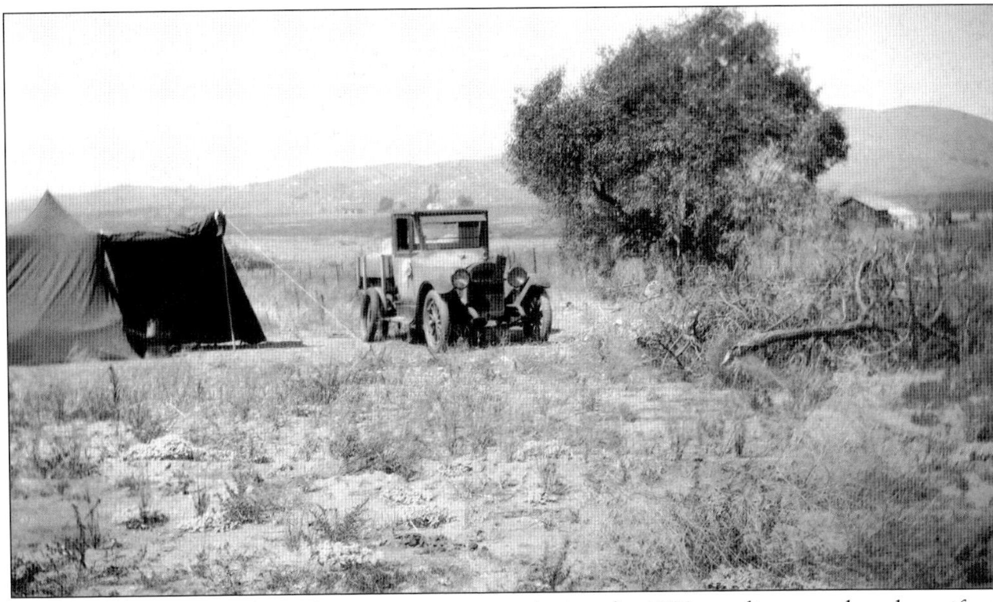

Archaeologists and anthropologists set up camps during the 1920s to dig up and study artifacts from the Spanish colonial period along El Camino Real. Some of what was discovered is currently housed in museums and at the International Heritage Center for people to enjoy and learn about the history of this Land of Enchantment.

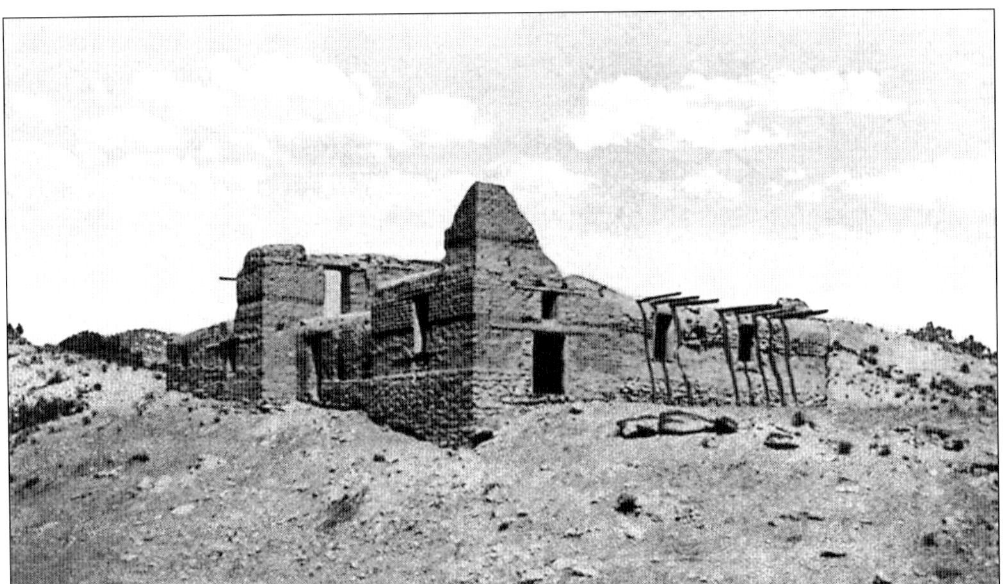

These ruins of a Spanish mission church are no longer extant. The location is unknown. Fortunately, a photographer caught this view for posterity. One of the values of photographers traveling out into isolated areas is historic preservation on film of a view into the past and memories of what was.

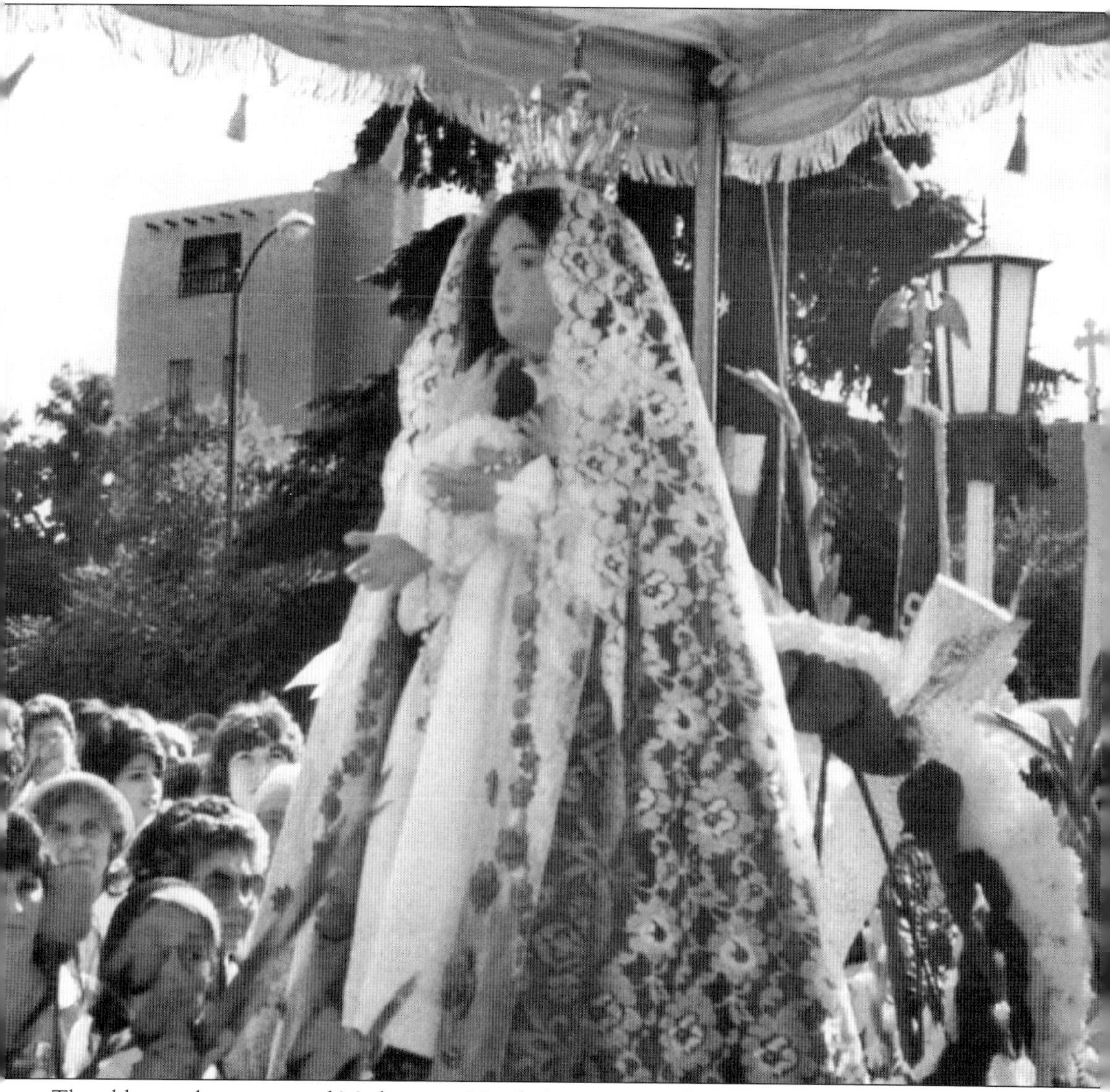

The oldest and most revered Madonna in North America is in Santa Fe. Experts date it between the 15th and 17th centuries. It is a wooden image brought to the capital city on El Camino Real in a missionary caravan by Fray Alonso de Benavidez in 1626. It is called *Nuestra Señora de la Santa Fe* (Our Lady of the Holy Faith) or *La Conquistadora* (Our Lady of the Conquest). A Catholic confraternity is assigned to protect the statue. The image survived the brutal 1680 Pueblo Indian Revolt, in which hundreds were massacred, including Indians and priests. The statue was returned to Santa Fe by Gov. Don Diego de Vargas. It is carried in procession to kick off an annual fiesta.

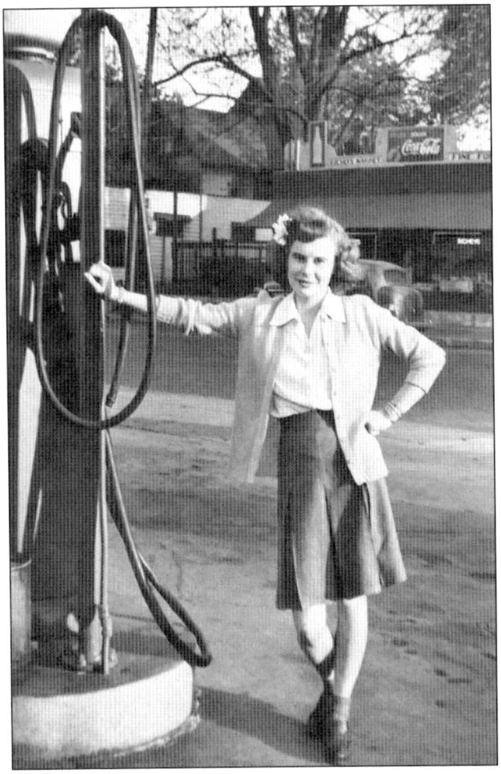

A 1950s gas station and a girl standing next to a gas pump show how time has changed everything on the famous road of El Camino Real. At one time, many markers designating the ancient road were set by the State of New Mexico, but over the years, the elements destroyed a number of them.

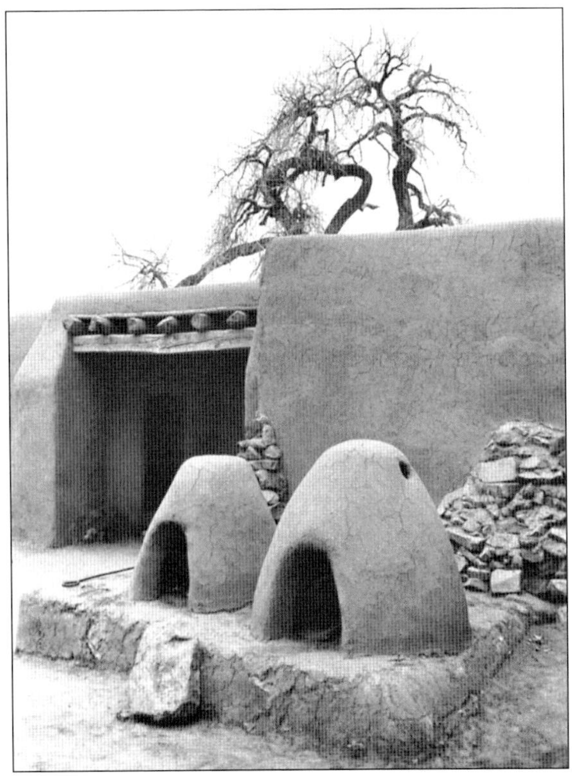

Many Americans arriving in New Mexico loved the Spanish style of architecture to the point of building lavish "Santa Fe Style" homes that incorporated the signature beehive ovens. This type of structure, and the ovens, actually originated in the Middle East.

Bernalillo, New Mexico, was a main stop on El Camino Real. The city continues to celebrate and embrace its long Spanish history and heritage on the Royal Road by marking certain areas. This marker is at the entrance to the city, and identifies the portion of El Camino Real that leads through the town.

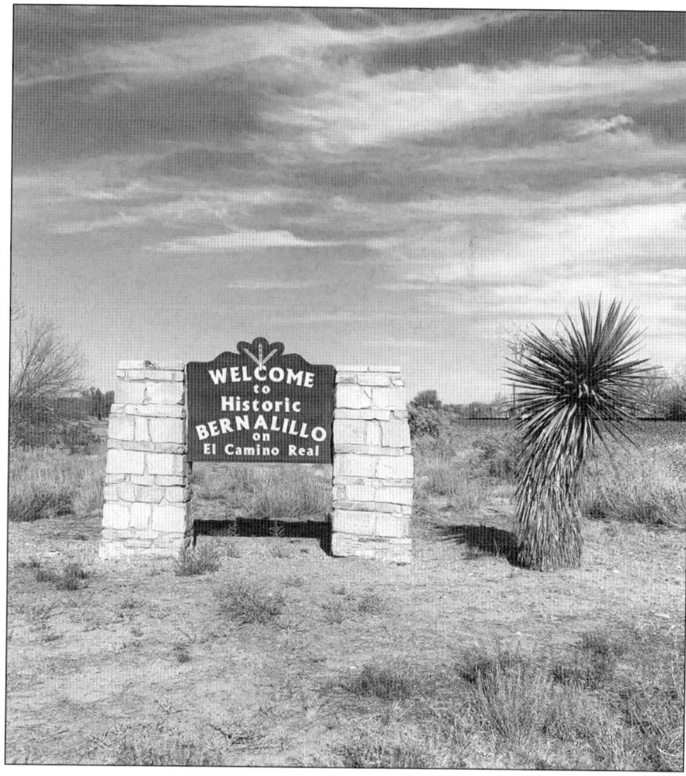

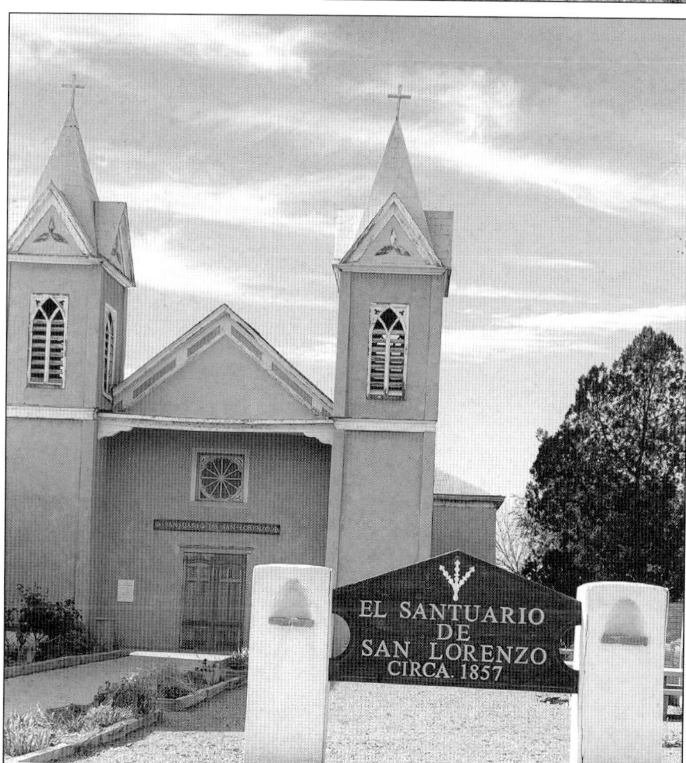

The San Lorenzo Sanctuary in Bernalillo was completed in 1857 and is now recognized as a religious landmark. The sanctuary has massive four-foot-thick adobe walls, vigas, and an earthen floor. Bernalillo was an important stopover on El Camino Real. Residents celebrate this history and commemorate its founding with Matachín dances and other celebrations of Spanish history.

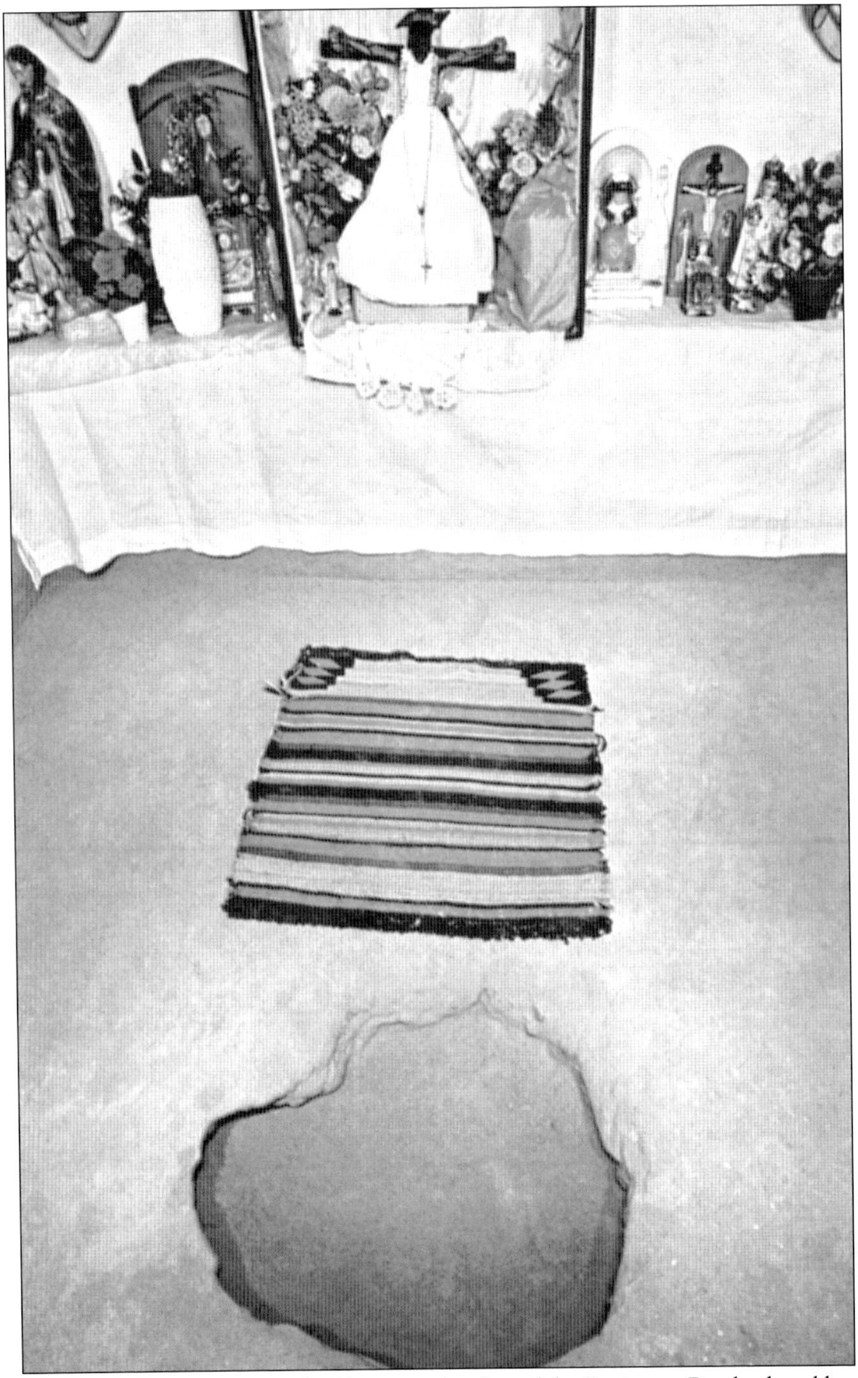

Sometime before 1819, Don Bernardo Abeyta, a member of the Penitente Brotherhood lay society, was doing his prayerful exercises in the hills. He discovered a half-buried wooden crucifix. In time, he built a chapel over the place to house the crucifix. This is known as the Santuario (sanctuary) de Chimayo. Now thousands of visitors to this internationally recognized pilgrimage site attest to the healing powers of the dirt where the crucifix was buried. This photograph shows the Healing Room with the hole of holy dirt, which supposedly is removed but never empties.

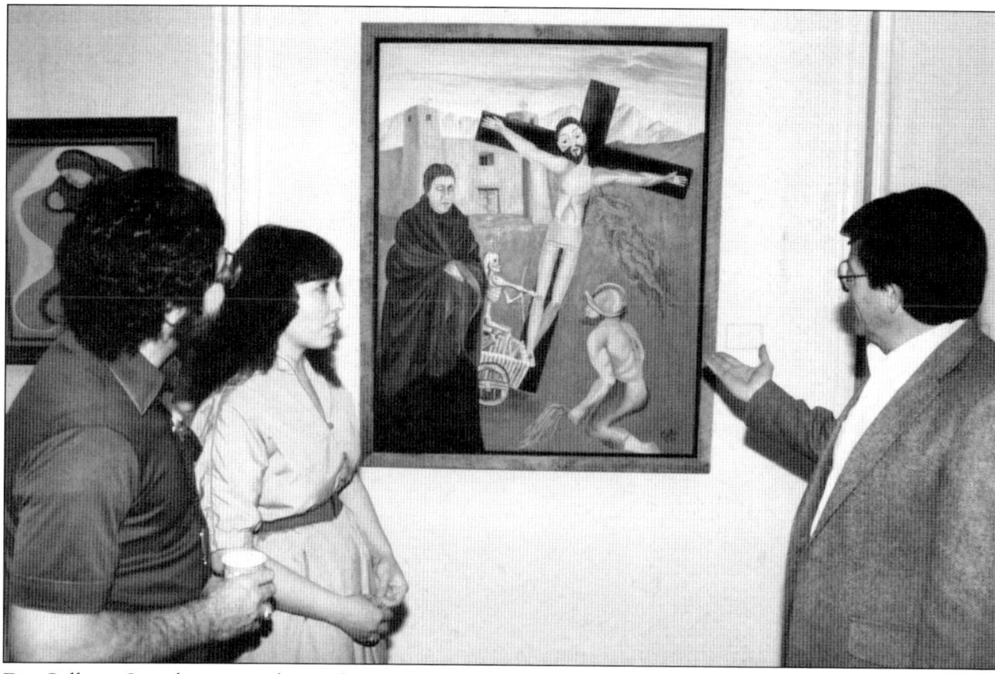

Dr. Gilbert Sánchez, president of New Mexico Highlands University, admires an award-winning oil and acrylic painting by Rosa María Calles. This painting, *Sacrificios, Sacrifices*, was part of a 1986 exhibition called Visions of El Camino Real at the campus gallery for professional and noted artists. The artist stated that she portrayed the struggles and hardships of the colonizers in New Mexico during the 18th century.

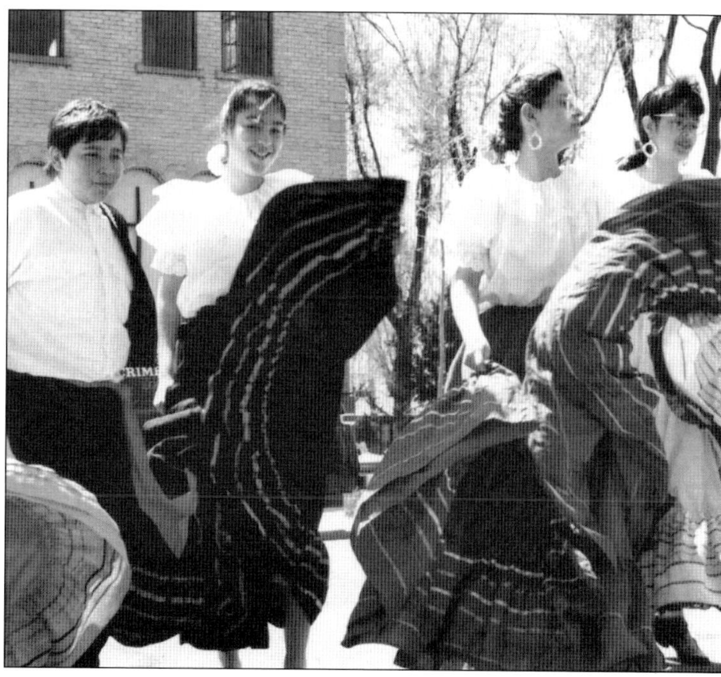

This group of *baila* dancers performed for the Nuestra Señora de los Dolores (Our lady of Sorrows) Church fiestas. Annual fiestas take place throughout New Mexico. This tradition dates to the early settlement. Performances take place throughout the state in many communities that recognize and honor the Spanish settlement.

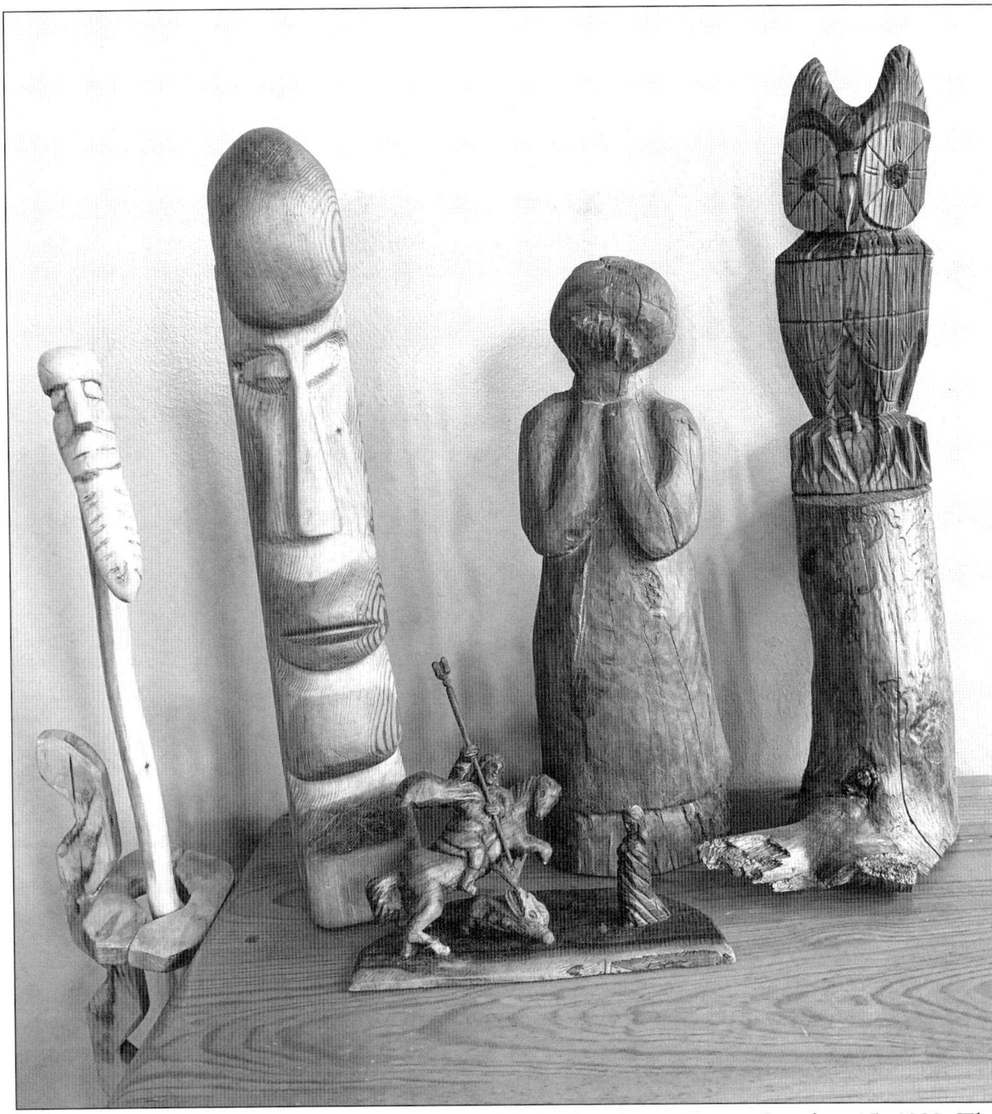

The Spanish Colonial Arts Society was established in Santa Fe on October 15, 1929. This important and vital group sought to preserve the colonial arts, which included religious arts, furniture, weaving, and other arts stemming from the early settlement of New Mexico. Music and dance were also included. Committee members feared the arts could be irretrievably lost. During the 1930s, the federal Works Progress Administration (WPA) was instrumental in preserving the arts in New Mexico. Well-known artists from the period are represented by these sculptures (from left to right): Patrocino Barela, *Old Man Cane* and *Pensamientos* (*Thoughts*); Celso Gallegos, *Weeping Woman* and *Saint George*; and José Dolores López, *Tecolote* (*Owl*). These WPA artists gained national and international recognition.

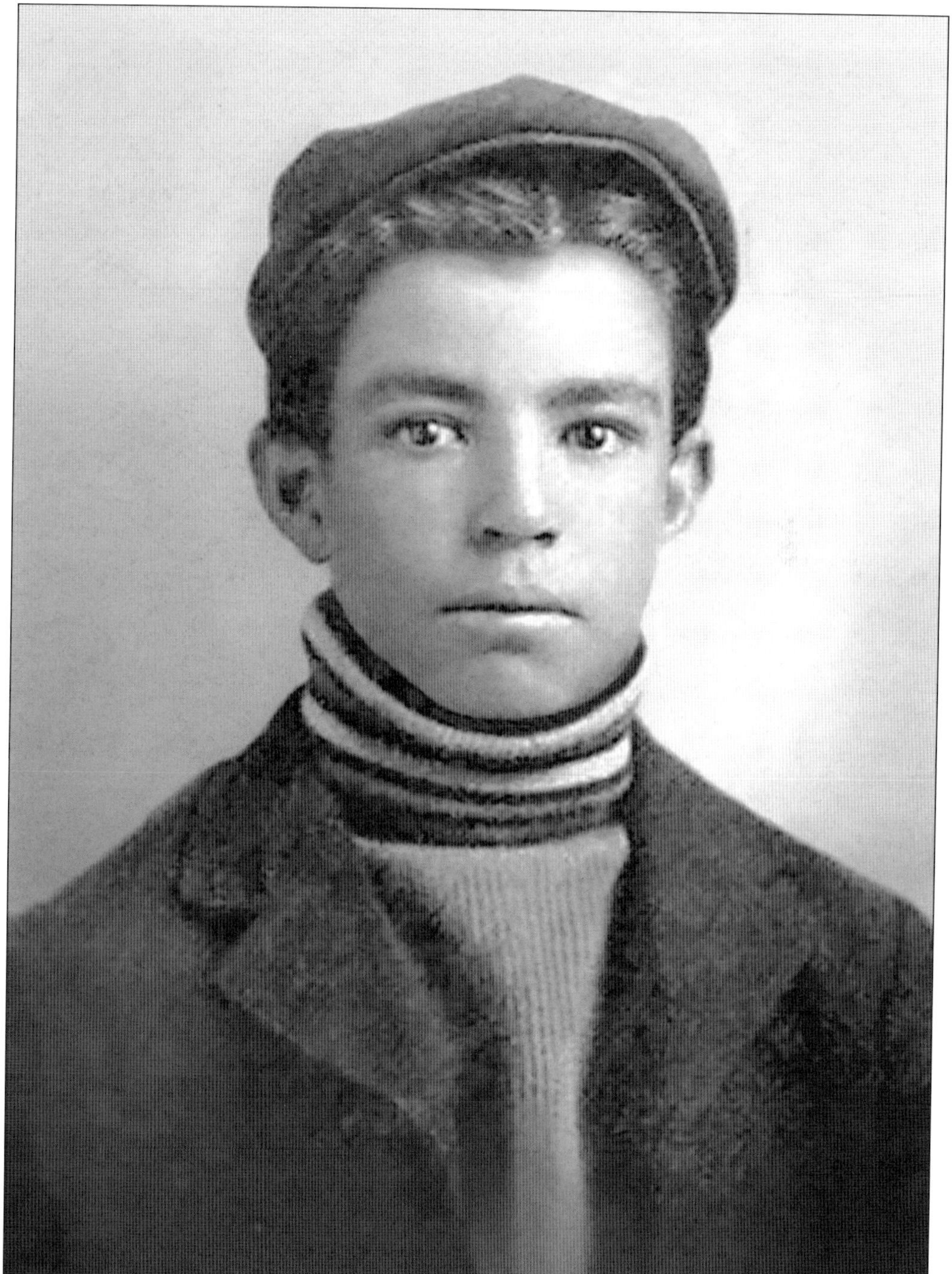

This photograph shows Dionicio "Dennis" Chávez as a teenager. He was born in Los Chávez, New Mexico, on April 8, 1888. He was the son of David Chávez and Paz Sanchez, daughter of Doña Barbara Chávez de Sanchez. He was from a prominent family with roots stemming from the 1598 settlers. Dennis Chávez became a US senator who was honored with a statue in Statuary Hall in Washington, DC, and a US postage stamp. He is recognized as a major Hispanic leader who inspired and motivated others with Spanish roots.

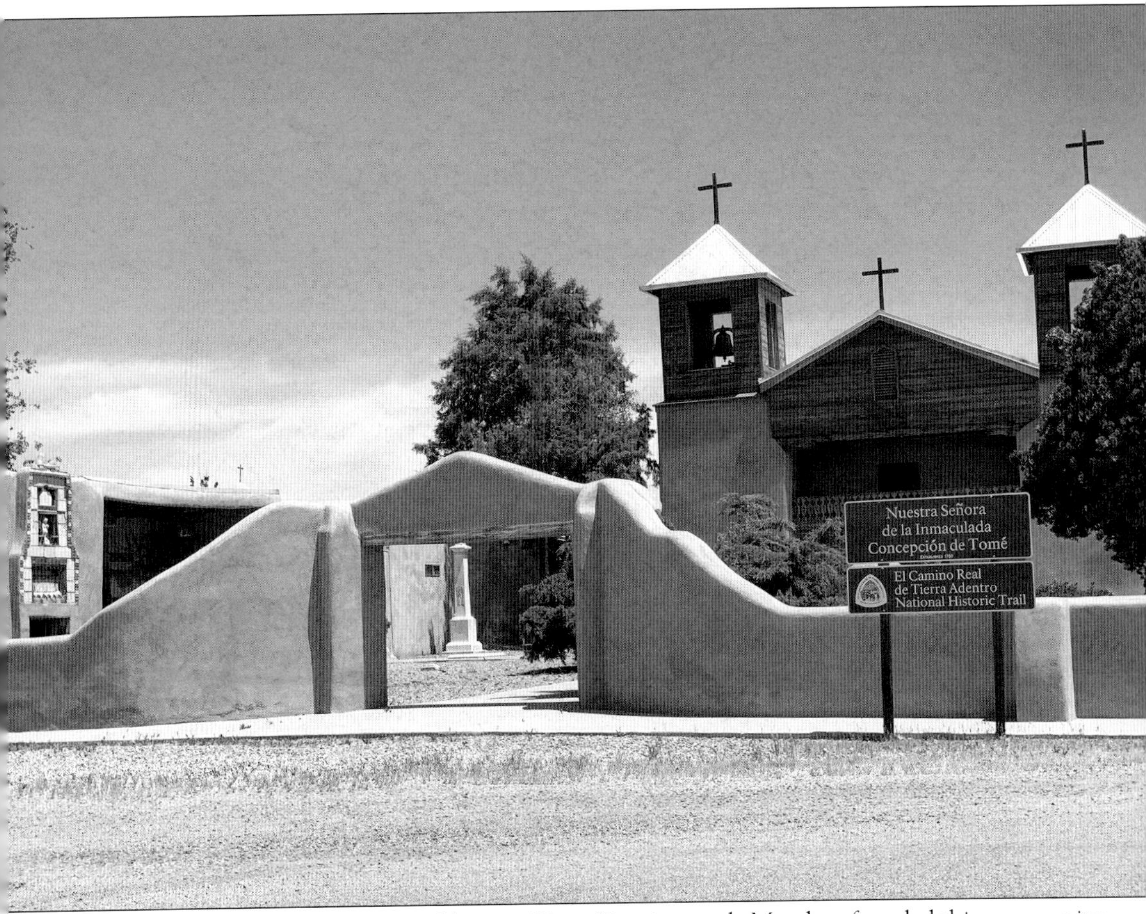

Tome, New Mexico, has a storied history. Tome Domínguez de Mendoza founded this community in the early 18th century. The official date is given as July 30, 1739, for Nuestra Señora de la Concepción de Tome Domínguez. A branch of the Santa Fe Presidio was stationed at Tome to help the villagers and travelers on El Camino Real. Those journeying to Santa Fe looked forward to refreshments, lodging, and entertainment in this town. Tome was one of the most important stops on the road. This region has several designated areas acknowledging the contributions of El Camino Real to history. There is a park in the main town where celebrations are held. The Immaculate Conception Church was built in the 18th century. An outdoor museum is nearby.

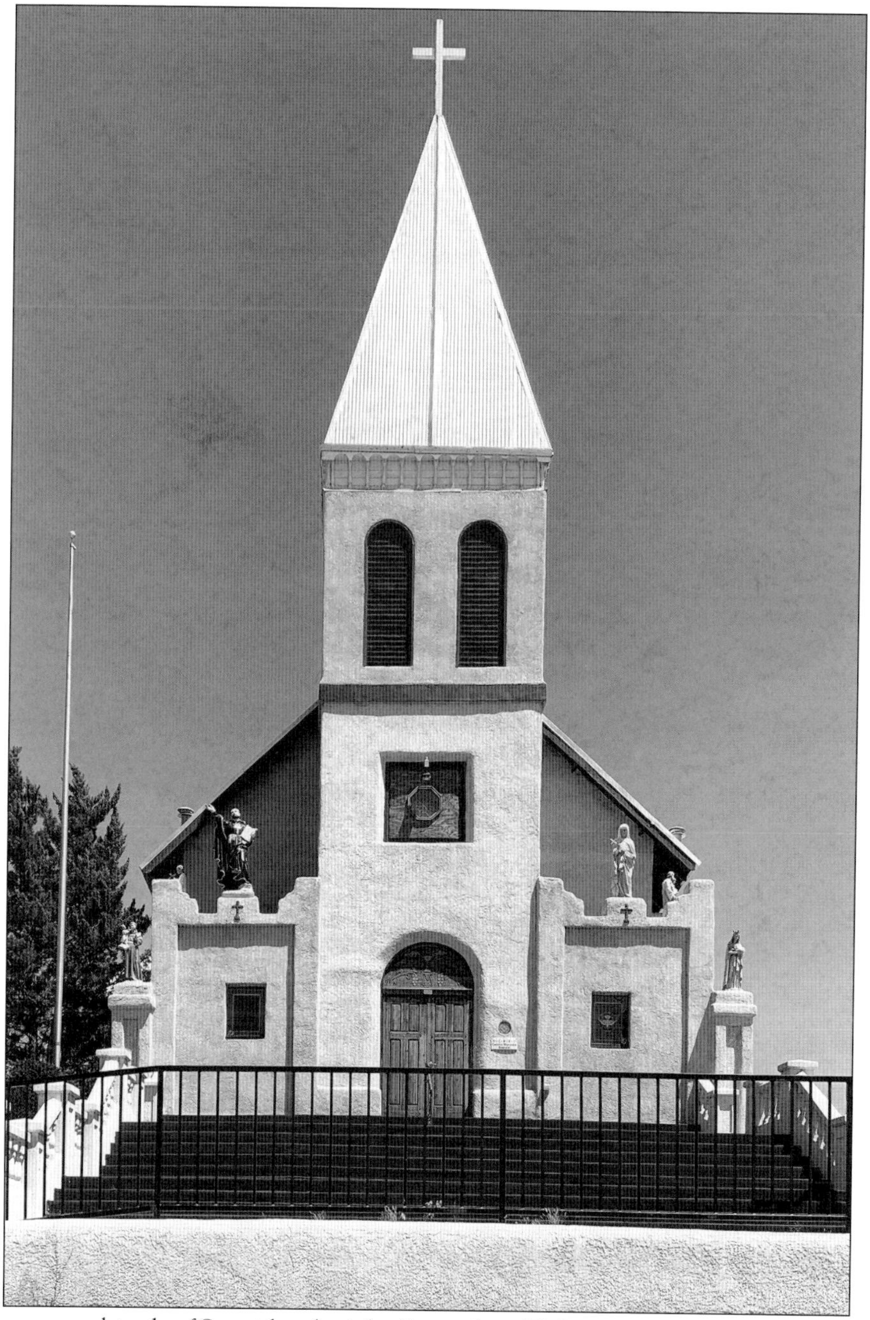

There were a multitude of Spanish colonial villages along El Camino Real in New Mexico. A few still exist, such as San José, Alameda, Atrisco, Ranchos de Albuquerque, Barelas, Los Poblanos, and Martínez Town–Santa Bárbara. These areas have been mostly absorbed by the sprawling city of Albuquerque. Mountain Road leads to Martínez Town–Santa Bárbara with its San Ignacio Church, built around 1849–1850. This road was once known as Carnuel Trail. The trail branched off of El Camino del Lado, which was a section of El Camino Real. Branches spreading out from the Royal Road to Santa Fe were found from the start to the end of the old road. El Camino Real was the main artery, with branches to towns and Indian villages.

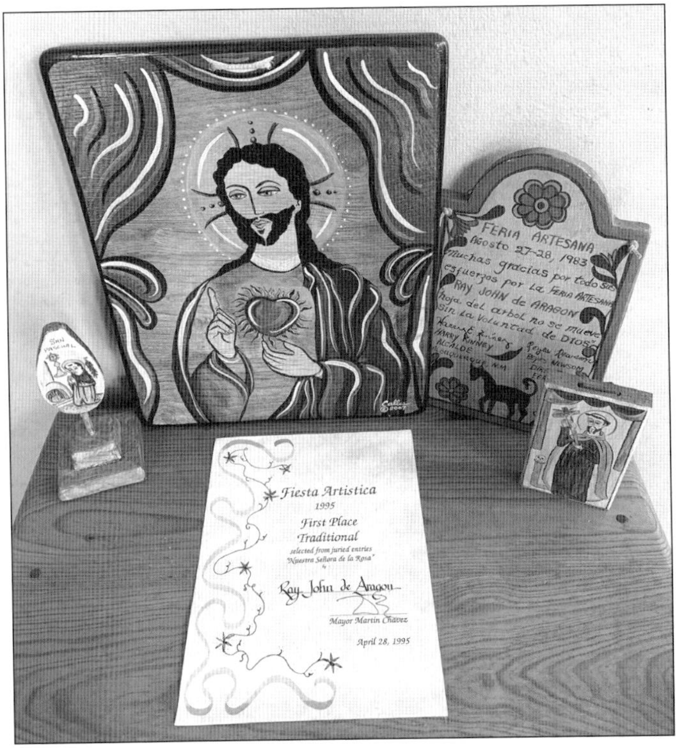

This photograph features, from left to right, San Pascual, patron saint of cooks, by Charlie Carrillo; El Sagrado Corazón (the Sacred Heart of Jesus); by Rosa María Calles; and a plaque and retablo of San Francisco (Saint Francis) by Marie Romero Cash.

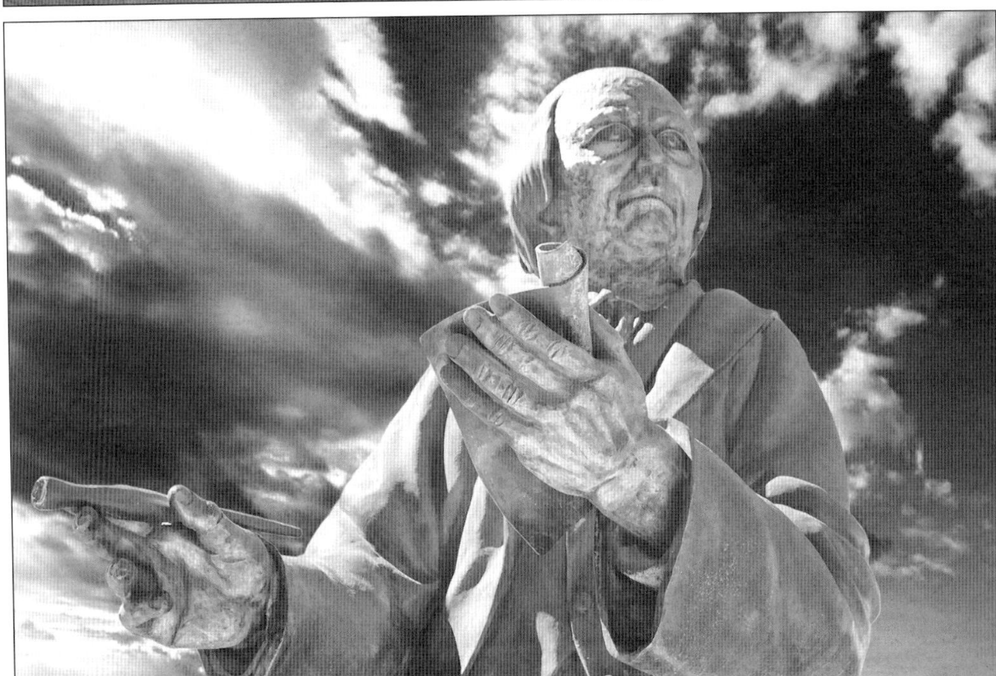

Internationally recognized sculptor Huberto Maestas created this 10-foot bronze sculpture of New Mexico's folk hero priest Presbítero Don Antonio José Martínez. The sculpture dominates the Taos Plaza and graphically represents the legacy of El Camino Real. The priest was a major figure of this region. (Photograph by Santiago Pacheco.)

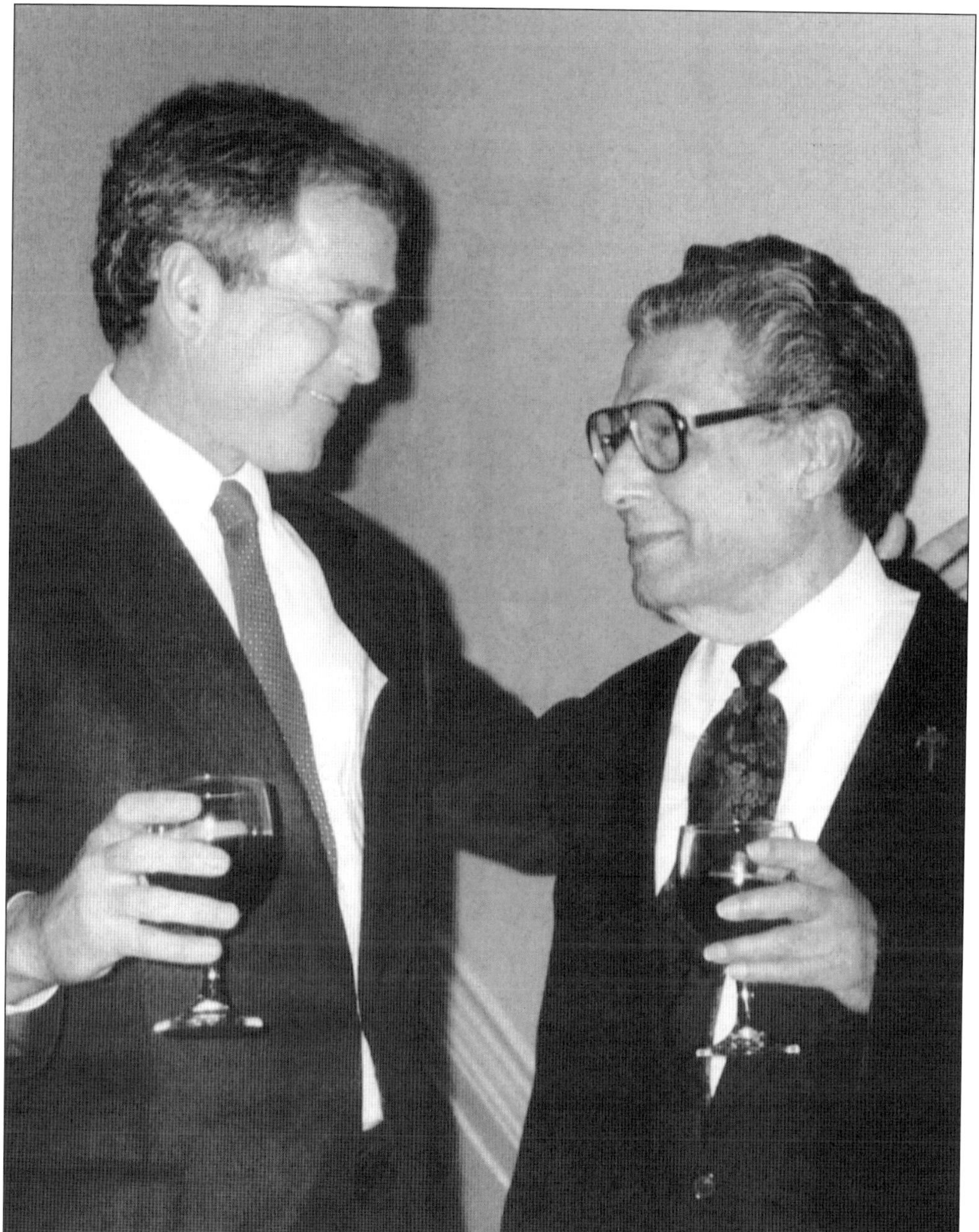

George W. Bush, former governor of Texas and 43rd US president, awarded artist José Cisneros with the National Humanities Medal in 2001. As noted by the National Endowment of the Humanities, Cisneros received the award because he "deepened the nation's understanding of the humanities, broadened our citizens' engagement with the humanities, or helped preserve and expand Americans' access to important resources in the Humanities." Cisneros also received the Americanism Award, the Western Book Award, and the Ohti Award, given by the government of Mexico. He was knighted by Pope John Paul II and by King Juan Carlos of Spain. (Courtesy of José Cisneros.)

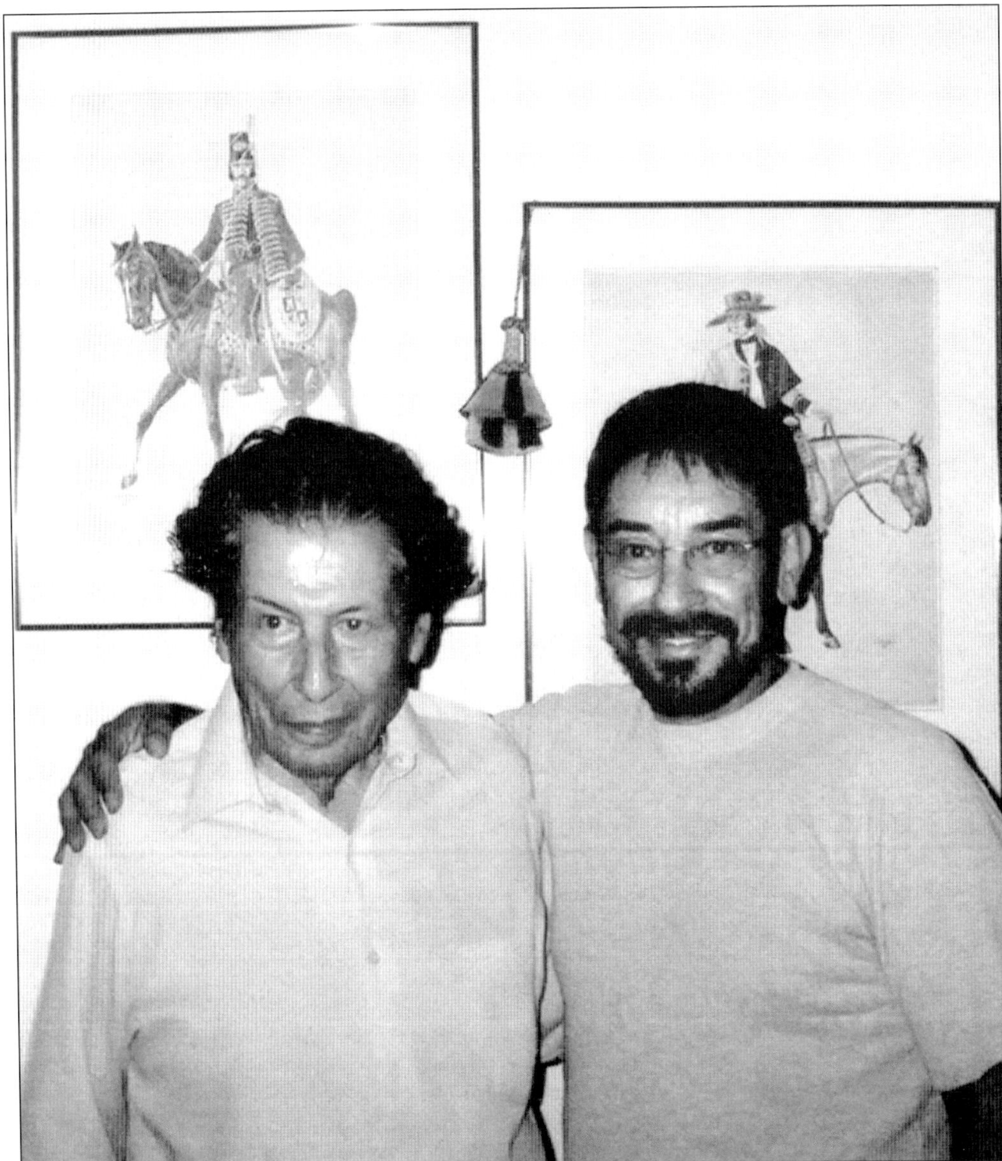

The author (right) poses with José Cisneros in 2002. The artist illustrated over 500 books during his illustrious career. He captured New Mexican and Southwestern history with renderings and details that brought important times to life. He spent countless hours researching clothing styles, trappings, firearms and armaments, and explicit items that showed the actual effects of people in history. Cisneros captured the early settlers of New Mexico and their personas as they persevered in the land while traveling and settling along El Camino Real de Tierra Adentro. (Photograph by Ramón Juan Carlos de Aragón.)

Bibliography

Albuquerque Bicentennial Commission. *Albuquerque Remembers.* Albuquerque, NM: American Revolution Bicentennial 1776–1976, 1977.

Anderson, Joan. *Spanish Pioneers of the Southwest.* New York, NY: E.P. Dutton, 1989.

Burke, James T. *This Miserable Kingdom: The Story of the Spanish Presence in New Mexico and the Southwest from the Beginning until the 18th Century.* Las Vegas, NM: Our Lady of Sorrows Church, 1973.

Chavez, Fray Angelico. *Origins of New Mexico Families: A Genealogy of the Spanish Colonial Period.* Santa Fe, NM: Museum of New Mexico Press, 1992.

De Varona, Frank, ed. *Hispanic Presence in the United States: Historical Beginnings.* Miami, FL: National Hispanic Quincentennial Commission, 1993.

Jordan, Louann, and St. George Cook. *El Rancho de las Golondrinas: Spanish Colonial Life in New Mexico.* Santa Fe, NM: Colonial New Mexico Historical Foundation, 1977.

Hammond, George P. *Coronado's Seven Cities.* Albuquerque, NM: US Coronado Exposition Commission, 1940.

Horgan, Paul. *Great River: The Rio Grande in North American History.* New York, NY: Farrar, Straus & Giroux & Rinehart, 1954.

Palmer, Gabrielle G., and Stephen L. Fosberg. *El Camino Real de Tierra Adentro.* Vol. II. Edited by June-el Piper. Cultural Resources Series No. 13. Santa Fe, NM: Bureau of Land Management, New Mexico State Office, 1999.

Perrigo, Lynn I. *Our Spanish Southwest.* Dallas, TX: Banks Upshaw and Company, 1960.

Ribera-Ortega. *La Conquistadora: America's Oldest Madonna.* Santa Fe, NM: Sunstone Press, 1975.

Shalkop, Robert L. *Reflections of Spain.* Colorado Springs, CO: The Taylor Museum, 1968.

Simmons, Marc. *The Last Conquistador: Juan de Onate and the Settling of the Far Southwest.* Norman, OK: University of Oklahoma Press, 1991.

Weber, David J. *The Edge of Empire: The Taos Hacienda of Los Martinez.* Santa Fe, NM: Museum of New Mexico Press, 1969.

West, John O. *Riders across the Centuries: The Biography of Jose Cisneros.* El Paso, TX: Texas Western Press, 1984.

Consistent with our mission to preserve history on a local level, this book was printed in South Carolina on American-made paper and manufactured entirely in the United States. Products carrying the accredited Forest Stewardship Council (FSC) label are printed on 100 percent FSC-certified paper.